U0731611

中英对照

J.K.罗琳的读书单

丛林故事

THE JUNGLE STORY

[英] 吉卜林○著

辛 静○译

上

《哈里·波特》作者J.K.罗琳

最喜爱的英美经典文学名著

中国书籍出版社

图书在版编目（CIP）数据

丛林故事／（英）吉卜林著；辛静译．—北京：中国
书籍出版社，2007.1
（J.K. 罗琳的读书单）
书名原文：The Jungle Story
ISBN 978 - 7 - 5068 - 1721 - 9

Ⅰ．丛 ... 　Ⅱ．①吉 ... ②辛 ... 　Ⅲ．①英语—汉语—
对照读物②童话—作品集—英国—近代
　　Ⅳ．H319.4：Ⅰ

中国版本图书馆 CIP 数据核字（2006）第 159971 号

责任编辑／毕　磊　李立云
责任印制／熊　力　武雅彬
封面设计／汇智泉文化设计公司
出版发行／中国书籍出版社
　　　　地　　址：北京市丰台区三路居路 97 号（邮编：100073）
　　　　电　　话：（010）52257142（总编室）　（010）52257154（发行部）
　　　　电子邮箱：chinabp@ vip. sina. com
经　　销／全国新华书店
印　　刷／三河市杨庄镇明华印装厂
开　　本／690 毫米×960 毫米　1/16
印　　张／31
字　　数／238 千字
版　　次／2013 年第 1 月第 2 版，2013 第 2 次印刷
定　　价／61. 80 元（上、中、下）

版权所有　翻印必究

目录

丛林的故事

Chapter 1 Mowgli's Brothers

Now Rann the Kite brings home the night
That Mang the Bat sets free—
The herds are shut in byre and hut
For loosed till dawn are we.
This is the hour of pride and power,
Talon and tush and claw.
Oh, hear the call! —Good hunting all
That keep the Jungle Law!

——**Night-Song in the Jungle**

It was seven o'clock of a very warm evening in the Seeonee hills when Father Wolf woke up from his day's rest, scratched himself, yawned, and spread out his paws one after the other to get rid of the sleepy feeling in their tips. Mother Wolf lay with her big gray nose dropped across her four tumbling, squealing cubs, and the moon shone into the mouth of the cave where they all lived. "Augrh! " said Father Wolf. "It is time to hunt again." He was

THE JUNGLE STORY

第一章 莫格里的兄弟们

现在风筝兰恩释放了黑夜，
蝙蝠曼尼带来了自由——
牛群都被关进了牛棚和茅屋，
因为我们要尽情放纵到黎明。
这是荣耀与权威的时刻，
亮出我们的尖牙、利爪和巨钳。
哦，听那召唤声——祝大家狩猎成功
遵守丛林法则的全体动物们！

——《丛林夜歌》

这是西奥尼山上一个暖融融的傍晚。狼爸爸休息了一整天，七点他从睡梦中醒来，搔了搔痒，打了个哈欠，逐个地伸展着他的爪子，以便驱散爪尖尚存的睡意。狼妈妈躺在那儿，灰色的大鼻子搭在她翻滚嬉闹的四只幼崽身上，月光照进他们生活的山洞洞口。"噢呜！"狼爸爸说，"又该去打猎了。"他正准备跑下山坡，一个拖着毛茸茸尾巴的小

tumble. v. 翻滚，打滚　　squeal vi (小孩、猪等)发出长声尖叫

003

going to spring down hill when a little shadow with a bushy tail crossed the threshold and whined : "Good luck go with you, O Chief of the Wolves. And good luck and strong white teeth go with noble children that they may never forget the hungry in this world."

It was the jackal—Tabaqui, the Dish-licker—and the wolves of India despise Tabaqui because he runs about making mischief, and telling tales, and eating rags and pieces of leather from the village rubbish-heaps. But they are afraid of him too, because Tabaqui, more than anyone else in the jungle, is apt to go mad, and then he forgets that he was ever afraid of anyone, and runs through the forest biting everything in his way. Even the tiger runs and hides when little Tabaqui goes mad, for madness is the most disgraceful thing that can overtake a wild creature. We call it hydrophobia, but they call it dewanee—the madness— and run.

"Enter, then, and look," said Father Wolf stiffly, "but there is no food here."

"For a wolf, no," said Tabaqui, "but for so mean a person as myself a dry bone is a good feast. Who are we, the Gidur-log [the jackal people], to pick and choose?" He scuttled to the back of the cave, where he found the bone of a buck with some meat on it, and

THE JUNGLE STORY

身影出现在洞口,用哀怨的声音说:"祝您好运啊,狼的首领。也祝福您高贵的孩子们,愿他们能长一副洁白坚硬的牙齿,但愿他们永不忘记这个世界上还有挨饿的。"

那是塔巴奇,一只专门吃残羹冷炙的豺。印度狼们都看不起塔巴奇,因为他总是到处挑拨离间、搬弄是非,在村子的垃圾堆里捡破烂吃。但是,印度狼们也都怕他,因为他比丛林里的其他动物都容易发疯。一发起疯来,他就忘了自己曾经怕过谁,在丛林里横冲直撞,见到什么咬什么。即使是老虎,一看到小塔巴奇犯了疯病,也要逃走躲起来,那是因为对于野生动物来说,得了疯病是最丢脸的事情了。我们称之为狂犬病,但动物们称它"达瓦尼"——也就是疯病——遇到得赶紧跑。

"那就进来看看吧",狼爸爸很不友好地说,"不过这儿没什么吃的。"

"对一头狼来说,是没什么可吃的了。"塔巴奇说,"但对我这样一个卑微的人来说,一块干骨头就是一顿美餐了。我们是什么东西呀?豺,哪能这么挑剔呢?"他急匆匆地跑到山洞里面,找到了一块还留着

---

whine *v.* 哀诉　despise *v.* 鄙视,藐视　rubbish-heap *n.* 垃圾堆
disgraceful *a.* 丢脸的,可耻的　overtake *v.* 突然侵袭　mean *a.* 卑鄙的,卑贱的
feast *n.* 盛宴　scuttle *v.* 急促奔跑

sat cracking the end merrily.

"All thanks for this good meal," he said, licking his lips. "How beautiful are the noble children! How large are their eyes! And so young too! Indeed, indeed, I might have remembered that the children of kings are men from the beginning."

Now, Tabaqui knew as well as anyone else that there is nothing so unlucky as to **compliment** children to their faces. It pleased him to see Mother and Father Wolf look uncomfortable.

Tabaqui sat still, rejoicing in the **mischief** that he had made, and then he said **spitefully**:

"Shere Khan, the Big One, has **shifted** his hunting grounds. He will hunt among these hills for the next month, so he has told me."

Shere Khan was the tiger who lived near the Waingunga River, twenty miles away.

"He has no right! " Father Wolf began angrily, "By the Law of the Jungle he has no right to change his quarters without due warning. He will frighten every head of game within ten miles, and I—I have to kill for two, these days."

"His mother did not call him Lungri [the **Lame One**] for nothing," said Mother Wolf quietly. "He has been lame in one foot

些肉的雄鹿骨头,坐在地上高兴得吧嗒吧哒啃了起来。

"多谢您的美食",他添了舔嘴巴说,"这些高贵的孩子多漂亮啊!瞧他们的眼睛,真大呀!又这么年轻!真的,真的,我就知道,大王的孩子一出生就这么气宇非凡!"

其实,塔巴尼和其他动物一样清楚地知道,当面称赞孩子们是很不妥当的做法。看到狼爸爸、狼妈妈不自在的表情,他心里暗自高兴。

塔巴尼一动不动地坐在那里,为自己刚才的恶作剧自鸣得意。然后,他不怀好意地说:

"大家伙萨克汗更换狩猎场了。他告诉我,下个月他将在这几座山上狩猎。"

萨克汗是住在20英里外维冈加河畔的一只老虎。

"他没这个权利!"狼爸爸生气地说,"根据丛林法则,他没有权力不事先通知就更换地盘。他会吓跑方圆10英里内的所有猎物,而我——我这两天得捕到双份的猎物才行。"

"他妈妈叫他'瘸腿'可不是没有原因的",狼妈妈平静地说,"他一生下来就瘸了一条腿,所以他只能猎杀耕牛。维冈加的村民都已经被

---

compliment *v.* 称赞,恭维　　mischief *n.*恶作剧,捣蛋　　spitefully *adv.* 恶意地
shift *v.* 替换,转移　　lame *a.* 跛的,瘸的

from his birth. That is why he has only killed cattle. Now the villagers of the Waingunga are angry with him, and he has come here to make our villagers angry. They will **scour** the jungle for him when he is far away, and we and our children must run when the grass is set alight. Indeed, we are very grateful to Shere Khan! "

"Shall I tell him of your gratitude?" said Tabaqui.

"Out! " snapped Father Wolf. "Out and hunt with **your** master. **Thou have** done harm enough for one night."

"I go," said Tabaqui quietly. "Ye can hear Shere Khan below in the thickets. I might have saved myself the message."

Father Wolf listened, and below in the **valley** that ran down to a little river, he heard the dry, angry, **snarly**, singsong whine of a tiger who has caught nothing and does not care if all the jungle knows it.

"The fool! " said Father Wolf. "To begin a night's work with that noise! Does he think that our buck are like his fat Waingunga bullocks?"

"H'sh. It is neither bullock nor buck he hunts tonight," said Mother Wolf. "It is Man."

The whine had changed to a sort of **humming** purr that seemed to come from every quarter of the compass. It was the noise that

THE JUNGLE STORY

他惹火了，现在他又要来惹我们的村民。到时候村民们定会到丛林搜寻他，而他却早逃走了。村民们定会放火烧野草，我们和孩子们就得逃命。我们还真得谢谢萨克汗了。"

"要我向他转达你们的谢意吗？"塔巴奇问道。

"滚出去！"狼爸爸怒气冲冲地说，"去和你的主子一起捕猎吧，你今天晚上做的坏事已经够多了。"

"我走，"塔巴奇不慌不忙地说，"你们听，萨克汗在下面灌木丛里走动呢。早知道我就不来告诉你们这个消息了。"

狼爸爸竖起耳朵倾听，在下面小河淌过的河谷里，有一只暴怒的老虎。他什么也没逮着，嘴里粗鲁地发出哼哼声，也不在乎整个丛林的动物们能否听到。

"傻瓜！"狼爸爸说，"哪有发出这么大声响开始干活的！他以为我们这里的公鹿像维冈加那些肥肥的小公牛一样蠢？"

"嘘！今晚他捕猎的既不是小公牛也不是公鹿，"狼妈妈说，"是人。"

哼哼声变成了低沉的呜呜声，似乎来自四面八方。这种声音常常会使露宿野外的樵夫和吉普赛人迷失方向，甚至有时使他们在逃跑时

---

scour n. 走遍(某地)搜寻   your pron. (古)你的   you pron (古)你   have (古)have
valley n. (山)谷   snarly adv. 咆哮的, 易怒的   humming adj. 发嗡嗡声的

丛林的故事

bewilders woodcutters and gypsies sleeping in the open, and makes them run sometimes into the very mouth of the tiger.

"Man! " said Father Wolf, showing all his white teeth. "Faugh! Are there not enough beetles and frogs in the **tanks** that he must eat Man, and on our ground too! "

The Law of the Jungle, which never orders anything without a reason, forbids every beast to eat Man except when he is killing to show his children how to kill, and then he must hunt outside the hunting grounds of his **pack** or tribe. The real reason for this is that man-killing means, sooner or later, the arrival of white men on elephants, with guns, and hundreds of brown men with gongs and rockets and torches. Then everybody in the jungle **suffers**. The reason the beasts give among themselves is that Man is the weakest and most defenseless of all living things, and it is **unsportsmanlike** to touch him. They say too—and it is true —that man-eaters become mangy, and lose their teeth.

The purr grew louder, and ended in the **full-throated** "Aaarh! " of the tiger's charge.

Then there was a howl—an untigerish howl—from Shere Khan.

THE JUNGLE STORY

把自己送进虎口。

"人!"狼爸爸咬牙切齿地说,"呸!池塘里的甲壳虫和青蛙不够他吃的了?他非要吃人不可?而且还是在我们的地盘上?"

丛林法则的规定从来都是不无道理的。它禁止任何一头野兽捕杀人,除非他在教自己的孩子如何捕猎。即使这样,也必须在他的家族或部落的狩猎地以外的地方行事。制定这条规定的真正原因是猎杀人类迟早会招来骑着大象、带着枪支的白人和成百上千的手持铜锣、火箭和火把的棕色皮肤的人。这样丛林里的所有动物都要遭罪。而动物们自己对这个规定的理解是:人类是所有生物中最软弱、最缺少防御能力的,所以对人类下手,是最卑鄙的。他们还说——这可是真的——吃人的动物会长疥癣,牙齿会脱落。

呜呜声越来越大,最后就变成了老虎扑食时发出的洪亮的吼叫声:"啊呜!"

接着萨克汗发出一声嚎叫——缺乏虎威的一声吼叫。"他没扑

---

tank n. 水池   pack n. 兽群   suffer v. 遭受苦难
unsportmanlike a. 没有风度的,不光明正大的   full-throated a. 声音洪亮的

"He has missed," said Mother Wolf. "What is it?"

Father Wolf ran out a few paces and heard Shere Khan muttering and mumbling savagely as he tumbled about in the scrub.

"The fool has had no more sense than to jump at a woodcutter's campfire, and has burned his feet," said Father Wolf with a grunt. "Tabaqui is with him."

"Something is coming up hill," said Mother Wolf, twitching one ear. "Get ready."

The bushes rustled a little in the thicket, and Father Wolf dropped with his haunches under him, ready for his leap. Then, if you had been watching, you would have seen the most wonderful thing in the world—the wolf checked in mid-spring. He made his bound before he saw what it was he was jumping at, and then he tried to stop himself. The result was that he shot up straight into the air for four or five feet, landing almost where he left ground.

"Man! ." he snapped. "A man's cub. Look! "

Directly in front of him, holding on by a low branch, stood a naked brown baby who could just walk—as soft and as dimpled a little atom as ever came to a wolf's cave at night. He looked up into

THE JUNGLE STORY

到，"狼妈妈说，"怎么回事？"

狼爸爸跑出几步，听到萨克汗在矮树丛里打着滚，一边粗鲁地咕哝着。

"这傻瓜居然跳到樵夫的篝火上，把脚烫伤了，"狼爸爸嘀咕着，"塔巴奇和他在一块儿。"

"有什么东西上山来了，"狼妈妈一只耳朵抽搐了一下，说道，"做好准备。"

灌木丛里发出沙沙的声响，狼爸爸蹲下身子，随即纵身一跃。接着，如果你注意看的话，你会看到世界上最令人惊叹的一幕——狼爸爸跳到半空中突然停止了。他还没弄清楚那是什么东西就跃了出去，于是就得设法制止自己。结果是他向空中跳到四至五英寸高，然后几乎就落在了他刚才跃起的地方。

"人！"他急促地说，"是个小孩！看！"

一个刚刚学会走路、全身赤裸的棕色皮肤的小娃娃，手里握着一根短小的树枝，就站在他的面前——还从来没有这样一个柔弱的、脸上带着小酒窝的小生命在黑夜里来到一头狼的洞穴里。他抬头看着狼爸爸，笑

---

mutter v. 咕哝，抱怨　　savagely adv. 粗鲁的，残暴的　　haunch n. 腰部，臀部
leap n. 跳跃　　check v. 突然停止

Father Wolf's face, and laughed.

"Is that a man's cub?" said Mother Wolf. "I have never seen one. Bring it here."

A Wolf accustomed to moving his own cubs can, if necessary, mouth an egg without breaking it, and though Father Wolf's jaws closed right on the child's back not a tooth even scratched the skin as he laid it down among the cubs.

"How little! How naked, and—how bold! " said Mother Wolf softly. The baby was pushing his way between the cubs to get close to the warm hide. "Ahai! He is taking his meal with the others. And so this is a man's cub. Now, was there ever a wolf that could boast of a man's cub among her children?"

"I have heard now and again of such a thing, but never in our pack or in my time," said Father Wolf. "He is altogether without hair, and I could kill him with a touch of my foot. But see, he looks up and is not afraid."

The moonlight was blocked out of the mouth of the cave, for Shere Khan's great square head and shoulders were thrust into the entrance. Tabaqui, behind him, was squeaking: "My lord, my lord, it

THE JUNGLE STORY

着。

"那个小娃娃是人吗？"狼妈妈说，"我还从没见过呢！带过来让我瞧瞧。"

狼总是习惯用嘴巴衔着他们的狼崽，如果必要的话，就是衔着一枚鸡蛋也不会弄碎的。虽然狼爸爸紧紧地咬住娃娃的背部，但当他把娃娃放在狼崽中时，一点也没有伤到娃娃的皮肤。

"多么娇小啊！身上滑溜溜的！而且——胆子还真大！"狼妈妈温柔地说。小娃娃拼命地挤到狼崽子中间，希望得到些温暖。"啊哈，他和他们一起吃起来了。原来这就是娃娃人呀。谁听说过一头狼的狼崽中会有个娃娃人呢？"

"我倒是听说过这样的事情，但在我们狼群里或是在我这一辈子里，还从来没发生过，"狼爸爸说，"他全身都没有毛，我只要用爪子轻轻一碰，他就会没命的。可是你看，他抬头看着我，一点也不害怕。"

洞口的月光突然被挡住了，萨克汗方方的大脑袋和肩膀拼命地要挤进洞口。塔巴奇跟在他身后，尖叫着："哦，我的天哪，我的上帝呀，他

---

hide *n.* 兽皮   square *a.* 方的   thrust *v.* 猛推，硬挤

went in here! "

"Shere Khan does us great honor," said Father Wolf, but his eyes were very angry. "What does Shere Khan need?"

"My quarry. A man's cub went this way," said Shere Khan. "Its parents have run off. Give it to me."

Shere Khan had jumped at a woodcutter's campfire, as Father Wolf had said, and was furious from the pain of his burned feet. But Father Wolf knew that the mouth of the cave was too narrow for a tiger to come in by. Even where he was, Shere Khan's shoulders and forepaws were cramped for want of room, as a man would be if he tried to fight in a barrel.

"The wolves are a free people," said Father Wolf. "They take orders from the head of the pack, and not from any striped cattle-killer. The man's cub is ours—to kill if we choose."

"You choose and you do not choose! What talk is this of choosing? By the bull that I killed, am I to stand nosing into your dog's den for my fair dues? It is I, Shere Khan, who speak! "

The tiger's roar filled the cave with thunder. Mother Wolf shook herself clear of the cubs and sprang forward, her eyes, like two green moons in the darkness, facing the blazing eyes of Shere

THE JUNGLE STORY

跑到这儿来了。"

"萨克汗可真是赏脸啊,"狼爸爸说,可是眼神里充满着愤怒,"不知道萨克汗想要什么呢?"

"我的猎物,一个人类幼崽跑到这儿来了,"萨克汗说,"它的父母跑掉了,把它交给我吧。"

正如狼爸爸刚才所说的,萨克汗跳到了樵夫的篝火上,至今还为烧伤的爪子痛得怒气未消。但狼爸爸知道这洞口很窄,老虎是钻不进来的。即使在洞口,萨克汗的肩膀和前爪也都被挤作一团,就像一个人在木桶里打架,伸展不开手脚。

"狼是自由的,"狼爸爸说,"他们只听从狼群首领的吩咐,而不听从那些身上带着条纹、专吃耕牛的家伙。人类的幼崽是我们的,要杀也要由我们来杀。"

"什么你们要杀不杀的?这是什么话?我以我杀的公牛发誓,难道还要我钻到你们的狗窝里来拿回我应得的东西吗?这可是我——萨克汗在发话!"

老虎的吼声如响雷般在洞里回响。狼妈妈抖开了幼崽们跳上前来,她的眼睛在黑暗中像两个发出绿光的月亮,正盯着萨克汗闪闪发

---

quarry n. 猎物   furious a. 狂怒的   striped adj. 有条纹的

Khan.

"And it is I, Raksha , who answers. The man's cub is mine, Lungri—mine to me! He shall not be killed. He shall live to run with the pack and to hunt with the pack; and in the end, look you, hunter of little naked cubs—frog-eater—fish-killer—he shall hunt you! Now get hence, or by the Sambhur that I killed (I eat no starved cattle), back you goest to your mother, burned beast of the jungle, lamer than ever you came into the world! Go! "

Father Wolf looked on amazed. He had almost forgotten the days when he won Mother Wolf in fair fight from five other wolves, when she ran in the pack and was not called The Demon for compliment's sake. Shere Khan might have faced Father Wolf, but he could not stand up against Mother Wolf, for he knew that where he was she had all the **advantage** of the ground, and would fight to the death. So he backed out of the cave mouth growling, and when he was clear he shouted:

"Each dog barks in his own yard! We will see what the pack will say to this **fostering** of man-cubs. The cub is mine, and to my teeth he will come in the end, O bush-tailed thieves! "

THE JUNGLE STORY

亮的眼睛。

"魔鬼，这是我，雷克莎，在回答你。人类的幼崽是我的，瘸子——他也是我的！谁也不能杀了他。他将和狼群一起奔跑，一起狩猎；你看看自己，一个猎杀赤裸裸的幼崽的家伙，一个吃青蛙、杀鱼的家伙，总有一天，他会来猎捕你！现在，你给我滚，否则我以我杀的大公鹿发誓(我可从来不吃挨饿的耕牛)，我会让你比你出生时瘸得更加厉害，滚回你妈那里，你这丛林里被火烧了的野兽，滚！"

狼爸爸惊奇地看着这一切。他已经忘记了他曾经公平地斗败了其他五头狼、赢得狼妈妈的那段岁月。狼妈妈当时在狼群里被称为"魔鬼"，那可不是别人称赞的话。萨克汗也许能对付狼爸爸，但是却可能对付不了狼妈妈，因为他知道，在这儿狼妈妈占据了有利的地形，而且她将战斗到生命的最后一刻。所以他吼叫着退出了洞口。到了洞外，他嚷道：

"每只狗都只会在自己的院子里汪汪叫！等着瞧吧，看狼群对你们收养人类幼崽的做法会怎么说！幼崽是我的，总有一天会落在我的嘴里的，长着蓬松尾巴的贼！"

---

advantage n. 优势   fostering n. 养育

丛林的故事

Mother Wolf threw herself down panting among the cubs, and Father Wolf said to her gravely:

"Shere Khan speaks this much truth. The cub must be shown to the pack. Will you still keep him, Mother?"

"Keep him! " she gasped. "He came naked, by night, alone and very hungry; yet he was not afraid! Look, he has pushed one of my babes to one side already. And that lame butcher would have killed him and would have run off to the Waingunga while the villagers here hunted through all our lairs in revenge! Keep him? Assuredly I will keep him. Lie still, little frog. O you Mowgli —for Mowgli the Frog I will call you—the time will come when you will hunt Shere Khan as he has hunted you."

"But what will our pack say?" said Father Wolf.

The Law of the Jungle lays down very clearly that any wolf may, when he marries, withdraw from the pack he belongs to. But as soon as his cubs are old enough to stand on their feet he must bring them to the Pack Council, which is generally held once a month at full moon, in order that the other wolves may identify them. After that inspection the cubs are free to run where they please, and until they have killed their first buck no excuse is

狼妈妈气喘吁吁地在狼崽中间躺下来,狼爸爸认真地对她说:

"萨克汗说的倒是实话。我们必须把这娃娃人交给狼群看看。你还要留着他吗,狼妈妈?"

"当然留着!"她喘着气说,"他晚上孤零零的,光着身子饿着肚子来到这里;可他居然不害怕! 看,他已经把我的一个狼崽挤到一边去了。再说,那个瘸腿的屠夫会把他杀了,然后逃回维冈加。接着村民就会来搜索我们的巢穴为他报仇。收留他吗? 我当然要收留他了。继续躺着,小青蛙。哦,你莫格里——我就叫你小青蛙莫格里吧——现在萨克汗猎捕你,总有一天,你会去猎捕他。"

"但我们的狼群会怎么说呢?"狼爸爸说。

丛林法则清楚地规定了,任何一头狼,只要结了婚,就可以退出他所属的狼群。但一旦他们的幼崽能够站立了,他就必须带着他们参加狼群大会,以便让其他的狼可以认识他们。狼群大会通常在每月满月的那一天举行。 经过检阅之后,幼崽们就可以随心所欲地奔跑了。在狼崽们猎杀到他们的第一头雄鹿之前,绝不允许狼群中任何成年狼杀

---

withdraw v. 撤回,收回   council n. 委员会,政务会

accepted if a grown wolf of the pack kills one of them. The punishment is death where the murderer can be found; and if you think for a minute you will see that this must be so.

Father Wolf waited till his cubs could run a little, and then on the night of the pack Meeting took them and Mowgli and Mother Wolf to the Council Rock—a hilltop covered with stones and boulders where a hundred wolves could hide. Akela, the great gray Lone Wolf, who led all the pack by strength and cunning, lay out at full length on his rock, and below him sat forty or more wolves of every size and color, from badger-colored veterans who could handle a buck alone to young black three-year-olds who thought they could. The Lone Wolf had led them for a year now. He had fallen twice into a wolf trap in his youth, and once he had been beaten and left for dead; so he knew the manners and customs of men. There was very little talking at the Rock. The cubs tumbled over each other in the center of the circle where their mothers and fathers sat, and now and again a senior wolf would go quietly up to a cub, look at him carefully, and return to his place on noiseless feet. Sometimes a mother would push her cub far out into the

THE JUNGLE STORY

害他们。否则，一旦抓住凶手，就要把他处死作为惩罚。如果你略加思索，你就会意识到必须这么做。

狼爸爸一直等到幼崽们能跑一点路了，才在举行狼群大会的晚上带着他们和莫格里、狼妈妈来到会议岩上——那是一个布满了石块、巨岩的小山头，那里藏得下一百头狼。阿克拉，独身的大灰狼，以他的力量和智慧领导着狼群。此时他正躺在岩石上，舒展着全身，在他下面躺着四十多头大大小小、毛色各异的狼。有能单独对付一头雄鹿、长着獾色皮毛的老狼，也有自以为可以单独对付一头雄鹿的三岁的年轻黑狼。独身狼领导狼群已经有一年了。在他年轻时，他曾经两次掉到捕狼的陷阱里去，还有一次差点被人揍死，后来以为他死了才被丢弃。因此他了解人类的风俗习惯。在岩石上，大家都很少说话。幼崽们在爸爸妈妈围坐起来的圈圈里翻滚嬉闹。不时地会有年长的老狼轻轻地走到一个幼崽的身边，仔细地观察一番，然后轻手轻脚地回到自己的位置上。有时，有些狼妈妈会把自己的幼崽在月光下高高地抛起，好让人家不

---

cunning *n.* 狡猾　　veteran *n.* 老兵,老战士

023

moonlight to be sure that he had not been overlooked.

Akela from his rock would cry: "You know the Law—you know the Law. Look well, O Wolves! " And the anxious mothers would take up the call: "Look—look well, O Wolves! "

At last—and Mother Wolf's neck bristles lifted as the time came—Father Wolf pushed "Mowgli the Frog," as they called him, into the center, where he sat laughing and playing with some pebbles that glistened in the moonlight.

Akela never raised his head from his paws, but went on with the monotonous cry: "Look well! " A muffled roar came up from behind the rocks—the voice of Shere Khan crying: "The cub is mine. Give him to me. What have the free people to do with a man's cub?" Akela never even twitched his ears. All he said was: "Look well, O Wolves! What have the free people to do with the orders of any save the free people? Look well! "

There was a chorus of deep growls, and a young wolf in his fourth year flung back Shere Khan's question to Akela: "What have the free people to do with a man's cub?" Now, the Law of the Jungle lays down that if there is any dispute as to the right of a cub to be accepted by the pack, he must be spoken for by at least two

THE JUNGLE STORY

会把他遗漏。

阿克拉在他那块岩石上大喊："你们都知道法则吧——都知道法则的。大伙都仔细看看！"然后焦急的妈妈们就会接着他的话说："是啊,大伙仔细看看！"

最后的时刻到了——狼妈妈脖子上的鬃毛都竖了起来——狼爸爸把"小青蛙莫格里"——他们是这样叫他的——推到了中间。莫格里坐在地上笑着,玩着几颗在月光下闪闪发亮的鹅卵石。

阿克拉的头一直都没从爪子里抬起来,继续着他千篇一律的吩咐："仔细看看吧！"从岩石后面传出一阵低沉的吼声——那是萨克汗在叫嚷："那个幼崽是我的。把他给我吧。自由的狼群要人类的幼崽有什么用呢?"阿克拉连耳朵都没有动一下,只是说："好好看看吧,各位。自由的狼群只会听从来自自由的狼群的命令,别人谁的命令也不会听的。好好看看吧。"

一片低沉的嚎叫声响起,一头四岁的年轻狼抛出萨克汗的问题问阿克拉："自由的狼群要如何对待一个人类的幼崽?"丛林法则规定,如果对于一个幼崽是否享有被狼群所接受的权利发生争议的话,他必须

---

monotonous *a.* 单调的　　save *prep.* 除……外

members of the pack who are not his father and mother.

"Who speaks for this cub?" said Akela. "Among the free people who speaks?" There was no answer and Mother Wolf got ready for what she knew would be her last fight, if things came to fighting.

Then the only other creature who is allowed at the pack Council—Baloo, the sleepy brown bear who teaches the wolf cubs the Law of the Jungle: old Baloo, who can come and go where he pleases because he eats only nuts and roots and honey—rose upon his hind quarters and grunted.

"The man's cub—the man's cub?" he said. "I speak for the man's cub. There is no harm in a man's cub. I have no gift of words, but I speak the truth. Let him run with the pack, and be entered with the others. I myself will teach him."

"We need yet another," said Akela. "Baloo has spoken, and he is our teacher for the young cubs. Who speaks besides Baloo?"

A black shadow dropped down into the circle. It was Bagheera the Black Panther, inky black all over, but with the panther markings showing up in certain lights like the pattern of watered silk. Everybody knew Bagheera, and nobody cared to cross his path;

得到除了他父母以外至少两个成员的支持。

"谁为这个娃娃说话？"阿克拉说，"自由的狼群中有谁要站出来说话？"没有人回答。狼妈妈为战斗做好了准备，她知道，如果事情发展到非打不可的话，这将是她最后的战斗。

这时，惟一被允许参加狼群大会的异类动物巴洛用后脚站起来咕哝着说话了——他是一头嗜睡的棕熊，专门教导狼崽们丛林法则的。老巴洛可以来去自由，因为他只吃坚果、树根和蜂蜜。

"人类的幼崽——人类的幼崽？"他说，"我支持他。人类的幼崽不会伤害谁。我不太会说话，但我说的是事实。让他和狼群一起奔跑吧，和其他狼一起加入狼群。我自己来教他。"

"我们还需要另外一个支持者。"阿克拉说，"巴洛算一个，他是我们狼崽们的老师。除了巴洛还有谁？"

一个黑影跳到圈子中央。那是黑豹巴格希拉，他全身长着漆黑的皮毛，在亮光下显现出波纹绸一样的豹纹。大家都认识巴格希拉，但没人敢招惹他，因为他像塔巴奇一般狡猾，像野水牛一般凶猛，像受伤的

---

grunt *v.* 咕哝地说　　gift *n.* 天赋，天资

丛林的故事

for he was as cunning as Tabaqui, as bold as the wild buffalo, and as reckless as the wounded elephant. But he had a voice as soft as wild honey dripping from a tree, and a skin softer than down.

"O Akela, and you the free people," he purred, "I have no right in your assembly, but the Law of the Jungle says that if there is a doubt which is not a killing matter in regard to a new cub, the life of that cub may be bought at a price. And the Law does not say who may or may not pay that price. Am I right?"

"Good! Good!" said the young wolves, who are always hungry. "Listen to Bagheera. The cub can be bought for a price. It is the Law."

"Knowing that I have no right to speak here, I ask for your leave."

"Speak then," cried twenty voices.

"To kill a naked cub is shame. Besides, he may make better sport for you when he is grown. Baloo has spoken in his behalf. Now to Baloo's word I will add one bull, and a fat one, newly killed, not half a mile from here, if you will accept the man's cub according to the Law. Is it difficult?"

There was a clamor of scores of voices, saying: "What matter? He will die in the winter rains. He will scorch in the sun. What harm

THE JUNGLE STORY

大象一般横冲直撞,但他的声音却有如树上滴的野蜂蜜般甜腻,毛皮比绒毛还要柔软。

"哦,阿克拉,还有自由的狼群。"他愉快地说:"我没有权利参加你们的大会。但是丛林法则规定了,如果对于一个小幼崽的归属产生疑问,而又不至于要杀死他,可以用价钱来买他的生命,而且法则并没有规定谁有权或者无权买,我说的对吗?"

"太对了!太对了!"那些总是饿着肚子的年轻狼说道,"听巴格希拉说吧。这幼崽可以用价钱买的,这是法则规定的。"

"我知道我没权利在这儿说话。我请求你们的批准。"

"说吧。"二十个声音一起喊了起来。

"杀死一个赤裸裸的幼崽是不光彩的。而且,当他长大了,可以为你们捕获更好的猎物。巴洛已经为他说过话了。现在除了巴洛的话,我再加上一头公牛,一头刚刚被捕杀的肥公牛,离这里只有半英里远。如果你们能按照法则接受这个人类幼崽的话,它就是你们的了。这很难吗?"

几十个声音喧嚷着:"这有什么啊?他可能会在冬天的雨里冻死,也可能在太阳下晒死。一个光着身子的小青蛙对我们能有什么害处

---

down *n.* 绒毛　　assembly *n.* 集会,集合　　leave *n.* 许可,同意　　shame *n.* 羞耻,耻辱
behalf *n.* 利益,方面　　scorch *v.* 烧焦,烤焦

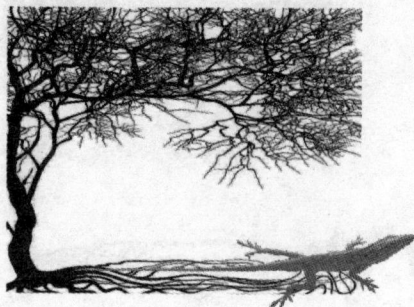

can a naked frog do us? Let him run with the pack. Where is the bull, Bagheera? Let him be accepted." And then came Akela's deep bay, crying: "Look well—look well, O Wolves! "

Mowgli was still deeply interested in the pebbles, and he did not notice when the wolves came and looked at him one by one. At last they all went down the hill for the dead bull, and only Akela, Bagheera, Baloo, and Mowgli's own wolves were left. Shere Khan roared still in the night, for he was very angry that Mowgli had not been handed over to him.

"Ay, roar well," said Bagheera, under his whiskers, "for the time will come when this naked thing will make you roar to another tune, or I know nothing of man."

"It was well done," said Akela. "Men and their cubs are very wise. He may be a help in time."

"Truly, a help in time of need; for none can hope to lead the pack forever," said Bagheera.

Akela said nothing. He was thinking of the time that comes to every leader of every pack when his strength goes from him and he gets feebler and feebler, till at last he is killed by the wolves and a new leader comes up—to be killed in his turn.

THE JUNGLE STORY

啊？让他和狼群一起奔跑吧。公牛在哪呢,巴格希拉？我们接受他。"接着又传来阿克拉低沉的喊声:"仔细看看吧,大家仔细看看吧!"

　　莫格里仍然被鹅卵石所深深地吸引着,他没有注意到群狼们一个接一个地走过来,仔细地看着他。最后他们都下山去寻找那头刚死的公牛了,只剩下阿克拉、巴格希拉、巴洛和莫格里家里的狼。萨克汗仍然在黑夜里咆哮着,没有把莫格里交给他,这让他十分生气。

　　"吼吧,就让你吼个够吧。"巴格希拉抖动着他的胡须说道。"总有一天,这个光溜溜的小家伙会让你用另外一种声调吼叫的,否则就算我对人类一无所知吧。"

　　"做得很好,"阿克拉说,"人类和他们的幼崽都是非常聪明的。到时候,他肯定能帮上我们的忙。"

　　"真的,在必要的时候可以做个帮手。因为谁也不可能永远领导狼群。"巴格希拉说。

　　阿克拉没有回答。他在想着,每个狼群的首领都会年老体衰,越来越虚弱,直到最后被其他的狼杀死,然后就会有一个新的头领出现,然后轮到他最后也被杀死。

---

whisker n. (动物)须

031

"Take him away," he said to Father Wolf, "and train him as befits one of the free people."

And that is how Mowgli was entered into the Seeonee Wolf Pack for the price of a bull and on Baloo's good words.

Now you must be content to skip ten or eleven whole years, and only guess at all the wonderful life that Mowgli led among the wolves, because if it were written out it would fill ever so many books. He grew up with the cubs, though they, of course, were grown wolves almost before he was a child. And Father Wolf taught him his business, and the meaning of things in the jungle, till every rustle in the grass, every breath of the warm night air, every note of the owls above his head, every scratch of a bat's claws as it roosted for a while in a tree, and every splash of every little fish jumping in a pool meant just as much to him as the work of his office means to a business man. When he was not learning he sat out in the sun and slept, and ate and went to sleep again. When he felt dirty or hot he swam in the forest pools; and when he wanted honey (Baloo told him that honey and nuts were just as pleasant to eat as raw meat) he climbed up for it, and that Bagheera showed him how to do. Bagheera would lie out on a branch and call, "Come along, Little

THE JUNGLE STORY

"带他走吧,"他对狼爸爸说,"把他训练成像自由的狼民一样合格的猎手。"

就这样,莫格里以一头公牛的价格和巴洛的一些好话进入了西奥尼的狼群。

现在你也许很乐意跳过十年或是十一年,自己去想象一下莫格里在狼群中度过的快乐时光,因为如果把它都写出来得写好几本书呢。他和狼崽们一起长大,当然在他变成一个少年以前,他们都已经长成成年的狼了。狼爸爸把他的本领,丛林里一切事物的含义都教会了他:从小草的沙沙声到夜晚温暖的空气,从他头上飞过的猫头鹰发出的每一声叫唤,到蝙蝠在树上休憩片刻爪子搔抓的声音。池塘里一条小鱼跃起发出的溅水声对他来说熟悉得就像商人了解他办公室的工作一样。当他不用学习的时候,他就躺在太阳底下睡觉,睡醒了吃,吃完了又睡;当他觉得身上脏了或是热了,就在森林中的水塘里游泳;当他想吃蜂蜜的时候(巴洛告诉他,蜂蜜、坚果有和生肉一样的美味),他就爬到树上去找,那是巴格西拉教他的。巴格西拉会躺在一根树杈上,对

---

skip v. 跳过,略过 roost v. 栖息 splash n. 飞溅

033

Brother," and at first Mowgli would cling like the sloth, but afterward he would fling himself through the branches almost as boldly as the gray ape. He took his place at the Council Rock, too, when the pack met, and then he discovered that if he stared hard at any wolf, the wolf would be forced to drop his eyes, and so he used to stare for fun. At other times he would pick the long thorns out of the pads of his friends, for wolves suffer terribly from thorns and burs in their coats. He would go down the hillside into the cultivated lands by night, and look very curiously at the villagers in their huts, but he had a mistrust of men because Bagheera showed him a square box with a drop gate so cunningly hidden in the jungle that he nearly walked into it, and told him that it was a trap. He loved better than anything else to go with Bagheera into the dark warm heart of the forest, to sleep all through the drowsy day, and at night see how Bagheera did his killing. Bagheera killed right and left as he felt hungry, and so did Mowgli—with one exception. As soon as he was old enough to understand things, Bagheera told him that he must never touch cattle because he had been bought into the pack at the price of a bull's life. "All the jungle is your," said Bagheera, "and you can kill everything that you are strong enough to kill; but

THE JUNGLE STORY

他喊："来吧，小兄弟！"最初，莫格里像树獭一样紧紧地抱着树，可后来他能像灰人猿那样勇敢地在树枝间跳跃了。他也参加狼群大会。开会的时候，他发现，只要他死命地盯着任何一头狼，那头狼总会被看得低下头去。 所以他总是拿这个来开玩笑。有时，狼总因为身上脚上扎到刺而吃尽苦头，他就帮他的朋友们把脚掌里的长刺拔出来。夜晚，他会下山到农田里，好奇地看着小屋里的村民。但莫格里不信任人类，因为有一次，他差点走入一个隐藏在树丛里的小方匣子中。匣子上装着会落下的匣门，巴格西拉告诉他那是陷阱。他最喜欢和巴格西拉走进森林黑暗温暖沉寂的深处，躺上一整天，然后夜晚的时候，看巴格西拉捕杀猎物。巴格西拉饥饿的时候，看到猎物就杀。莫格里也是一样——只有一个例外。当莫格里长大能懂事了，巴格西拉告诉他他永远不能猎杀公牛，因为他是以一头公牛的代价被狼群接受的。"整个丛林都是你的，"巴格西拉说，"你可以猎杀所有你能杀的猎物，但为了买下你的那头公牛，你必须做到永远不杀、不吃公牛，无论小牛还是老牛。这是

---

cling *v.* 紧紧靠着　　coat *n.* 皮毛　　cultivate *v.* 耕种
drowsy *a.* 沉寂的　　your *pron.* (古)你的东西

035

丛林的故事

for the sake of the bull that bought you you must never kill or eat any cattle young or old. That is the Law of the Jungle." Mowgli obeyed faithfully.

And he grew and grew strong as a boy must grow who does not know that he is learning any lessons, and who has nothing in the world to think of except things to eat.

Mother Wolf told him once or twice that Shere Khan was not a creature to be trusted, and that some day he must kill Shere Khan. But though a young wolf would have remembered that advice every hour, Mowgli forgot it because he was only a boy—though he would have called himself a wolf if he had been able to speak in any human tongue.

Shere Khan was always crossing his path in the jungle, for as Akela grew older and feebler the lame tiger had come to be great friends with the younger wolves of the pack, who followed him for scraps, a thing Akela would never have allowed if he had dared to push his authority to the proper bounds. Then Shere Khan would flatter them and wonder that such fine young hunters were content to be led by a dying wolf and a man's cub. "They tell me," Shere Khan would say, "that at Council you dare not look him between

THE JUNGLE STORY

丛林法则规定的。"莫格里一直遵守这个规定。

于是，莫格里就像别的男孩子一样长大了。他不知道他正在学习知识，除了吃东西，他不用思考任何事情。

狼妈妈几次对他说，萨克汗是一个不可信赖的家伙，总有一天，他得杀了萨克汗。虽然这是一头小狼必须每时每刻记住的忠告，但是莫格里却忘了狼妈妈的话，因为他毕竟只是个小男孩——即使他会说人类的语言，他也会把自己称为一头狼。

他常常在丛林里遇到萨克汗。随着阿克拉日渐衰老，这个瘸腿的老虎和狼群中年轻的狼们交上了朋友，这些狼总是跟在他身后，吃他丢下的残羹冷炙。如果阿克拉真的敢于实施自己的权力的话，他是不会允许这样的事情发生的。而且萨克汗总是会奉承他们，并且质疑如此年轻力壮的猎手怎么会甘于服从一头垂死的老狼和一个人类崽子的领导。"他们告诉我，"萨克汗会说，"狼群大会的时候你们都不敢和

---

flatter *v.* 奉承

037

the eyes." And the young wolves would growl and bristle.

Bagheera, who had eyes and ears everywhere, knew something of this, and once or twice he told Mowgli in so many words that Shere Khan would kill him some day. Mowgli would laugh and answer: "I have the pack and I have you; and Baloo, though he is so lazy, might strike a blow or two for my sake. Why should I be afraid?"

It was one very warm day that a new **notion** came to Bagheera—born of something that he had heard. Perhaps Ikki the Porcupine had told him; but he said to Mowgli when they were deep in the jungle, as the boy lay with his head on Bagheera's beautiful black skin, "Little Brother, how often have I told you that Shere Khan is your enemy?"

"As many times as there are nuts on that palm," said Mowgli, who, naturally, could not count. "What of it? I am sleepy, Bagheera, and Shere Khan is all long tail and loud talk—like Mao, the Peacock."

"But this is no time for sleeping. Baloo knows it; I know it; the pack know it; and even the foolish, foolish deer know. Tabaqui has told you too."

THE JUNGLE STORY

他对视。"然后,年轻的狼们就会全身鬃毛竖起,愤愤不已。

巴格西拉消息十分灵通,对这件事情也有所耳闻。有几次他也费尽口舌告诉莫格里有一天萨克汗会要了他的命,莫格里就会笑着说,"我有狼群和你,还有巴洛,虽说懒惰,也会帮我和他斗的,我有什么可担心的?"

一天,天气暖暖的,巴格西拉突然有了一个新的想法——这个想法来源于他听到的一些事情。也许是豪猪伊基告诉过他的。当他们在丛林深处,男孩把头靠在巴格西拉俊亮的黑色豹皮上的时候,他对莫格里说:"小兄弟,萨克汗是你的敌人,这我对你说了多少回了?"

"说过的次数就像棕榈树上的坚果这么多吧,"莫格里说,当然,他不会数数。"怎么了啊?我很困了,巴格西拉,萨克汗是不是像孔雀玛奥那样,有着长长的尾巴,还爱吹牛?"

"但现在可不是睡觉的时候。巴洛知道这事,我知道,狼群知道,甚至连最最愚蠢的鹿都知道,塔巴奇也告诉过你。"

---

notion *n.* 想法

丛林的故事

"Ho! ho! " said Mowgli. "Tabaqui came to me not long ago with some rude talk that I was a naked man's cub and not fit to dig pig-nuts. But I caught Tabaqui by the tail and swung him twice against a palm-tree to teach him better manners."

"That was foolishness, for though Tabaqui is a mischief-maker, he would have told you of something that **concerned** you closely. Open those eyes, Little Brother. Shere Khan dare not kill you in the jungle. But remember, Akela is very old, and soon the day comes when he cannot kill his buck, and then he will be leader no more. Many of the wolves that looked you over when you was brought to the Council first are old too, and the young wolves believe, as Shere Khan has taught them, that a man-cub has no place with the pack. In a little time you will be a man."

"And what is a man that he should not run with his brothers?" said Mowgli. "I was born in the jungle. I have obeyed the Law of the Jungle, and there is no wolf of ours from whose paws I have not pulled a thorn. Surely they are my brothers! "

Bagheera stretched himself at full length and half shut his eyes. "Little Brother," said he, "feel under my jaw."

Mowgli put up his strong brown hand, and just under

THE JUNGLE STORY

"嘀嘀，"莫格里说，"不久前，塔巴奇来找我还说了些难听的话，说我是光着身子的人类崽子，不配挖落花生吃。但我一把抓住塔巴奇的尾巴，朝棕榈树上甩了两下，让他规矩点。"

"那样做太愚蠢了，虽说塔巴奇是个捣蛋鬼，但他会告诉你一些和你密切相关的事情。睁大你的眼睛，小兄弟。萨克汗不敢在丛林里杀你。但是你要记住，阿克拉已经老了，等到有一天他杀不了一头雄鹿，他就不再是首领了。许多在你第一次被带到狼群大会时审视你的狼也都已经老了。而年轻的狼们相信，正如萨克汗教他们的，一个人类的崽子在狼群里是没有立足之地的。很快你就要长大成人了。"

"长大成人就不能和其他的兄弟们一起奔跑了？"莫格里说，"我是在丛林里出生的。我一直遵守着丛林法则，这里每一头狼，我都帮他们拔过脚上的刺。他们当然是我的兄弟了！"

巴格西拉舒展了他的身子，半闭着眼睛。"小兄弟，"他说，"来摸摸我的下巴底下。"

莫格里伸出他那强壮的棕色的手。在巴格西拉光滑的下巴下面，

concerned *a.* 相关的

Bagheera's silky chin, where the giant **rolling** muscles were all hid by the glossy hair, he came upon a little **bald** spot.

"There is no one in the jungle that knows that I, Bagheera, carry that mark—the mark of the **collar**; and yet, Little Brother, I was born among men, and it was among men that my mother died—in the cages of the king's palace at Oodeypore. It was because of this that I paid the price for you at the Council when you was a little naked cub. Yes, I too was born among men. I had never seen the jungle. They fed me behind bars from an iron pan till one night I felt that I was Bagheer a—the Panther— and no man's plaything, and I broke the silly lock with one blow of my paw and came away. And because I had learned the ways of men, I became more terrible in the jungle than Shere Khan. Is it not so?"

"Yes," said Mowgli, "all the jungle fear Bagheera—all except Mowgli."

"Oh, you are a man's cub," said the Black Panther very tenderly. "And even as I returned to my jungle, so you must go back to men at last—to the men who are your brothers—if you are not killed in the Council."

THE JUNGLE STORY

光泽的毛皮底下是起伏的肌肉。他摸到一块光秃秃的地方。

"丛林里没有一个知道我,巴格西拉,身上带着这个记号——带过颈圈的记号。还有,小兄弟,我是在人类中出生的,我妈妈也是在人类中死去的——死在奥德波王宫的笼子里。这就是为什么当我在狼群大会上看到你这个弱小的赤裸裸的娃娃时,我付出代价保住了你。是的,我也是在人类中出生的。那时我从来没有见过丛林。他们把我关在笼子里,用铁盘给我喂食。直到有一天,我觉得我是巴格西拉——一头豹子——不是人类的玩物,我就用爪子打碎了那把愚蠢的锁,离开了那儿。正是因为我了解人类的习性,在丛林里他们觉得我比萨克汗更可怕,不是吗?"

"是的,"莫格里说,"丛林里所有的动物都怕巴格西拉——除了莫格里。"

"哦,你是人类的娃娃,"黑豹温柔地说,"就像我最终回到了丛林里,你最后也必然要回到人类中——回到你的兄弟们中去——如果你在狼群大会上没有被他们杀死的话。"

·   rolling *a.* 起伏的   bald *a.* 光秃秃的   collar *n.* 领圈

丛林的故事

"But why—but why should they wish to kill me?" said Mowgli.

"Look at me," said Bagheera. And Mowgli looked at him steadily between the eyes. The big panther turned his head away in half a minute.

"That is why," he said, shifting his paw on the leaves. "Not even I can look you between the eyes, and I was born among men, and I love you, Little Brother. The others they hate you because their eyes cannot meet your; because you are wise; because you have pulled out thorns from their feet—because you are a man."

"I did not know these things," said Mowgli sullenly, and he frowned under his heavy black eyebrows.

"What is the Law of the Jungle? Strike first and then give tongue. By your very carelessness they know that you are a man. But be wise. It is in my heart that when Akela misses his next kill—and at each hunt it costs him more to pin the buck—the pack will turn against him and against you. They will hold a jungle Council at the Rock, and then—and then—I have it! " said Bagheera, leaping up. "Go you down quickly to the men's huts in the valley, and take some of the Red Flower which they grow there, so that when the time comes you mayest have even a stronger friend than I or Baloo

THE JUNGLE STORY

"但是,为什么? 为什么他们想要杀我呢? "莫格里说。

"看着我,"巴格西拉说。于是他们四目相对。只过了半分钟,大黑豹就把头扭开了。

"这就是原因。" 他一边说着一边用爪子在树叶上磨蹭,"即使是我,也无法与你对视,小兄弟,我可是在人类中出生的,而且我是爱你的。其他人恨你,因为他们的眼睛不敢与你对视,因为你聪明,因为你帮他们拔脚上的刺,因为你是人类。"

"我不知道这些事情,"莫格里愠怒地说,他皱起浓黑的眉毛。

"丛林法则是怎么说的? 先动手再动口。他们看你粗枝大叶的就知道你是人。你可要放聪明点啊。我心里明白,如果阿克拉下次没有逮到他的猎物——现在每次打猎他要逮住一头雄鹿已经越来越困难了——狼群就会起来反对他,反对你了。他们会在岩石上举行丛林大会,然后——然后——我有办法了。"巴格西拉跳起来说道。"你快下山到山谷中人类住的小屋里,拿些他们种在那里的红花。这样到时候,你就拥有比我或是巴洛或是狼群里爱你的那些狼更加强大的朋友了。快

---

steadily *adv*. 稳固地,不变地   shift *v*. 移动   sullenly *adv*. 愠怒地
frown *v*. 皱眉   pin *v*. 把……困住   leap *v*. 跳越

or those of the pack that love you. Get the Red Flower."

By Red Flower Bagheera meant fire, only no **creature** in the jungle will call fire by its proper name. Every beast lives in deadly fear of it, and invents a hundred ways of describing it.

"The Red Flower?" said Mowgli. "That grows outside their huts in the **twilight**. I will get some."

"There speaks the man's cub," said Bagheera proudly. "Remember that it grows in little pots. Get one swiftly, and keep it by you for time of need."

"Good! " said Mowgli. "I go. But art you sure, O my Bagheera."—he slipped his arm around the splendid neck and looked deep into the big eyes—"Art you sure that all this is Shere Khan's doing?"

"By the Broken Lock that freed me, I am sure, Little Brother."

"Then, by the Bull that bought me, I will pay Shere Khan full tale for this, and it may be a little over," said Mowgli, and he bounded away.

"That is a man. That is all a man," said Bagheera to himself, lying down again. "Oh, Shere Khan, never was a blacker hunting than that frog-hunt of your ten years ago! "

Mowgli was far and far through the forest, running hard, and

THE JUNGLE STORY

去拿些红花。"

巴格西拉所说的红花其实是火。丛林里没有一个动物能准确地称它为火。每个野兽对火都万分恐惧,于是发明了百种描述它的方式。

"红花?"莫格里说,"是傍晚开在他们小屋外的那些吗?我去拿点来。"

"这才是娃娃人说的话。"巴格西拉骄傲地说。"记住它长在小盆子里。快去拿一盆回来,留着它以备日后所需。"

"好的!"莫格里说,"我去,但你能肯定吗,喔,我的巴格西拉。"——他把手臂缠在巴格西拉漂亮的脖子上,深深地凝望着他的大眼睛——"你能肯定这都是萨克汗在搞鬼?"

"以使我获得自由的破锁发誓,我肯定,小兄弟。"

"那么,我以买我的那头公牛发誓,我会让萨克汗为此付出代价的,或许还要更多。"莫格里边说边跳着跑开了。

"这才是人啊,他是个大人了。"巴格西拉自言自语地说,他又重新躺了下来。"噢,萨克汗,从来没有哪次打猎能比你十年前那次捕青蛙更加倒霉了。"

莫格里飞快地跑呀跑,穿过了森林,他的心情无比激动。当傍晚的

---

creature *n.* 生物,动物　　twilight *n.* 暮色,曙光

his heart was hot in him. He came to the cave as the evening mist rose, and drew breath, and looked down the valley. The cubs were out, but Mother Wolf, at the back of the cave, knew by his breathing that something was troubling her frog.

"What is it, Son?" she said.

"Some bat's **chatter** of Shere Khan," he called back. "I hunt among the plowed fields tonight," and he plunged downward through the bushes, to the stream at the bottom of the valley. There he **checked,** for he heard the yell of the pack hunting, heard the bellow of a hunted Sambhur, and the snort as the buck turned at **bay.** Then there were wicked, bitter howls from the young wolves: "Akela! Akela! Let the Lone Wolf show his strength. Room for the leader of the pack! Spring, Akela! "

The Lone Wolf must have sprung and missed his hold, for Mowgli heard the snap of his teeth and then a yelp as the Sambhur knocked him over with his forefoot.

He did not wait for anything more, but **dashed** on; and the yells grew **fainter** behind him as he ran into the croplands where the villagers lived.

THE JUNGLE STORY

薄雾升起的时候,他跑到了山洞。他大口喘着气,看着山下的山谷。狼
崽们都出去了,但是待在洞里边的狼妈妈从他的呼吸中就知道有事情
烦着她的小青蛙。

"怎么了,儿子?"她问道。

"是萨克汗喋喋不休地说了些蠢
话。"他回答说,"我今晚去耕地打猎。"
说着,他就下山冲进了灌木丛里,一直
跑到谷底的小溪边。在那里他突然停
下了,因为他听见狼群打猎的叫嚷声,
听到被捕猎的大公鹿的狂叫声和被困后发出的粗重的鼻息声。接着是
年轻狼们不怀好意地叫嚷声:"阿克拉!阿克拉!让独身狼显显他的威
力。给我们狼群的首领让路吧!跳!阿克拉!"

独身狼想必是纵身一跃,但没逮住他的猎物,因为莫格里听到他
的牙齿喀嚓一声折断的声音,然后大公鹿用前蹄撞倒了阿克拉,阿克
拉发出痛苦的一声大叫。

他听不下去了,继续往前冲。随着他跑进了村民们居住的庄稼地
里,他身后的叫喊声,变得越来越轻,慢慢地消失了。

---

mist *n.* 薄雾   chatter *n.* 喋喋不休   check *v.* 突然停止
bay *n.* 走投无路的处境   dash *v.* 猛冲,飞奔   faint *a.* 微弱的,不明显的

丛林的故事

"Bagheera spoke truth," he panted, as he nestled down in some cattle fodder by the window of a hut. "Tomorrow is one day both for Akela and for me."

Then he pressed his face close to the window and watched the fire on the hearth. He saw the husbandman's wife get up and feed it in the night with black lumps. And when the morning came and the mists were all white and cold, he saw the man's child pick up a wicker pot plastered inside with earth, fill it with lumps of red-hot charcoal, put it under his blanket, and go out to tend the cows in the byre.

"Is that all?" said Mowgli. "If a cub can do it, there is nothing to fear." So he strode round the corner and met the boy, took the pot from his hand, and disappeared into the mist while the boy howled with fear.

"They are very like me," said Mowgli, blowing into the pot as he had seen the woman do. "This thing will die if I do not give it things to eat"; and he dropped twigs and dried bark on the red stuff. Halfway up the hill he met Bagheera with the morning dew shining like moonstones on his coat.

"Akela has missed," said the Panther. "They would have killed

050

　　"巴格西拉说的是真的。"他喘着气在小屋窗户下堆着的牛饲料上舒服地躺了下来,"明天对阿克拉和我都很重要。"

　　然后他把脸贴着窗户,看到了壁炉里的火。他看到农夫的妻子夜里起来把一块块黑色的东西扔到壁炉里。早晨来临了,雾蒙蒙的,还很冷,他看到农夫的孩子拿起一个柳条编的抹了灰泥的小盆,往里面添了些火红的木炭,把它放到自己的毯子底下,然后走到牛棚里喂牛去了。

　　"就是这样啊?"莫格里说,"如果一个小孩也能做,没什么好害怕的。"于是,他大踏步地转过屋角,走到男孩面前,从他手里夺过小盆,然后消失在晨雾里,留下在身后吓得号啕大哭的男孩。

　　"他们和我很像。"莫格里自言自语道,一边对着小盆吹气,他看到农夫的妻子刚才就是这样做的。"如果我不给它东西吃,它会死的。"于是他就朝这红红的东西上扔些小树枝和干树皮。走到半路的时候,他碰到巴格西拉,他身上还带着晨露,在他的皮毛上像月长石一样闪闪发亮。

　　"阿克拉没有逮住他的猎物。"黑豹说,"他们本来昨天晚上就要杀

him last night, but they needed you also. They were looking for you on the hill."

"I was among the plowed lands. I am ready. See!" Mowgli held up the fire-pot.

"Good! Now, I have seen men thrust a dry branch into that stuff, and presently the Red Flower blossomed at the end of it. Art you not afraid?"

"No. Why should I fear? I remember now—if it is not a dream—how, before I was a Wolf, I lay beside the Red Flower, and it was warm and pleasant."

All that day Mowgli sat in the cave tending his fire pot and dipping dry branches into it to see how they looked. He found a branch that satisfied him, and in the evening when Tabaqui came to the cave and told him rudely enough that he was wanted at the Council Rock, he laughed till Tabaqui ran away. Then Mowgli went to the Council, still laughing.

Akela the Lone Wolf lay by the side of his rock as a sign that the leadership of the pack was open, and Shere Khan with his following of scrap-fed wolves walked to and fro openly being flattered. Bagheera lay close to Mowgli, and the fire pot was

THE JUNGLE STORY

了他，但他们还想连你一块杀。刚才他们在山上找你呢。"

"我刚才在耕地里。我准备好了，看！"莫格里举起了火盆。

"很好！我曾经见过人们把干树枝投到这东西里，然后树枝的一头就会盛开红色的花了。你不害怕吗？"

"不害怕。我为什么要害怕？我现在想起来了——如果那不是一个梦的话——在我成为一头狼之前，我曾经躺在红花的旁边，又温暖又舒适。"

那一整天，莫格里就坐在山洞里照料着他的火盆，不断地把干树枝扔到火盆里，看他们烧起来的样子。他找到一根令他满意的树枝。傍晚，当塔巴奇来山洞里找他，粗鲁地通知他去岩石开狼群大会时，他仰天大笑，吓得塔巴奇赶紧逃走了。然后莫格里就动身去狼群大会了，一路上依然大笑着。

独身狼阿克拉躺在他的岩石旁边，表明狼群的首领现在空缺。萨克汗和那群吃他剩食的跟班来来回回地踱着步，神气十足。巴格西拉躺在莫格里的旁边，火盆放在莫格里的膝盖上。等大伙都到齐了，萨克

---

blossom *v.* 开花

053

between Mowgli's knees. When they were all gathered together, Shere Khan began to speak—a thing he would never have dared to do when Akela was in his **prime**.

"He has no right," whispered Bagheera. "Say so. He is a dog's son. He will be frightened."

Mowgli sprang to his feet. "Free People," he cried, "does Shere Khan lead the pack? What has a tiger to do with our leadership?"

"Seeing that the leadership is yet open, and being asked to speak—" Shere Khan began.

"By whom?" said Mowgli. "Are we all jackals, to **fawn** on this cattle butcher? The leadership of the pack is with the pack alone."

There were yells of "Silence, you man's cub! " "Let him speak. He has kept our Law"; and at last the **seniors** of the pack **thundered**: "Let the Dead Wolf speak." When a leader of the pack has missed his kill, he is called the Dead Wolf as long as he lives, which is not long.

Akela raised his old head **wearily**:—

"Free People, and you too, jackals of Shere Khan, for twelve seasons I have led you to and from the kill, and in all that time not one has been trapped or **maimed**. Now I have missed my kill. Ye

THE JUNGLE STORY

汗开始说话了——要是在阿克拉的全盛时期，他根本没胆量这样做。

"他没这个权利。"巴格西拉小声说，"就这么说。他是个狗崽子，他会被吓倒的。"

莫格里跳了起来。"自由的狼群，"他喊道，"萨克汗是我们的首领吗？一只老虎和我们选首领有什么关系？"

"因为你们的首领空缺，而且我是被邀请来发言的——"萨克汗说。

"谁邀请你的？"莫格里说，"难道我们都是豺，得讨好你这个杀耕牛的屠夫吗？狼群选领导是狼群自己的事情。"

这时响起了一片叫嚷声："住嘴，你这个人崽子。""让他说，他一直遵守着我们的法则，"最后是老狼们的怒喝声："让'死狼'说话吧。"当狼群的首领没有捕捉到他的猎物时，只要他还活着就被称为"死狼"，当然他也活不了多久了。

阿克拉艰难地抬起他的头：——

"自由的狼群，还有你们，萨克汗的豺狗们，在过去的12个季节里，我带领你们到处打猎，在这期间，没有一头狼被陷阱捕住或是受了重伤。现在我没捕到我的猎物，你们心里明白这是谁设下的圈套。你们故

---

prime *n.* 全盛时期，壮年　　fawn *v.* 奉承，讨好　　senior *a.* 较年长的
thunder *v.* 怒喝；厉声说出　　wearily *adv.* 疲倦地　　maim *v.* 使残疾；使负重伤

know how that plot was made. Ye know how you brought me up to an untried buck to make my weakness known. It was cleverly done. Your right is to kill me here on the Council Rock, now. Therefore, I ask, who comes to make an end of the Lone Wolf? For it is my right, by the Law of the Jungle, that you come one by one."

There was a long hush, for no single wolf cared to fight Akela to the death. Then Shere Khan roared: "Bah! What have we to do with this toothless fool? He is doomed to die! It is the man-cub who has lived too long. Free People, he was my meat from the first. Give him to me. I am weary of this man-wolf folly. He has troubled the jungle for ten seasons. Give me the man-cub, or I will hunt here always, and not give you one bone. He is a man, a man's child, and from the marrow of my bones I hate him! "

Then more than half the pack yelled: "A man! A man! What has a man to do with us? Let him go to his own place."

"And turn all the people of the villages against us?" clamored Shere Khan. "No, give him to me. He is a man, and none of us can look him between the eyes."

Akela lifted his head again and said, "He has eaten our food. He has slept with us. He has driven game for us. He has broken no

THE JUNGLE STORY

意把我引到年轻力壮的公鹿跟前,好让大伙看到我的虚弱。做得很聪明。你们现在有权利在这会议岩上把我杀死。但是我要问,由谁来结束独身狼的生命呢？根据丛林法则，我有权利让你们一个个过来跟我打。"

接着是很长时间的一段沉默,因为没有一头狼愿意和阿克拉拼个你死我活。然后萨克汗咆哮着说:"呸！我们干吗要理这个没牙的笨蛋呢?他注定得死！倒是这个人崽子活了这么久了。自由的狼群,他从一开始就是我的口中肉。把他交给我,我对这个愚蠢的既是人又是狼的家伙已经厌烦透了。他给丛林惹麻烦已经将近十个季节了。把这个人崽子交给我,否则我就一直在这里狩猎,一块骨头也不会给你们剩下。他是人,人类的孩子,我对他恨之入骨。"

接着超过一半的狼喊着:"人！人！人到我们这里来干什么?让他回到他自己的地方去。"

"难道你们要让整个村子的人和我们作对?"萨克汗嚷道,"不,把他给我。他是个人,我们没有谁敢正视他的眼睛。"

阿克拉又一次抬起他的头说,"他和我们一起吃,一起睡,他为我

---

plot *n.* 秘密计划;计谋　　hush *n.* 沉默　　marrow *n.* 骨髓

word of the Law of the Jungle."

"Also, I paid for him with a bull when he was accepted. The worth of a bull is little, but Bagheera's honor is something that he will perhaps fight for," said Bagheera in his gentlest voice.

"A bull paid ten years ago! " the pack snarled. "What do we care for bones ten years old?"

"Or for a pledge?" said Bagheera, his white teeth bared under his lip. "Well are you called the Free People! "

"No man's cub can run with the people of the jungle," howled Shere Khan. "Give him to me! "

"He is our brother in all but blood," Akela went on, "and you would kill him here! In truth, I have lived too long. Some of you are eaters of cattle, and of others I have heard that, under Shere Khan's teaching, you go by dark night and snatch children from the villager's doorstep. Therefore I know you to be cowards, and it is to cowards I speak. It is certain that I must die, and my life is of no worth, or I would offer that in the man-cub's place. But for the sake of the Honor of the pack,—a little matter that by being without a leader you have forgotten,—I promise that if you let the man-cub go to his own place, I will not, when my time comes to die, bare one

们追逐猎物。他从来没有违反过丛林法则。"

"还有，我付了一头牛的代价才让你们接受他。一头牛是不值什么，但是巴格西拉也许会为了他的荣耀而和你们大战一场。"巴格西拉用他最温柔的声音说。

"一头十年前的牛。"狼群嚎叫起来，"我们怎么会把十年前的牛骨头放在心上？"

"那么誓言呢？"巴格西拉问道，他的嘴巴底下露出了白牙。"这就是所谓的自由的狼群吗？"

"不能让一个人崽子和丛林的动物一起奔跑，"萨克汗叫嚣着，"把他给我！"

"他虽然和我们的血统不同，但他是我们的兄弟，"阿克拉继续说，"而你们却要在这里杀死他！说实话，我活得太久了。你们当中有些成了吃耕牛的狼，还有一些，我听说，在萨克汗的教唆下，趁着黑夜，从村民家门口叼走小孩。所以我知道你们是胆小鬼，我这是和胆小鬼们在说话。当然，我一定会死，我的命值不了什么，否则我会用它来换人娃娃的命。但是为了狼群的名誉——这件小事，因为没有了首领，你们可

---

pledge *n.* 誓言　　snatch *v.* 攫取，绑架

tooth against you. I will die without fighting. That will at least save the pack three lives. More I cannot do; but if you will, I can save you the shame that comes of killing a brother against whom there is no fault—a brother spoken for and bought into the pack according to the Law of the Jungle."

"He is a man—a man—a man!" snarled the pack. And most of the wolves began to gather round Shere Khan, whose tail was beginning to switch.

"Now the business is in your hands," said Bagheera to Mowgli. "We can do no more except fight."

Mowgli stood upright—the fire pot in his hands. Then he stretched out his arms, and yawned in the face of the Council; but he was furious with rage and sorrow, for, wolflike, the wolves had never told him how they hated him. "Listen you! " he cried. "There is no need for this dog's jabber. Ye have told me so often tonight that I am a man (and indeed I would have been a wolf with you to my life's end) that I feel your words are true. So I do not call you my brothers any more, but sag [dogs], as a man should. What you will do, and what you will not do, is not yours to say. That matter is with

THE JUNGLE STORY

能已经忘记了——如果你们让这个人娃娃回到他自己的地方,那么当我的死期到来的时候,我保证牙都不会对你们龇一下,打的时候我一定不反抗。这至少能使狼群里的三头狼免于一死。再多我恐怕做不到,但是如果你们这么做的话,我可以使你们避免蒙上杀死一个无辜兄弟的耻辱,一个依据丛林法则,有动物替他说话,并且有动物付出代价赎买他进狼群的兄弟。"

"他是个人——一个人——人哪!"狼群大声地嚷嚷着。大多数的狼开始聚集在萨克汗周围,萨克汗的尾巴都开始摇了起来。

"现在事情就看你的了。"巴格西拉对莫格里说,"只能打一场了。"

莫格里笔直地站了起来,手里端着火盆。然后他伸开双臂,对着大会打了个哈欠,但是他的心里充满了愤怒和悲伤,因为这些狼真狡猾,从来没有告诉过他,他们这么仇恨他。"听着!"他叫嚷道,"你们不用再唧唧喳喳地说个没完没了。你们今天晚上已经告诉我太多次我是人了,(实际上,本来我这辈子都将和你们一起做一头狼),现在我觉得你们说的是真的。所以我不再称你们是我的兄弟了,而是像人那样,叫你

---

yawn v. 打哈欠　　furious a. 狂怒的

me; and that we may see the matter more plainly, I, the man, have brought here a little of the Red Flower which you, dogs, fear."

He flung the fire pot on the ground, and some of the red coals lit a tuft of dried moss that flared up, as all the Council drew back in terror before the leaping flames.

Mowgli thrust his dead branch into the fire till the twigs lit and crackled, and whirled it above his head among the cowering wolves.

"Thou art the master," said Bagheera in an undertone. "Save Akela from the death. He was ever your friend."

Akela, the grim old wolf who had never asked for mercy in his life, gave one piteous look at Mowgli as the boy stood all naked, his long black hair tossing over his shoulders in the light of the blazing branch that made the shadows jump and quiver.

"Good! " said Mowgli, staring round slowly. "I see that you are dogs. I go from you to my own people—if they be my own people. The jungle is shut to me, and I must forget your talk and your companionship. But I will be more merciful than you are. Because I was all but your brother in blood, I promise that when I am a man among men I will not betray you to men as you have betrayed me." He kicked the fire with his foot, and the sparks flew up. "There

THE JUNGLE STORY

们狗。你们要做什么，不做什么，不是你们说了就算，这事由我做主。我们把事情说得更明白些吧，我，一个人，带来了一些你们这群狗害怕的东西，红花！"

他把火盆扔到地上，火红的木炭点燃了一簇干苔藓，烧了起来。跳动的火焰吓得大会上所有的狼都往后退。

莫格里把枯树枝放到火上点燃了，发出哔哔啪啪的响声。他把树枝在头上回旋，周围的狼都吓得缩成一团。

"现在你说了算。"巴格西拉低声说，"救救阿克拉的命，他至始至终都是你的朋友。"

阿克拉，坚强的老狼，一生中都没有求乞过别人的怜悯。现在他用惹人哀怜的目光看着莫格里。男孩莫格里赤身裸体站着，他的长长的黑发在熊熊燃烧的树枝的光亮下在肩头飘动。许多身影随着火光跳动、颤抖着。

"太好了！"莫格里慢慢地环视着周围说道。"我看出来了，你们的确是狗。我要离开你们回到我自己的人当中去——如果他们是我的自己人的话。丛林已经对我关上门了，我必须忘记和你们的谈话和友谊，但是我会比你们更加仁慈。因为我除了血统以外，曾经算是你们的兄弟。我保证，当我成为人类中的一员时，我不会像你们出卖我那样出卖

---

plainly *adv.* 清楚地，明白地　　undertone *n.* 低声，小声　　quiver *v.* 颤抖　　spark *n.* 火星

shall be no war between any of us in the pack. But here is a debt to pay before I go." He strode forward to where Shere Khan sat blinking stupidly at the flames, and caught him by the tuft on his chin. Bagheera followed in case of accidents. "Up, dog! " Mowgli cried. "Up, when a man speaks, or I will set that coat ablaze! "

Shere Khan's ears lay flat back on his head, and he shut his eyes, for the blazing branch was very near.

"This cattle-killer said he would kill me in the Council because he had not killed me when I was a cub. Thus and thus, then, do we beat dogs when we are men. Stir a whisker, Lungri, and I ram the Red Flower down your gullet! " He beat Shere Khan over the head with the branch, and the tiger whimpered and whined in an agony of fear.

"Pah! Singed jungle cat—go now! But remember when next I come to the Council Rock, as a man should come, it will be with Shere Khan's hide on my head. For the rest, Akela goes free to live as he pleases. Ye will not kill him, because that is not my will. Nor do I think that you will sit here any longer, lolling out your tongues as though you were somebodies, instead of dogs whom I drive out— thus! Go!" The fire was burning furiously at the end of the branch,

THE JUNGLE STORY

你们。"他用脚踢了下火堆,火星飞了起来。"我们和狼群之间将不会有战争。但是在我走之前,还有一笔帐没有算。"他大踏步走向萨克汗,他正傻坐在那里对着火焰眨眼睛。莫格里一把抓住他下巴上的一簇胡须。巴格西拉紧跟着他,以防有意外发生。"起来,"莫格里叫到,"起来,这是人的命令,否则我把你的虎皮都烧了!"

萨克汗的耳朵耷拉在脑袋上,闭上了眼睛,因为燃烧的树枝已经离他很近了。

"这个杀耕牛的家伙说在我小时候他没能杀了我,所以要在狼群大会上杀了我。那么,一下,再来一下,我们人就是这么打狗的。瘸子,你敢动一下胡须,我就把红花塞到你喉咙里去。"他用树枝敲打着萨克汗的脑袋,老虎被恐惧折磨得发出哀叫声。

"哼!被烧焦的丛林野猫——滚吧!但是记住,下次等我作为一个人到会议岩来的时候,头上一定会顶着萨克汗的虎皮。至于其他的事情,阿克拉可以任由它自由地生活。你们不能杀死他,因为我不允许。我也不愿让你们继续坐在这里,伸出舌头,好像你们是多么重要,而不是我要赶走的一群狗。滚吧!"火焰在树枝的一头熊熊地燃烧着,莫格里把它绕着圈到处挥动着,火星溅到狼的皮毛上,他们惨叫着跑开了。

---

agony *n.* 痛苦,折磨   loll *v.* (舌头等)伸出外面   somebody *n.* 重要人物,有名气的人

丛林的故事

and Mowgli struck right and left round the circle, and the wolves ran howling with the sparks burning their fur. At last there were only Akela, Bagheera, and perhaps ten wolves that had taken Mowgli's part. Then something began to hurt Mowgli inside him, as he had never been hurt in his life before, and he caught his breath and sobbed, and the tears ran down his face.

"What is it? What is it?" he said. "I do not wish to leave the jungle, and I do not know what this is. Am I dying, Bagheera?"

"No, Little Brother. That is only tears such as men use," said Bagheera. "Now I know you are a man, and a man's cub no longer. The jungle is shut indeed to you henceforward. Let them fall, Mowgli. They are only tears." So Mowgli sat and cried as though his heart would break; and he had never cried in all his life before.

"Now," he said, "I will go to men. But first I must say farewell to my mother." And he went to the cave where she lived with Father Wolf, and he cried on her coat, while the four cubs howled miserably.

"Ye will not forget me?" said Mowgli.

"Never while we can follow a trail," said the cubs. "Come to the foot of the hill when you are a man, and we will talk to you; and

THE JUNGLE STORY

最后只剩下阿克拉、巴格西拉和站在莫格里这边的十多头狼。突然,莫格里身体里什么地方开始痛了起来,他一生中还从来没有这么痛过,他哽咽了,啜泣了起来,眼泪从脸上流了下来。

"这是什么?这是什么?"他说,"我不想离开丛林,我不知道这是什么。我要死了吗?巴格西拉?"

"不是的,小兄弟。这是人类才有的眼泪。"巴格西拉说。"现在我可以确定你是大人了,不再是小孩了。从今以后,丛林真的对你关上了大门。让他们流下来,莫格里,只是眼泪而已。"于是,莫格里坐在那里大声地哭着,好像他的心都要碎了。在他的一生中,他还从来没有哭过。

"现在,"他说,"我要到人类中去了。但是我得先和妈妈告别。"他回到狼妈妈和狼爸爸居住的山洞,趴在她的身上痛哭,四只小狼悲凄地嚎叫着。

"你们不会忘了我吧?"莫格里说。

"我们可以嗅到你的足迹,不会忘记你的。"狼崽们说,"当你成为人了,你可以到山脚下来和我们聊天,晚上我们可以跟你去庄稼地里

---

henceforward *adv.* 从今以后　　farewell *n.* 告别　　trail *n.* 足迹

067

丛林的故事

we will come into the croplands to play with you by night."

"Come soon! " said Father Wolf. "Oh, wise little frog, come again soon; for we be old, your mother and I."

"Come soon," said Mother Wolf, "little naked son of mine. For, listen, child of man, I loved you more than ever I loved my cubs."

"I will surely come," said Mowgli. "And when I come it will be to lay out Shere Khan's hide upon the Council Rock. Do not forget me! Tell them in the jungle never to forget me! "

The dawn was beginning to break when Mowgli went down the hillside alone, to meet those mysterious things that are called men.

THE JUNGLE STORY

玩耍。"

　　"快点来啊！"狼爸爸说，"噢，聪明的小青蛙，可要快点来；我和你的狼妈妈都已经老了。"

　　"快点来啊，"狼妈妈说，"我光溜溜的小青蛙。听着，人娃娃，我爱你胜过爱我自己的狼崽们。"

　　"我一定会来的，"莫格里说，"等我来的时候，我要在会议岩上铺上萨克汗的毛皮。不要忘了我！告诉丛林里的动物们不要忘了我。"

　　当莫格里独自走下山坡的时候，天快亮了。他要去见那些所谓的神秘的人。

Chapter 2 Hunting-Song of the Seeonee Pack

As the dawn was breaking the Sambhur belled,

Once, twice and again!

And a doe leaped up, and a doe leaped up,

From the pond in the wood where the wild deer sup.

This I, scouting alone, beheld,

Once, twice and again!

As the dawn was breaking the Sambhur belled,

Once, twice and again!

And a wolf stole back, and a wolf stole back,

To carry the word to the waiting pack,

And we sought and we found and we bayed on his track,

Once, twice and again!

As the dawn was breaking the Wolf Pack yelled,

THE JUNGLE STORY

第二章　西奥尼狼群狩猎之歌

天将破晓,大公鹿在鸣叫,

一次,两次,反反复复!

一头母鹿跃起,一头母鹿跃起,

从野鹿喝水的丛林的池塘里跃起。

我在这里,独自侦察,凝目注视,

一次,两次,反反复复!

天将破晓,大公鹿在鸣叫,

一次,两次,反反复复!

一头狼悄悄地回来,一头狼悄悄地回来,

给等候的狼群带回了消息,

沿着他的足迹,我们寻找,我们发现,我们嚎叫,

一次,两次,反反复复!

天将破晓,狼群在嚎叫,

---

scout *v.* 侦察　　behold *v.* 看,注视

丛林的故事

Once, twice and again!
Feet in the jungle that leave no mark!

Eyes that can see in the dark—the dark!
Tongue—give tongue to it! Hark! O hark!
Once, twice and again!

THE JUNGLE STORY

一次,两次,反反复复!
爪子在丛林里飞奔却不留下印记!

眼睛穿透破晓前的黑暗——那黑暗!
向着猎物嚎叫——大声地嚎叫!听!噢,听!
一次,两次,反反复复!

Chapter 3 Kaa's Hunting

His spots are the joy of the Leopard: his horns are the Buffalo's pride.

Be clean, for the strength of the hunter is known by the **gloss** of his hide.

If you find that the Bullock can toss you, or the heavy-browed Sambhur can gore;

Ye need not stop work to **inform** us: we knew it ten seasons before.

Oppress not the cubs of the stranger, but **hail** them as Sister and Brother,

For though they are little and fubsy, it may be the Bear is their mother.

"There is none like to me! " says the Cub in the pride of his earliest kill;

But the jungle is large and the Cub he is small.

Let him think and be still.

Maxims of Baloo

THE JUNGLE STORY

第三章　蟒蛇卡阿捕猎

斑点是豹子的快乐；犄角是水牛的骄傲。

要遵守法则，因为从光泽的皮毛上可以看出猎手的力量。

如果你发现小公牛能把你抛起，或者浓眉的大公鹿能用鹿角抵你；

你不必停下工作来告诉我们：我们十个季节之前就已经知晓。

不要欺负陌生的娃娃，要像对待兄弟姐妹一样招呼他们，

因为虽然他们又小又胖，但熊也许就是他们的妈妈。

"我是多么与众不同！"人娃娃第一次捕杀了猎物后得意地说。

但是丛林是广袤的，而人娃娃还小。

让他思考，保持沉默。

　　　　　　　　　　　　　　　　　　——巴洛箴言

---

gloss *n.* 光泽　　　inform *v.* 通知,告知　　　hail *v.* 招呼　　　maxim *n.* 座右铭,箴言

丛林的故事

All that is told here happened some time before Mowgli was turned out of the Seeonee Wolf Pack, or revenged himself on Shere Khan the tiger. It was in the days when Baloo was teaching him the Law of the Jungle. The big, serious, old brown bear was delighted to have so quick a pupil, for the young wolves will only learn as much of the Law of the Jungle as applies to their own pack and tribe, and run away as soon as they can repeat the Hunting Verse—"Feet that make no noise; eyes that can see in the dark; ears that can hear the winds in their lairs, and sharp white teeth, all these things are the marks of our brothers except Tabaqui the Jackal and the Hyaena whom we hate." But Mowgli, as a man-cub, had to learn a great deal more than this. Sometimes Bagheera the Black Panther would come lounging through the jungle to see how his pet was getting on, and would purr with his head against a tree while Mowgli recited the day's lesson to Baloo. The boy could climb almost as well as he could swim, and swim almost as well as he could run. So Baloo, the Teacher of the Law, taught him the Wood and Water Laws: how to tell a rotten branch from a sound one; how to speak politely to the wild bees when he came upon a hive of

THE JUNGLE STORY

　　这里讲述的故事是发生在莫格里被赶出西奥尼狼群之前的,或者说是在他向老虎萨克汗报仇之前的故事。那是在巴洛教他丛林法则的那些日子里。这个胖胖的严肃的老棕熊很高兴有这个聪明的学生,因为狼崽子们只愿意学习适用在他们自己狼群、部落里的丛林法则,一旦他们能背诵捕猎诗了,他们就跑开了。——"脚下没有声音,眼睛透视黑夜,耳朵能听穴中风,白白的牙齿锋又利,所有这些都是我们兄弟的特征,除了豺狗塔巴奇和我们憎恨的鬣狗。"但是,莫格里,这个人娃娃,要学习的东西就比这多多了。有时候,黑豹巴格西拉漫步穿过丛林,来看看他的宝贝学得怎么样了。当莫格里向巴洛背诵今天学习的内容时,巴格西拉总是把头靠在树上,发出呼呼的声音。这个男孩子爬树像他游泳一样快,游泳又像他跑步一样快。因此,巴洛,这个丛林法则老师,又教他树林和水的法则:如何区分一根烂树枝和一根好树枝;当他在离地面五十英尺的地方碰上蜂窝,如何礼貌地和野蜜蜂打招呼;当他正午在树枝上打扰了蝙蝠曼尼时,应该怎么道歉;在他跳下水

---

lounge *v.* 闲荡　　**recite** *v.* 背诵;朗诵

them fifty feet above ground; what to say to Mang the Bat when he disturbed him in the branches at midday; and how to warn the water-snakes in the pools before he splashed down among them. None of the Jungle People like being disturbed, and all are very ready to fly at an **intruder**. Then, too, Mowgli was taught the Strangers' Hunting Call, which must be repeated aloud till it is answered, whenever one of the Jungle-people hunts outside his own grounds. It means, translated, "Give me **leave** to hunt here because I am hungry." And the answer is, "Hunt then for food, but not for pleasure."

All this will show you how much Mowgli had to learn by heart, and he grew very tired of saying the same thing over a hundred times. But, as Baloo said to Bagheera, one day when Mowgli had been cuffed and run off in a temper, "A man's cub is a man's cub, and he must learn all the Law of the Jungle."

"But think how small he is," said the Black Panther, who would have spoiled Mowgli if he had had his own way. "How can his little head carry all your long talk?"

"Is there anything in the jungle too little to be killed? No. That is why I teach him these things, and that is why I hit him, very

THE JUNGLE STORY

池之前,如何警告水中的水蛇注意。没有一个丛林成员喜欢被打扰,当有入侵者来临时,全都做好了飞走的准备。于是,他又教莫格里陌生者打猎时如何喊叫, 这是当丛林成员在自己的狩猎地以外的地方打猎时,必须大声喊的,直到有人回答。这个喊叫的意思就是说:"请允许我在这儿打猎,因为我饿了。"回答是:"那么为食物打猎吧,不能为了好玩而打猎。"

所有的这些都能向你证明,莫格里记住了多少东西,他对于上百遍地重复相同的东西感到非常厌倦了。但是,一天当莫格里挨了巴掌,气呼呼地跑掉时,巴洛对巴格西拉说:"人娃娃就是人娃娃,他必须学会所有的丛林法则。"

"但是想想他还这么小,"黑豹说(如果他一直这样对莫格里的话,一定会把他宠坏的)。"他这个小脑袋怎么能装下你所有的长篇大论呢?"

"这个丛林里有什么动物会因为太小而不会被杀?不可能。这就是

<hr>

intruder *n.* 入侵者　　leave *n.* 许可

softly, when he forgets."

"Softly! What dost you know of softness, old Iron-feet?" Bagheera grunted. "His face is all bruised today by your— softness. Ugh."

"Better he should be bruised from head to foot by me who love him than that he should come to harm through ignorance," Baloo answered very earnestly. "I am now teaching him the Master Words of the Jungle that shall protect him with the birds and the Snake People, and all that hunt on four feet, except his own pack. He can now claim protection, if he will only remember the words, from all in the jungle. Is not that worth a little beating?"

"Well, look to it then that you dost not kill the man-cub. He is no tree trunk to sharpen your blunt claws upon. But what are those Master Words? I am more likely to give help than to ask it" —Bagheera stretched out one paw and admired the steel-blue, ripping-chisel talons at the end of it—"still I should like to know."

"I will call Mowgli and he shall say them—if he will. Come, Little Brother! "

"My head is ringing like a bee tree," said a sullen little voice over their heads, and Mowgli slid down a tree trunk very angry and

为什么我要教他这些东西,为什么他忘记的时候我要轻轻地打他。"

"轻轻地打! 你这个老铁爪,知道什么是轻轻地?"巴格西拉嘀咕着,"今天他的脸就因为你轻轻地打全都青了。哼! "

"宁可让他被爱他的我打得从头到脚都青了,也比因为无知而受到伤害好吧。"巴洛真诚地说,"现在我正在教他丛林密语,这能使他在除了自己的种群之外,在鸟类、蛇类和四只脚着地捕猎的动物那里得到保护。如果他记住了这些密语,他可以从丛林中所有的动物那里寻求保护。这轻轻的一顿打还不值得吗?"

"那么,小心点,别打死了人娃娃。他可不是给你磨钝爪子的树干。但是,什么是丛林密语啊?我不问密语就会帮他一把了。"——巴格西拉伸出一个爪子,欣赏着他那铁青色、凿子般的爪尖——"但是,我还是想知道那是什么。"

"我叫莫格里来,如果他愿意的话,让他来说。来,小兄弟! "

"我的头像是有蜜蜂筑巢的蜂树一样嗡嗡地响,"一个闷闷不乐的声音在他们头上响起,莫格里气乎乎地从树干上滑下来,滑到地上的

---

ignorance *n.* 无知　　earnestly *adv.* 诚挚地　　claim *v.* 要求,索取
admire *v.* 赞美,钦佩

indignant, adding as he reached the ground: "I come for Bagheera and not for you, fat old Baloo! "

"That is all one to me," said Baloo, though he was hurt and grieved. "Tell Bagheera, then, the Master Words of the Jungle that I have taught you this day."

"Master Words for which people?" said Mowgli, delighted to show off. "The jungle has many tongues. I know them all."

"A little you knowest, but not much. See, O Bagheera, they never thank their teacher. Not one small wolfling has ever come back to thank old Baloo for his teachings. Say the word for the Hunting-People, then—great scholar."

"We be of one blood, you and I," said Mowgli, giving the words the Bear accent which all the Hunting People use.

"Good. Now for the birds."

Mowgli repeated, with the Kite's whistle at the end of the sentence.

"Now for the Snake-People," said Bagheera.

The answer was a perfectly indescribable hiss, and Mowgli kicked up his feet behind, clapped his hands together to applaud himself, and jumped on to Bagheera's

THE JUNGLE STORY

时候又补充了一句:"我是为了巴格西拉来的,可不是为了你,肥老巴洛!"

"这对我来说是一样的,"巴洛说,虽然他感到受了伤害,也挺难受的,"那么告诉巴格西拉今天我教你的丛林密语。"

"哪个种群的丛林密语?"莫格里问,高兴地想显摆一下,"丛林里有那么多种语言,我都懂。"

"你知道一些,不是很多。看,哦,巴格西拉,他们从来不感谢他们的老师。从没有一只小狼回来谢谢老巴洛教给他知识。那么就说说捕猎兽群的密语吧,伟大的学者。"

"我们是同一血统的,你和我。"莫格里用熊的腔调说,捕猎的兽群都用这种腔调。

"很好,现在说鸟类的密语。"

莫格里说了,最后结尾处还加上了一声鸢的啸叫。

"现在说蛇类的密语。"巴格西拉说。

这次是一个难以形容的咝咝声。莫格里把腿往后踢起,拍着手为自己鼓掌,然后跳到巴格西拉的背上。他斜坐在一边,用脚后跟在黑豹

---

indignant *adj.* 愤怒的,愤慨的   grieve *v.* 悲痛,伤心   indescribable *a.* 难以形容地
applaud *v.* 鼓掌

back, where he sat **sideways**, drumming with his heels on the glossy skin and making the worst faces he could think of at Baloo.

"There there! That was worth a little bruise," said the brown bear tenderly. "Some day you will remember me." Then he turned aside to tell Bagheera how he had begged the Master Words from Hathi the Wild Elephant, who knows all about these things, and how Hathi had taken Mowgli down to a pool to get the Snake Word from a water-snake, because Baloo could not pronounce it, and how Mowgli was now reasonably safe against all accidents in the jungle, because neither snake, bird, nor beast would hurt him.

"No one then is to be feared," Baloo wound up, patting his big furry stomach with pride.

"Except his own tribe," said Bagheera, under his breath; and then aloud to Mowgli, "Have a care for my ribs, Little Brother! What is all this dancing up and down?"

Mowgli had been trying to make himself heard by pulling at Bagheera's shoulder fur and kicking hard. When the two listened to him he was shouting at the top of his voice, "And so I shall have a tribe of my own, and lead them through the branches all day long."

THE JUNGLE STORY

有光泽的皮毛上打着拍子,还对巴洛做着最难看的鬼脸。

"嗯,不错!那一点点淤青还是值得的。"棕熊柔声说,"总有一天,你会记得我的。"然后他转向巴格西拉,告诉他自己是如何请求知道一切密语的大象海蒂,把密语告诉他的;海蒂是如何带着莫格里去池塘,从一条水蛇那里得到蛇类的密语的,因为巴洛发不出这个音;莫格里是如何在丛林里经历了大大小小的意外后仍然平平安安的,因为不管是蛇类、鸟类还是野兽都不会伤害他。

"这样就不用怕谁了。"巴洛蜷起身子,骄傲地拍着他肥肥的、毛绒绒的肚子。

"除了他自己的种群,"巴格西拉低声说。然后他又大声对莫格里说,"小心我的肋骨,小兄弟!这跳上跳下的是在干什么?"

莫格里为了让他们俩听见他说话,拼命地扯着巴格西拉肩膀上的毛,不停地踢着腿。当他俩听他说话时,莫格里高声地喊道,"所以我要有一个我自己的部落,带着他们整天在树林里穿梭。"

---

sideways adv. 斜向一边

丛林的故事

"What is this new folly, little dreamer of dreams?" said Bagheera.

"Yes, and throw branches and dirt at old Baloo," Mowgli went on. "They have promised me this. Ah! "

"Whoof ! " Baloo's big paw scooped Mowgli off Bagheera's back, and as the boy lay between the big fore-paws he could see the Bear was angry.

"Mowgli," said Baloo, "you have been talking with the Bandar-log—the Monkey People."

Mowgli looked at Bagheera to see if the Panther was angry too, and Bagheera's eyes were as hard as jade stones.

"You have been with the Monkey People—the gray apes—the people without a law—the eaters of everything. That is great shame."

"When Baloo hurt my head," said Mowgli (he was still on his back), "I went away, and the gray apes came down from the trees and had pity on me. No one else cared." He snuffled a little.

"The pity of the Monkey People!" Baloo snorted. "The stillness of the mountain stream! The cool of the summer sun! And then, man-cub?"

THE JUNGLE STORY

"这是什么骇人听闻的傻话啊,异想天开的梦想者?"巴格西拉说。

"是的，他们还答应我，"莫格里继续说,"要向老巴洛扔树枝、污泥。哈！"

"噗！"巴洛的大爪子把莫格里从巴格西拉的背上拨了下来。男孩躺在他的大脚爪间,他看出那头熊生气了。

"莫格里,"巴洛说,"你一直在和那群猴子商量吧。"

莫格里看着巴格西拉,想瞧瞧豹子是不是也生气了,但巴格西拉的眼睛像玉石一样冰冷。

"你和猴子们在一块——那些灰猿——没有法律的种族——他们什么都吃。那可真是丢脸。"

"刚才巴洛打我的头,"莫格里说(他仍然躺在地上),"我跑开了。灰猿们从树上跑下来,只有他们同情我,没人在乎我了。"他抽抽了鼻子。

"猴子的同情！"巴洛哼了一声,"就像山涧的溪水静止了,夏天的太阳变凉了！然后呢,人娃娃?"

jade *n.* 玉

087

丛林的故事

"And then, and then, they gave me nuts and pleasant things to eat, and they—they carried me in their arms up to the top of the trees and said I was their blood brother except that I had no tail, and should be their leader some day."

"They have no leader," said Bagheera. "They lie. They have always lied."

"They were very kind and bade me come again. Why have I never been taken among the Monkey People? They stand on their feet as I do. They do not hit me with their hard paws. They play all day. Let me get up! Bad Baloo, let me up! I will play with them again."

"Listen, man-cub," said the Bear, and his voice rumbled like thunder on a hot night. "I have taught you all the Law of the Jungle for all the peoples of the jungle—except the Monkey-Folk who live in the trees. They have no law. They are outcasts. They have no speech of their own, but use the stolen words which they overhear when they listen, and peep, and wait up above in the branches. Their way is not our way. They are without leaders. They have no remembrance. They boast and chatter and pretend that they are a

THE JUNGLE STORY

"然后,然后,他们给我坚果和好吃的东西,他们,他们抬着我一直到树顶,说我是他们同一血脉的兄弟,只是我没有尾巴,还说我有一天会成为他们的首领。"

"他们没有首领,"巴格西拉说,"他们撒谎,他们总是撒谎。"

"他们很友善的,还邀请我再去呢。为什么你从来没带我去过猴群那里?他们和我一样能站立,他们不用硬爪子打我。他们整天都在玩。让我起来!坏巴洛,让我起来!我要再去和他们玩!"

"听着,人娃娃,"棕熊吼道,他的声音就像炎热的晚上打的闷雷。"我已经教会了你丛林中所有种群的丛林法则——除了住在树上的猴群。因为他们没有法则,他们是被驱逐出去的。他们没有自己的语言,而是用那些他们在树上呆着偷听偷窥时听到的话交流。他们的生活方式和我们不一样。他们没有首领,没有记忆力,喋喋不休地吹牛,假装他们是伟大的种群,要在丛林里做伟大的事情,但是树上掉个果子就会让他们大笑一通,然后把所有的事情都忘记了。我们丛林里的动物

---

bid *v.* 邀请   outcast *n.* 被遗弃者   overhear *v.* 偷听,无意中听到
remembrance *n.* 记忆力   boast *v.* 吹牛

089

great people about to do great affairs in the jungle, but the falling of a nut turns their minds to laughter and all is forgotten. We of the jungle have no **dealings** with them. We do not drink where the monkeys drink; we do not go where the monkeys go; we do not hunt where they hunt; we do not die where they die. Hast you ever heard me speak of the Bandar-log till today?"

"No," said Mowgli in a whisper, for the forest was very still now Baloo had finished.

"The Jungle-people put them out of their mouths and out of their minds. They are very many, evil, dirty, shameless, and they desire, if they have any fixed desire, to be noticed by the Jungle People. But we do not notice them even when they throw nuts and filth on our heads."

He had hardly spoken when a shower of nuts and twigs spattered down through the branches; and they could hear coughings and howlings and angry jumpings high up in the air among the thin branches.

"The Monkey-People are forbidden," said Baloo, "forbidden to the Jungle-people. Remember."

"Forbidden," said Bagheera, "but I still think Baloo should have warned you against them."

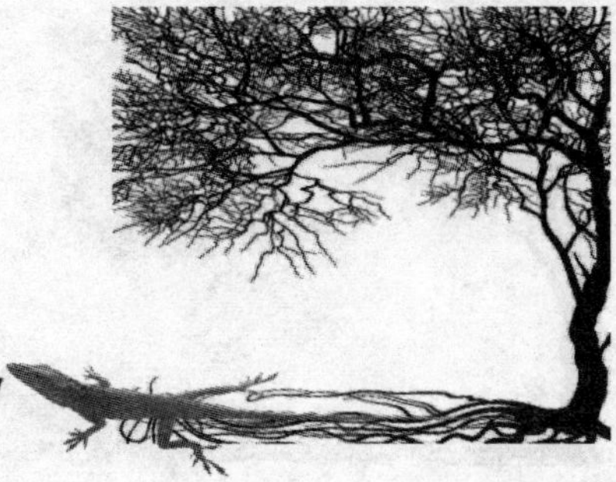

THE JUNGLE STORY

从来不和他们来往。我们不在猴子喝水的地方喝水;我们不去猴子去的地方;我们不在猴子猎食的地方猎食;我们不在猴子死的地方死。直到今天你有没有听我说起过猴子?"

"没有,"莫格里低声说,巴洛已经说完了,所以整个树林都静悄悄的。

"丛林动物把他们从自己的口中赶了出去,也把他们从自己的脑海中赶了出去。他们数量巨多,非常邪恶、肮脏、无耻,如果他们还有什么不变的愿望的话,那就是他们非常希望引起<u>丛林动物</u>的注意。但是即使他们在我们头上扔坚果、脏东西,我们也不会注意他们。"

他还没说完,一阵坚果、小树枝就从树上透过树枝的缝隙撒了下来,他们听到在高处细细的树枝间的咳嗽声、哀嚎声和猴子生气地上窜下跳的声音。

"丛林兽民不许和猴子来往,"巴洛说,"记住!"

"对,不许,"巴格西拉说,"但是我还是认为巴洛早就该警告你了。"

---

dealing *n*. 来往

"I—I? How was I to guess he would play with such dirt. The Monkey People! Faugh! "

A fresh shower came down on their heads and the two trotted away, taking Mowgli with them. What Baloo had said about the monkeys was perfectly true. They belonged to the tree-tops, and as beasts very seldom look up, there was no occasion for the monkeys and the Jungle-people to cross each other's path. But whenever they found a sick wolf, or a wounded tiger, or bear, the monkeys would torment him, and would throw sticks and nuts at any beast for fun and in the hope of being noticed. Then they would howl and shriek senseless songs, and invite the Jungle-people to climb up their trees and fight them, or would start furious battles over nothing among themselves, and leave the dead monkeys where the Jungle-people could see them. They were always just going to have a leader, and laws and customs of their own, but they never did, because their memories would not hold over from day to day, and so they compromised things by making up a saying, "What the Bandar-log think now the jungle will think later," and that comforted them a great deal. None of the beasts could reach them, but on the other hand none of the beasts would notice them, and that was why

THE JUNGLE STORY

"我——我？我怎么猜得到他会和这些卑鄙的家伙玩。猴群！呸！"

又是一阵雨一样的东西砸了下来,他们两个带上莫格里快步走开了。巴洛所说的关于猴群的一切都是千真万确的。他们住在树的顶端,因为野兽们很少会抬头看,猴子和丛林兽民也没什么机会在路上相遇。但是一旦他们发现一头生病的狼、受伤的老虎或者熊,猴子们就会折磨他;或者为了好玩,引起其他动物的注意,他们会向任何一头野兽扔树枝和坚果。然后啸叫着,尖声地唱些毫无意义的歌,引丛林兽民爬上树和他们打架;或者他们自己彼此之间会毫无缘故地进行激烈的打斗,把死猴子留在丛林兽民能看到的地方。他们总希望有个首领、有自己的法律和习俗,但他们从来都没有这样去做,因为他们的记忆力往往保持不了一天。所以他们总会编造一种说法来解释,"猴子们现在所想的,丛林兽民以后会想到的。"这给了他们极大的安慰。没有兽民能够得着他们,另一方面也没有兽民会注意到他们,这就是为什么当莫

---

torment v. 折磨　　furious a. 猛烈的,强烈的　　compromise v. 妥协,让步

丛林的故事

they were so pleased when Mowgli came to play with them, and they heard how angry Baloo was.

They never meant to do any more—the Bandar-log never mean anything at all; but one of them invented what seemed to him a brilliant idea, and he told all the others that Mowgli would be a useful person to keep in the tribe, because he could weave sticks together for protection from the wind; so, if they caught him, they could make him teach them. Of course Mowgli, as a woodcutter's child, **inherited** all sorts of **instincts**, and used to make little huts of fallen branches without thinking how he came to do it. The Monkey-People, watching in the trees, considered his play most wonderful. This time, they said, they were really going to have a leader and become the wisest people in the jungle —so wise that everyone else would notice and envy them. Therefore they followed Baloo and Bagheera and Mowgli through the jungle very quietly till it was time for the midday nap, and Mowgli, who was very much ashamed of himself, slept between the Panther and the Bear, **resolving** to have no more to do with the Monkey People.

The next thing he remembered was feeling hands on his legs and arms—hard, strong, little hands—and then a swash of branches

格里去和他们玩的时候,他们会如此高兴,他们也听到了巴洛有多生气。

　　他们从来没有打算多做点事情——猴子根本就不会打算。但是他们中有一只猴子想出了一个自以为了不起的主意,他告诉其他猴子,莫格里留在猴子部落里将会成为一个有用的人,因为他会把小树枝编起来挡风,所以,如果猴子们抓住了他,可以让莫格里教他们。当然,莫格里作为一个樵夫的孩子,继承了樵夫所有的天赋,他总是用落在地上的树枝搭起一个小棚子,尽管他没有想过他怎么会这样做的。猴群在树上看着他,认为他干得太棒了。这次,他们说,他们真的要有一位首领了,马上要变成丛林里最聪明的种群了——聪明得让每一个动物都注意到他们,嫉妒他们。因此他们静悄悄地跟着巴洛、巴格西拉和莫格里穿过丛林一直到中午午睡的时候。内心感到十分羞愧的莫格里,躺在豹子和熊的中间,心里暗暗下了决心,再也不和猴民们来往了。

　　接下来莫格里记得的事情是,他感觉到有一些手放在他的手臂和

---

inherit *v.* 继承　　instinct *n.* 本能,天赋　　resolve *v.* 决心

in his face, and then he was staring down through the swaying boughs as Baloo woke the jungle with his deep cries and Bagheera bounded up the trunk with every tooth bared. The Bandar-log howled with triumph and scuffled away to the upper branches where Bagheera dared not follow, shouting: "He has noticed us! Bagheera has noticed us. All the Jungle-people admire us for our skill and our cunning." Then they began their flight; and the flight of the Monkey-People through tree-land is one of the things nobody can describe. They have their regular roads and crossroads, up hills and down hills, all laid out from fifty to seventy or a hundred feet above ground, and by these they can travel even at night if necessary. Two of the strongest monkeys caught Mowgli under the arms and swung off with him through the treetops, twenty feet at a bound. Had they been alone they could have gone twice as fast, but the boy's weight held them back. Sick and giddy as Mowgli was he could not help enjoying the wild rush, though the glimpses of earth far down below frightened him, and the terrible check and jerk at the end of the swing over nothing but empty air brought his heart between his teeth. His escort would rush him up a tree till he felt

THE JUNGLE STORY

腿上——一些粗糙的、强壮的小手——然后有树枝在脸上一阵拍打，接着他透过摇晃的树枝往下看，巴洛低沉的吼叫似乎把整个丛林都唤醒了，他龇牙咧嘴往树上跳。猴子们胜利地欢呼着，急匆匆地跑到巴格西拉不敢跟上来的高高的树枝上，高声喊着："他注意到我们了！巴格西拉注意到我们了！所有的丛林兽民都钦佩我们的本领和智慧。"接着他们开始了树间行走，猴子在树间的行走是一件没有人能描述的事情。他们在山上山下都有自己固定的道路和支路，全都在离地面五十到七十或者一百英尺的地方，这样，必要的时候即使在晚上，他们也能行走。两只最强壮的猴子抓住莫格里的手臂，带着他荡过一个个枝头，一下子能跳过二十英尺。如果他们自己跳的话，可以比现在快两倍，但男孩的体重妨碍了他们。虽然莫格里感到头晕恶心，虽然瞥一眼远远在下面的地面让他害怕，虽然这种在空旷的空中摇荡后突然停下和它带来的往前的冲力使他的心提到了嗓子眼，但他还是情不自禁地喜欢这种狂奔。他的护送者把他推到一棵树上，直到他觉得树顶最柔嫩的

---

triumph *n.* 胜利　　escort *n.* 护卫队,护送者

the thinnest topmost branches crackle and bend under them, and then with a cough and a whoop would fling themselves into the air outward and downward, and bring up, hanging by their hands or their feet to the lower limbs of the next tree. Sometimes he could see for miles and miles across the still green jungle, as a man on the top of a mast can see for miles across the sea, and then the branches and leaves would lash him across the face, and he and his two guards would be almost down to earth again. So, bounding and crashing and whooping and yelling, the whole tribe of Bandar-log swept along the tree-roads with Mowgli their prisoner.

For a time he was afraid of being dropped. Then he grew angry but knew better than to struggle, and then he began to think. The first thing was to send back word to Baloo and Bagheera, for, at the pace the monkeys were going, he knew his friends would be left far behind. It was useless to look down, for he could only see the topsides of the branches, so he stared upward and saw, far away in the blue, Rann the Kite balancing and wheeling as he kept watch over the jungle waiting for things to die. Rann saw that the monkeys were carrying something, and dropped a few hundred yards to find

THE JUNGLE STORY

树枝在他们身下吱吱嘎嘎地作响,树枝都弯了,然后随着一声咳嗽和高喊,他们把自己在空中荡了起来,然后突然停下,用手或者脚挂在旁边一颗树的矮枝上。有时候他能越过郁郁葱葱的丛林看到连绵数里外的地方,就像一个站在桅杆顶端的人能看到海上数里以外的地方。接着有树枝、树叶打在他的脸上,他和他的两个守卫差点又到了地上。就这样跳跃着,碰撞着,欢呼着,嚎叫着,整个猴群带着他们的囚犯莫格里在树道上一路狂奔。

有一阵子,他害怕会掉下去。然后他生起气来,但他知道不能挣扎,于是他开始思考。首先要做的是捎话给巴洛和巴格西拉,因为按照猴子们现在的前进速度,他知道他的朋友们被远远地抛在了后面。往下看是没有用的,因为他只能看到树顶,所以他只好抬头往上看,看到远远的蓝天中,鸢鹰兰恩正在丛林上方回旋,盯着丛林,等待他的猎物。兰恩看到猴子们抬着个什么东西,于是飞下了几百英尺,想看看他

---

pace *n.* 速度

099

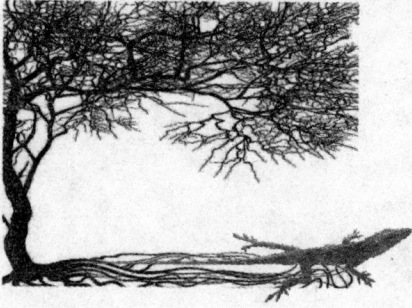

丛林的故事

out whether their load was good to eat. He whistled with surprise when he saw Mowgli being dragged up to a treetop and heard him give the Kite call for—"We be of one blood, you and I." The waves of the branches closed over the boy, but Chil balanced away to the next tree in time to see the little brown face come up again. "Mark my trail! " Mowgli shouted. "Tell Baloo of the Seeonee Pack and Bagheera of the Council Rock."

"In whose name, Brother?" Rann had never seen Mowgli before, though of course he had heard of him.

"Mowgli, the Frog. Man-cub they call me! Mark my tra-il! "

The last words were shrieked as he was being swung through the air, but Rann nodded and rose up till he looked no bigger than a speck of dust, and there he hung, watching with his telescope eyes the swaying of the treetops as Mowgli's escort whirled along.

"They never go far," he said with a chuckle. "They never do what they set out to do. Always pecking at new things are the Bandar-log. This time, if I have any eye-sight, they have pecked down trouble for themselves, for Baloo is no fledgling and Bagheera can, as I know, kill more than goats."

So he rocked on his wings, his feet gathered up under him, and waited.

THE JUNGLE STORY

们抬的是不是好吃的。当他看到莫格里被拖到树顶,听到他发出鸢鹰的呼叫——"我们是同一血脉的,你和我",兰恩发出惊奇地啸叫。起伏的树枝淹没了男孩,但是鸢鹰朝着第二棵树飞去,正好看见那张棕色的小脸又出现了。"记住我的路线,"莫格里喊道,"告诉西奥尼狼群的巴洛和会议岩的巴格西拉。"

"以谁的名义,兄弟?"兰恩以前从来没见过莫格里,当然尽管他听说过莫格里的名字。

"青蛙莫格里。他们叫我人娃娃!记住我的路——线!"

最后几个字是尖叫着喊出来的,因为他被荡到了半空中。但是兰恩点了点头,高高地飞起,直到他看上去像个小黑点。他停在那里,用他望远镜般的眼睛盯着莫格里护送者急速前进时晃起的树枝。

"他们永远走不远,"他笑着说,"他们从不会去做他们打算好的事情。猴子们总是不停地找新鲜的事情去做。这次,如果我没看走眼的话,他们是给自己找了个大麻烦了,因为巴洛可不是个初出茅庐的,而巴格西拉,据我所知,可不止会猎杀山羊。"

所以他挥动着翅膀,把双脚收起,等待着。

---

speck *n.* 斑点　　rock *v.* 摇动,摆动

丛林的故事

Meantime, Baloo and Bagheera were furious with rage and **grief**. Bagheera climbed as he had never climbed before, but the thin branches broke beneath his weight, and he slipped down, his claws full of bark.

"Why did you not warn the man-cub?" he roared to poor Baloo, who had set off at a **clumsy** trot in the hope of overtaking the monkeys. "What was the use of half slaying him with blows if you didst not warn him?"

"Haste! O haste! We—we may catch them yet!" Baloo panted.

"At that speed! It would not tire a wounded cow. Teacher of the Law—cub-beater—a mile of that rolling to and fro would burst you open. Sit still and think! Make a plan. This is no time for chasing. They may drop him if we follow too close."

"Arrula! Whoo! They may have dropped him already, being tired of carrying him. Who can trust the Bandar-log? Put dead bats on my head! Give me black bones to eat! Roll me into the hives of the wild bees that I may be stung to death, and bury me with the Hyaena, for I am most miserable of bears! Arulala! Wahooa! O

THE JUNGLE STORY

与此同时,巴洛和巴格西拉正暴跳如雷。从来没有爬过树的巴格西拉爬上了树,但是细细的树枝承受不了他的体重而折断了,他滑了下来,爪子里都是树皮。

"你为什么不警告人娃娃?"他对可怜的巴洛吼着,巴洛笨拙地快跑着,希望能赶上猴子。"你不警告他,只用拳头把他打个半死有什么用呢?"

"快点!哦,快点!我们——我们也许还能赶上他们!"巴洛喘着气说。

"就这样的速度!一头受伤的母牛都不会累。丛林法则的老师——打娃娃的家伙——那样来来回回地跑一英里能把你累得散架子了。坐下来想一想!制定一个计划。没时间追了,如果我们追得太紧,他们会把他扔下来的。"

"唉呀呀!呜!他们可能已经把他扔下树了,因为带着他太累了。谁能相信那些猴子啊?把死蝙蝠放在我头上吧!给我烂骨头吃吧!把我拖到野蜜蜂窝里,让我被蜜蜂蜇死吧!把我和鬣狗一起埋了吧!因为我是头最可怜的熊啊!唉呀呀!呜呼!哦,莫格里,莫格里!我为什么没有警告你小心这些猴子,而是打了你的头?现在我可能把今天上的课

---

grief *n.* 悲痛,悲伤   clumsy *a.* 笨拙的

103

丛林的故事

Mowgli, Mowgli! Why did I not warn you against the Monkey-Folk instead of breaking your head? Now perhaps I may have knocked the day's lesson out of his mind, and he will be alone in the jungle without the Master Words."

Baloo clasped his paws over his ears and rolled to and fro moaning.

"At least he gave me all the Words correctly a little time ago," said Bagheera impatiently. "Baloo, you have neither memory nor respect. What would the jungle think if I, the Black Panther, curled myself up like Ikki the Porcupine, and howled?"

"What do I care what the jungle thinks? He may be dead by now."

"Unless and until they drop him from the branches in sport, or kill him out of idleness, I have no fear for the man-cub. He is wise and well taught, and above all he has the eyes that make the Jungle-people afraid. But (and it is a great evil) he is in the power of the Bandar-log, and they, because they live in trees, have no fear of any of our people." Bagheera licked one forepaw thoughtfully.

"Fool that I am! Oh, fat, brown, root-digging fool that I am," said Baloo, uncoiling himself with a jerk, "it is true what Hathi the

THE JUNGLE STORY

从他脑袋里都敲出来了,如果他忘记了丛林密语,就只能孤零零一个人在丛林里了。"

巴洛用爪子抓着他的耳朵,晃来晃去地呜咽着。

"至少刚才他还能准确地对我说出这些丛林密语。"巴格西拉不耐烦地说,"巴洛,你既没记性又不尊重人。如果我黑豹像豪猪伊基那样把自己蜷起来嚎叫,丛林的动物会怎么想?"

"我才不在乎丛林的动物会怎么想呢? 他现在可能已经死了。"

"除非他们把他从树上扔下来扔着玩,或者出于懒惰杀了他,否则我一点也不担心人娃娃。他既聪明又接受了良好的教育,最重要的是他有让丛林动物都害怕的眼睛。但是(这可是一个大不幸),他落在猴子的手里,而他们因为住在树上,不怕我们任何动物。"巴格西拉若有所思地舔了舔一只前爪。

"我真是个笨蛋! 哦,我这个挖树根的棕色傻胖子,"巴洛说着,猛地伸展开身子,"野象海蒂说过:'一物降一物',这是千真万确的。他们

---

moan v. 呜咽,呻吟　　impatiently adv. 不耐烦地　　idleness n. 懒惰

丛林的故事

Wild Elephant says: 'To each his own fear'; and they, the Bandar-log, fear Kaa the Rock Snake. He can climb as well as they can. He steals the young monkeys in the night. The whisper of his name makes their wicked tails cold. Let us go to Kaa."

"What will he do for us? He is not of our tribe, being footless—and with most evil eyes," said Bagheera.

"He is very old and very cunning. Above all, he is always hungry," said Baloo hopefully. "Promise him many goats."

"He sleeps for a full month after he has once eaten. He may be asleep now, and even were he awake what if he would rather kill his own goats?" Bagheera, who did not know much about Kaa, was naturally suspicious.

"Then in that case, you and I together, old hunter, might make him see reason." Here Baloo rubbed his faded brown shoulder against the Panther, and they went off to look for Kaa the Rock Python.

They found him stretched out on a warm ledge in the afternoon sun, admiring his beautiful new coat, for he had been in retirement for the last ten days changing his skin, and now he was very splendid—darting his big blunt-nosed head along the ground, and

THE JUNGLE STORY

猴子怕的就是蟒蛇卡阿。他和他们一样能爬树。他在晚上偷小猴子。轻声地说他的名字都能把猴子邪恶的尾巴吓得冰凉。我们去找卡阿。"

"他会为我们做什么？他不是我们部落的,没有脚——而且有着最邪恶的眼睛。"巴格西拉说。

"他很老了,而且非常狡猾。最重要的是,他总是饿着肚子。"巴洛充满希望地说,"答应给他许多山羊就行了。"

"他吃完一次东西要睡上整整一个月呢。他现在也可能在睡觉,即使他醒着,如果他情愿自己猎杀山羊,该怎么办呢?"巴格西拉不太了解卡阿,自然充满了怀疑。

"那样的话,你和我一起,老猎手,让他明白明白道理。"巴洛用他褪了色的棕色肩膀蹭了一下豹子,他们就出发去找蟒蛇卡阿了。

他们找到他的时候,他正在午后的太阳下,躺在暖暖的岩石上欣赏着自己美丽的蛇皮。最近的十天里,他一直躲在这里休息、蜕皮。现在他真是绚烂夺目——他那长着嗅觉迟钝的鼻子的脑袋贴着地面,迅速地游动着,他把三十英寸长的身体卷成许多古怪的结和曲线,他想

---

suspicious *a.* 怀疑地　　fade *v.* 褪色　　retirement *n.* 退隐　　blunt *a.* 钝的

丛林的故事

twisting the thirty feet of his body into fantastic knots and curves, and licking his lips as he thought of his dinner to come.

"He has not eaten," said Baloo, with a grunt of relief, as soon as he saw the beautifully mottled brown and yellow jacket. "Be careful, Bagheera! He is always a little blind after he has changed his skin, and very quick to strike."

Kaa was not a poison snake—in fact he rather despised the poison snakes as cowards—but his strength lay in his hug, and when he had once lapped his huge coils round anybody there was no more to be said. "Good hunting! " cried Baloo, sitting up on his haunches. Like all snakes of his breed Kaa was rather deaf, and did not hear the call at first. Then he curled up ready for any accident, his head lowered.

"Good hunting for us all," he answered. "Oho, Baloo, what dost you do here? Good hunting, Bagheera. One of us at least needs food. Is there any news of game afoot? A doe now, or even a young buck? I am as empty as a dried well."

"We are hunting," said Baloo carelessly. He knew that you must not hurry Kaa. He is too big.

THE JUNGLE STORY

着即将到来的晚餐,舔了舔舌头。

"他还没吃过呢。"巴洛一看到他漂亮的综黄色外套,就松了口气。"小心点,巴格西拉! 他蜕皮以后总是有点盲目,而且会快速进攻。"

卡阿不是一条毒蛇——实际上他相当鄙视毒蛇,认为他们是胆小鬼——不过他的力量在于他的怀抱,一旦他把什么东西抱在他巨大的盘起的蛇蜷里,那就不用多说了。"打猎顺利!"巴洛蹲在那里喊道。像他所有的同类一样,卡阿的耳朵相当得聋,一开始并没有听见那声叫喊。于是他蜷起身子,低下头,准备应对任何突发的事情。

"大家都打猎顺利。"他回答道,"哦,巴洛,你怎么在这里啊? 打猎顺利,巴格西拉。我们当中至少有一个需要食物。有猎物在附近活动的消息吗? 一只雌兔还是一头小公鹿? 我肚里空空地像一口枯井了。"

"我们正在打猎呢。"巴洛漫不经心地说。他知道对卡阿不能着急,他太大了。

despise *v.* 鄙视,藐视　breed *n.* 品种,种族

109

"Give me **permission** to come with you," said Kaa. "A blow more or less is nothing to you, Bagheera or Baloo, but I—I have to wait and wait for days in a wood-path and climb half a night on the mere chance of a young ape. Psshaw! The branches are not what they were when I was young. Rotten twigs and dry boughs are they all."

"Maybe your great weight has something to do with the matter," said Baloo.

"I am a fair length—a fair length," said Kaa with a little pride. "But for all that, it is the fault of this new-grown timber. I came very near to falling on my last hunt—very near indeed—and the noise of my slipping, for my tail was not tight wrapped around the tree, waked the Bandar-log, and they called me most evil names."

"Footless, yellow earth-worm," said Bagheera under his whiskers, as though he were trying to remember something.

"Sssss! Have they ever called me that?" said Kaa.

"Something of that kind it was that they shouted to us last moon, but we never noticed them. They will say anything—even that you have lost all your teeth, and will not face anything bigger than a kid, because (they are indeed shameless, these Bandar-log)—

110

THE JUNGLE STORY

"请允许我和你们一起去吧。"卡阿说,"一次出击对你们,巴格西拉或者巴洛来说,不算什么,但是我——我得在树林里的小路上等上好几天,还要爬上半夜,只为了能碰到一只小猿猴。唉!这些树枝和我年轻时的那些都不一样了,尽是些烂细枝、干树枝了。"

"也许这和你巨大的体重有点关系。"巴洛说。

"我的身子的确是相当长——相当长,"卡阿带点儿骄傲地说,"但是尽管如此,还是这新长的树木的错。上次打猎我差点就扑到猎物了——真的就差一点点——因为尾巴没有紧紧地缠着树,我滑下去的声音吵醒了猴子们,他们就用最恶毒的名字称呼我。"

"没脚的黄土虫,"巴格西拉在胡子下面说,好像在努力地回忆着什么事情。

"嘶!他们是这样叫我的?"卡阿问。

"上个月他们就对我们喊这样的话了,但是我们从来不理他们。他们什么都说得出——即使会说你掉光了牙齿,说你不敢面对比小山羊大的东西了,因为(他们这些猴子,真的很无耻)——因为你害怕公山

---

permission *n.* 允许

111

because you are afraid of the he-goat's horns," Bagheera went on sweetly.

Now a snake, especially a **wary** old python like Kaa, very seldom shows that he is angry, but Baloo and Bagheera could see the big swallowing muscles on either side of Kaa's throat ripple and bulge.

"The Bandar-log have shifted their grounds," he said quietly. "When I came up into the sun today I heard them whooping among the tree-tops."

"It—it is the Bandar-log that we follow now," said Baloo, but the words stuck in his throat, for that was the first time in his memory that one of the Jungle-people had owned to being interested in the doings of the monkeys.

"Beyond doubt then it is no small thing that takes two such hunters—leaders in their own jungle I am certain—on the trail of the Bandar-log," Kaa replied courteously, as he **swelled** with curiosity.

"Indeed," Baloo began, "I am no more than the old and sometimes very foolish Teacher of the Law to the Seeonee wolf-cubs, and Bagheera here—"

THE JUNGLE STORY

羊的犄角,"巴格西拉继续和蔼地说。

现在一条蛇,尤其是像卡阿这样谨慎、年迈的蟒蛇,很少会流露出他的火气,但巴洛和巴格西拉可以看到卡阿喉咙两边用来吞咽的巨大的肌肉在颤抖,鼓了起来。

"猴子们换了地盘了。"他轻轻地说,"今天出来晒太阳的时候,我听到他们在树顶上高声说的。

"我们现在就是在追踪猴子们。"巴洛说,但是这些话却卡在了他的喉咙里,因为这是他记忆中第一次有丛林兽民显露出对猴子的所作所为感兴趣。

"毫无疑问,让两位丛林的打猎首领来追踪猴子的足迹,这件事,我敢肯定,一定小不了。"卡阿礼貌地回答,似乎他也充满了好奇。

"的确,"巴洛说,"我不过是西奥尼狼群年老的、有时候还很愚蠢的丛林法则老师,而这位巴格拉——"

---

wary *a.* 谨慎的　　swell *v.* 充满　　curiosity *n.* 好奇心

"Is Bagheera," said the Black Panther, and his jaws shut with a snap, for he did not believe in being **humble**. "The trouble is this, Kaa. Those nut-stealers and pickers of palm leaves have stolen away our man-cub of whom you have perhaps heard."

"I heard some news from Ikki (his quills make him presumptuous) of a man-thing that was entered into a wolf pack, but I did not believe. Ikki is full of stories half heard and very badly told."

"But it is true. He is such a man-cub as never was," said Baloo. "The best and wisest and boldest of man-cubs—my own pupil, who shall make the name of Baloo famous through all the jungles; and besides, I—we—love him, Kaa."

"Ts! Ts! " said Kaa, weaving his head to and fro. "I also have known what love is. There are tales I could tell that—"

"That need a clear night when we are all well fed to praise properly," said Bagheera quickly. "Our man-cub is in the hands of the Bandar-log now, and we know that of all the Jungle-people they fear Kaa alone."

"They fear me alone. They have good reason," said Kaa. "Chattering, foolish, vain—vain, foolish, and chattering, are the monkeys. But a man-thing in their hands is in no good luck. They

THE JUNGLE STORY

　　"是巴格西拉,"黑豹说,他的下巴啪的一下合上了,因为他不相信谦卑有用。"麻烦是这样的,卡阿。这些偷坚果、摘棕树叶子的家伙偷走了我们的人娃娃,你也许听说过他吧。"

　　"我从伊基那里听说过这事(他那身刺让他挺骄傲的),说一个人或是什么东西跑到狼群里来了,但我不相信。伊基满肚子都是道听途说的故事,但讲故事又讲得很糟糕。"

　　"但是这事是真的。他是个前所未有的人娃娃,"巴洛说,"是最优秀、最聪明、最勇敢的人娃娃——我的学生,他会让我巴洛的名字扬名整个丛林,而且,我——我们——爱他,卡阿。"

　　"嘶!嘶!"卡阿一边说,一边来回地动着他的头。"我也知道爱是什么。我还能说得出一些故事呢——"

　　"那得需要一个晴朗的夜晚,我们都吃得饱饱的,然后再来赞美爱情一番。"巴格西拉赶紧说,"我们的人娃娃现在在猴子们的手里,而据我们所知,在所有的丛林兽民里他们只怕卡阿一个。"

　　"他们只怕我,是有充足的理由的。"卡阿说,"那些猴子又吵又傻又自负——又自负又傻又吵。但是一个人落在他们的手里,可就倒霉

---

humble *a.* 谦卑的

115

丛林的故事

grow tired of the nuts they pick, and throw them down. They carry a branch half a day, meaning to do great things with it, and then they snap it in two. That man-thing is not to be envied. They called me also—'yellow fish' was it not?"

"Worm—worm—earth-worm," said Bagheera, "as well as other things which I cannot now say for shame."

"We must remind them to speak well of their master. Aaa-ssp! We must help their **wandering** memories. Now, whither went they with the cub?"

"The jungle alone knows. Toward the **sunset**, I believe," said Baloo. "We had thought that you wouldst know, Kaa."

"I? How? I take them when they come in my way, but I do not hunt the Bandar-log, or frogs—or green scum on a water-hole, for that matter."

"Up, Up! Up, Up! Hillo! Illo! Illo, look up, Baloo of the Seeonee Wolf Pack! "

Baloo looked up to see where the voice came from, and there was Rann the Kite, sweeping down with the sun shining on the upturned flanges of his wings. It was near Rann's bedtime, but he

THE JUNGLE STORY

了。如果他们拿坚果拿得厌烦了，就把它们扔掉了；他们抬着根树枝大半天，打算拿它派大用处，但接着就把它折断了；那个人或是什么东西不值得羡慕了，他们也叫我——黄鱼，是吗？"

"虫子——虫子——泥地里的虫子，"巴格西拉说，"还有其他的一些现在我都不好意思说。"

"我们必须提醒他们对主子要好好说话。阿——嘶！我们必须帮他们纠正错乱的记忆。现在他们带着人娃娃去哪里了？"

"只有丛林知道。我想，朝着太阳下山的地方去了。"巴洛说，"我们原本以为你会知道，卡阿。"

"我？我怎么会知道？他们从我这儿经过，我就抓住他们，但是我不去猎捕猴子或者青蛙——或是为了那种事到水洞里找寻绿浮藻。"

"上面，上面！上面，上面！喂！喂！喂，抬头，西奥尼狼群的巴洛！"

巴洛抬头找寻声音来自何处，鸢鹰兰恩正俯冲下来，他那向上翘起的翅膀的边缘上闪耀着太阳的光辉。那时已经将近兰恩睡觉的时间了，但是他搜索了整个丛林，寻找那头熊，但是由于茂密的树叶而没找

wandering *a.* 漫无目的的   sunset *n.* 日落

117

had **ranged** all over the jungle looking for the Bear and had missed him in the thick **foliage**.

"What is it?" said Baloo.

"I have seen Mowgli among the Bandar-log. He bade me tell you. I watched. The Bandar-log have taken him beyond the river to the monkey city—to the Cold Lairs. They may stay there for a night, or ten nights, or an hour. I have told the bats to watch through the dark time. That is my message. Good hunting, all you below! "

"Full gorge and a deep sleep to you, Rann," cried Bagheera. "I will remember you in my next kill, and put aside the head for you alone, O best of kites! "

"It is nothing. It is nothing. The boy held the Master Word. I could have done no less," and Rann circled up again to his **roost**.

"He has not forgotten to use his tongue," said Baloo with a chuckle of pride. "To think of one so young remembering the Master Word for the birds too while he was being pulled across trees! "

"It was most firmly driven into him," said Bagheera. "But I am proud of him, and now we must go to the Cold Lairs."

THE JUNGLE STORY

到他。

"什么事?"巴洛问。

"我在猴群中看到莫格里了,他恳求我给你稍个信。我观察过了,猴子们带着他穿过河,往猴子城——寒穴去了。他们可能会在那儿过一夜,或者十夜,或者一个小时。我已经让蝙蝠在天黑的时候盯着他们了。这就是我要捎给你们的口信。愿你们下面所有的人打猎顺利!"

"也祝你吃饱睡好,兰恩,"巴格西拉喊道,"下次打猎的时候我会记得你的,我会把猎物的头留起来,只留给你,最棒的鸢鹰!"

"这没什么!没什么!那男孩知道丛林密语。我非得这么帮他不可。"兰恩盘旋着飞上了天,回他的栖息地去了。

"他没忘记使用他的舌头。"巴洛骄傲地笑着说,"想想看,这么小个人,当他被拽着穿过树林的时候,还记起了鸟儿的丛林密语。"

"那些密语都被他牢牢地记住了," 巴格西拉说,"我为他骄傲,现在我们必须去寒穴了。"

---

range *v.* 搜寻　　foliage *n.* 叶子　　roost *n.* 栖息地

119

丛林的故事

They all knew where that place was, but few of the Jungle People ever went there, because what they called the Cold Lairs was an old deserted city, lost and buried in the jungle, and beasts seldom use a place that men have once used. The wild boar will, but the hunting tribes do not. Besides, the monkeys lived there as much as they could be said to live anywhere, and no self-respecting animal would come within eyeshot of it except in times of drought, when the half-ruined tanks and reservoirs held a little water.

"It is half a night's journey—at full speed," said Bagheera, and Baloo looked very serious. "I will go as fast as I can," he said anxiously.

"We dare not wait for you. Follow, Baloo. We must go on the quick-foot—Kaa and I."

"Feet or no feet, I can keep abreast of all your four," said Kaa shortly. Baloo made one effort to hurry, but had to sit down panting, and so they left him to come on later, while Bagheera hurried forward, at the quick panther-canter. Kaa said nothing, but, strive as Bagheera might, the huge Rock-python held level with him. When they came to a hill stream, Bagheera gained, because he

THE JUNGLE STORY

他们都知道那地方在哪里，但是几乎没有丛林兽民会去那里，因为他们称为寒穴的地方是个古老废弃的城市，一座在丛林中迷失湮没的城市，而且野兽很少使用人类曾经居住过的地方。野猪会，但是狩猎的动物不会。而且，猴子住在那里和他们住在其他任何地方一样。没有一个有自尊的动物会到这个眼睛看得到的城镇来，除了干旱时节，那时几乎毁坏的水池和水库里都只剩下一点水了。

"全速前进的话，也得跑上半夜了。"巴格西拉说，巴洛的表情看上去十分严肃。"我会尽快地跑。"他急切地说。

"我们可不敢等你。跟上，巴洛。我们必须快点走——卡阿和我。"

"不管有脚还是没脚，我都可以和你的四只脚并肩而行。"卡阿立刻说。巴洛使劲地跑，但是一会儿就不得不坐下来喘气了。于是，他们留下他在后面追赶，而巴格西拉以豹子慢跑的步子赶着路。卡阿没说什么，但是尽管巴格西拉在努力地跑，大蟒蛇还是能和他并驾齐驱。当他们跑到一条山间小河的时候，巴格西拉领先了，因为他一跳就越过

---

deserted a. 废弃的　　reservoir n. 水库
abreast adv. 并列地,并肩地　　shortly adv. 立刻

121

bounded across while Kaa swam, his head and two feet of his neck clearing the water, but on level ground Kaa made up the distance.

"By the Broken Lock that freed me," said Bagheera, when twilight had fallen, "you are no slow goer! "

"I am hungry," said Kaa. "Besides, they called me speckled frog."

"Worm—earth-worm, and yellow to boot."

"All one. Let us go on," and Kaa seemed to pour himself along the ground, finding the shortest road with his steady eyes, and keeping to it.

In the Cold Lairs the Monkey-People were not thinking of Mowgli's friends at all. They had brought the boy to the Lost City, and were very much pleased with themselves for the time. Mowgli had never seen an Indian city before, and though this was almost a heap of ruins it seemed very wonderful and splendid. Some king had built it long ago on a little hill. You could still trace the stone causeways that led up to the ruined gates where the last splinters of wood hung to the worn, rusted hinges. Trees had grown into and out of the walls; the battlements were tumbled down and decayed, and wild creepers hung out of the windows of the towers on the

122

THE JUNGLE STORY

了小河,而卡阿得游过去,他的头和两英尺脖子露在水面上。但是上了岸以后,卡阿很快就赶上了落后的距离。

"我以赋予我自由的、被我砸碎的锁发誓,"巴格西拉在黄昏来临时说道,"你跑得一点都不慢。"

"我饿了,"卡阿说,"而且,他们叫我有斑点的青蛙。"

"虫子——地上的虫子,而且全身都是黄的。"

"都一样,我们继续走吧。"卡阿用镇静的眼睛搜寻着最近的路,然后像是倒在地上的水一样快速地游去。

在寒穴,猴子们压根没考虑莫格里的朋友们。他们把男孩带到了废城,眼下正洋洋得意着呢。莫格里以前从未看到过一座印度城,虽然这里几乎是一堆废墟,但似乎还是非常令人惊叹,壮丽非凡。很久以前一位国王在一座小山上建造了它。你依然能看到那些石头筑造的堤道通往已经毁坏的大门,大门上那些残余的木头碎片挂在磨损了的、生锈了的铰链上;树木长得高过了墙,墙里墙外都有;城墙坍塌、毁坏了;

---

steady *a.* 镇静地   rusted *a.* 生锈的   decay *v.* 腐烂

walls in bushy hanging clumps.

A great roofless palace crowned the hill, and the marble of the courtyards and the fountains was split, and stained with red and green, and the very cobblestones in the courtyard where the king's elephants used to live had been thrust up and apart by grasses and young trees. From the palace you could see the rows and rows of roofless houses that made up the city looking like empty honeycombs filled with blackness; the shapeless block of stone that had been an idol in the square where four roads met; the pits and dimples at street corners where the public wells once stood, and the shattered domes of temples with wild figs sprouting on their sides. The monkeys called the place their city, and pretended to despise the Jungle-people because they lived in the forest. And yet they never knew what the buildings were made for nor how to use them. They would sit in circles on the hall of the king's council chamber, and scratch for fleas and pretend to be men; or they would run in and out of the roofless houses and collect pieces of plaster and old bricks in a corner, and forget where they had hidden them, and fight and cry in scuffling crowds, and then break off to play up and down the terraces of the king's garden, where they would shake the

THE JUNGLE STORY

爬山虎从塔楼的窗户里挂出来,浓密地一团团地长在墙上。

　　一座巨大的无顶的官殿覆盖了整个山头,庭院里的大理石和水池都裂开了,长满了红色、绿色的斑点。御用大象曾经住过的庭院里,那些大鹅卵石都突了出来,被野草和小树分开了。从官殿那里,你可以看到一排排没有屋顶的房子,这让整个城市看上去像个长满了黑洞洞的蜂窝;你还能看见在四条道路交汇的广场上那块没有形状的大石头;还有街道角落里的坑坑洼洼,那里以前是公用的水井;还有那些已经毁坏了的圆顶庙宇,旁边长满了无花果。猴子们认为这个地方是他们的城市,假装看不起丛林兽民,因为他们住在森林里。尽管他们永远不知道这些建筑物用来干什么或者该怎么使用它们。他们在国王会议室的大厅里围坐成一圈,捉着跳蚤,假装自己是人;或者他们在没有房顶的屋子里跑进跑出,把灰泥和旧砖头收集到角落里,然后就忘了他们把那些东西放在哪里了,于是他们就打架、喊叫,混战成一团。然后又

---

　　crown v. 覆盖……的顶部　　chamber n. 房间,会议室　　scratch v. 搔,抓

rose trees and the oranges in sport to see the fruit and flowers fall. They explored all the passages and dark tunnels in the palace and the hundreds of little dark rooms, but they never remembered what they had seen and what they had not; and so drifted about in ones and twos or crowds telling each other that they were doing as men did. They drank at the tanks and made the water all muddy, and then they fought over it, and then they would all rush together in mobs and shout: "There is no one in the jungle so wise and good and clever and strong and gentle as the Bandar-log." Then all would begin again till they grew tired of the city and went back to the tree-tops, hoping the Jungle-people would notice them.

Mowgli, who had been trained under the Law of the Jungle, did not like or understand this kind of life. The monkeys dragged him into the Cold Lairs late in the afternoon, and instead of going to sleep, as Mowgli would have done after a long journey, they joined hands and danced about and sang their foolish songs. One of the monkeys made a speech and told his **companions** that Mowgli's **capture marked** a new thing in the history of the Bandar-log, for Mowgli was going to show them how to weave sticks and canes

会突然停下来,到国王花园的露台上跑上跑下地玩耍,他们会摇晃玫瑰树和橘子树来玩,看着果子和花掉下来。他们探索了官殿里所有的走廊和黑漆漆的地道,几百间小黑房间,但是他们永远也不记得哪些曾看过了,哪些没看过,所以总是单独地或者两两地、成群地到处乱跑,互相告知。他们像人类那样做事情。他们在水池里喝水,把水弄得脏兮兮的,然后就在那里面打架。他们会成群地冲过来,喊叫着:"丛林里再没有其他动物像猴子一样聪明、优秀、机智、健壮和温柔了。"接着他们又会重头再来一遍,直到他们对这座城感到厌倦了,就又回到树顶上,希望丛林兽民会注意到他们。

　　莫格里是按照丛林法则训练出来的, 他不喜欢也不理解这种生活。猴子们把他拖到寒穴的时候已经是傍晚时分了,通常莫格里在走了这么远的路之后都会睡一觉,但是猴子们却拉起手来跳着舞,唱着那些傻傻的歌。其中有一只猴子发表了演说,他告诉他的同伴们,抓住莫格里标志着猴子历史上的一个新的开始,因为莫格里会教他们如何用树枝和藤条来挡雨防寒。莫格里捡了一些爬山虎,开始编了起来,猴

---

companion *n.* 同伴　　capture *n.* 捕获,俘虏　　mark *v.* 标明,标志

together as a protection against rain and cold. Mowgli picked up some creepers and began to work them in and out, and the monkeys tried to **imitate**; but in a very few minutes they lost interest and began to pull their friends' tails or jump up and down on all fours, coughing.

"I wish to eat," said Mowgli. "I am a stranger in this part of the jungle. Bring me food, or give me leave to hunt here."

Twenty or thirty monkeys bounded away to bring him nuts and wild pawpaws. But they fell to fighting on the road, and it was too much trouble to go back with what was left of the fruit. Mowgli was sore and angry as well as hungry, and he roamed through the empty city giving the Strangers' Hunting Call from time to time, but no one answered him, and Mowgli felt that he had reached a very bad place indeed. "All that Baloo has said about the Bandar-log is true," he thought to himself. "They have no Law, no Hunting Call, and no leaders—nothing but foolish words and little picking thievish hands. So if I am **starved** or killed here, it will be all my own fault. But I must try to return to my own jungle. Baloo will surely beat me, but that is better than chasing silly rose leaves with the Bandar-log."

No sooner had he walked to the city wall than the monkeys

子们设法模仿,但是没过几分钟,他们就失去了兴趣,开始去拉伙伴们的尾巴或是四条腿跳上跳下的,还发出咯咯的咳嗽声。

"我想吃东西,"莫格里说,"我在这个地方是个陌生人。给我拿点吃的来,或者允许我在这里打猎。"

二三十只猴子跳开去给他拿坚果和野生巴婆果。但是在路上他们就开始打了起来,而且带着剩下的果子回来也太麻烦了。莫格里又气又饿,他在空荡荡的城市里漫步,不时地发出陌生人狩猎时的呼叫,但是没有人回答他。莫格里觉得他真的到了一个糟糕透顶的地方。"巴洛所说的关于猴子的一切都是真的。"他心里暗想,"他们没有法律,没有狩猎呼叫,也没有首领——什么都没有,除了可笑的言论和偷东西的小手。所以如果我在这里饿死或者被杀死,都是我自己的错。但是我必须设法回到我自己的丛林去。巴洛肯定会揍我,但是这总比和猴子们追寻愚蠢的玫瑰花瓣好。"

他刚走到城墙边,猴子们就把他拖了回去,还告诉他,他不知道自

---

imitate *v.* 模仿   starve *v.* 饿死;挨饿

丛林的故事

pulled him back, telling him that he did not know how happy he was, and pinching him to make him **grateful**. He set his teeth and said nothing, but went with the shouting monkeys to a terrace above the red sandstone reservoirs that were half-full of rain water. There was a ruined summer-house of white marble in the center of the terrace, built for queens dead a hundred years ago. The domed roof had half fallen in and blocked up the underground passage from the palace by which the queens used to enter. But the walls were made of screens of marble tracery—beautiful milk-white fretwork, set with agates and cornelians and jasper and lapis lazuli, and as the moon came up behind the hill it shone through the open work, casting shadows on the ground like black velvet embroidery. Sore, sleepy, and hungry as he was, Mowgli could not help laughing when the Bandar-log began, twenty at a time, to tell him how great and wise and strong and gentle they were, and how foolish he was to wish to leave them. "We are great. We are free. We are wonderful. We are the most wonderful people in all the jungle! We all say so, and so it must be true," they shouted. "Now as you are a new listener and can carry our words back to the Jungle-people so that they may notice us in future, we will tell you all about our most

130

已有多幸福。他们拧他，让他表示感谢。他紧咬牙关，一声不吭，然后跟着大喊大叫的猴子来到红沙石蓄水池上方的露台，那蓄水池里有半池的雨水。露台的中央有个废弃的白色大理石花园凉亭，是为一百多年前去世的王后们建造的。圆屋顶有一半塌了下来，挡住了地下通道。以前王后们就是经过那个通道从官殿里进出的。不过那些墙是由大理石窗花格围屏组成的——漂亮的乳白色浮雕，镶嵌着玛瑙、红玉髓、碧玉和天青石。当月亮从山后爬上来的时候，月光透过浮雕屏风，把影子投射在地上，就像是黑色的天鹅绒绣品。虽然莫格里又生气又瞌睡又饿，但是当二十只猴子一起对他说，他们是多么伟大、优秀、健壮和温柔，莫格里想要离开他们的想法是多么愚蠢时，他还是忍不住笑了起来。"我们是伟大的，我们是自由的，我们是很棒的，我们是整个丛林里最棒的种群！我们都这么说，所以这必定是真的。"他们大喊道，"现在既然你是第一次听到，你可以把我们的话转告丛林兽民们，这样以后他们就可能注意到我们

---

grateful *a.* 感激的，感谢的

excellent selves." Mowgli made no objection, and the monkeys gathered by hundreds and hundreds on the terrace to listen to their own speakers singing the praises of the Bandar-log, and whenever a speaker stopped for want of breath they would all shout together: "This is true; we all say so." Mowgli nodded and blinked, and said "Yes" when they asked him a question, and his head spun with the noise. "Tabaqui the Jackal must have bitten all these people," he said to himself, "and now they have madness. Certainly this is dewanee, the madness. Do they never go to sleep? Now there is a cloud coming to cover that moon. If it were only a big enough cloud I might try to run away in the darkness. But I am tired."

That same cloud was being watched by two good friends in the ruined ditch below the city wall, for Bagheera and Kaa, knowing well how dangerous the Monkey-People were in large numbers, did not wish to run any risks. The monkeys never fight unless they are a hundred to one, and few in the jungle care for those odds.

"I will go to the west wall," Kaa whispered, "and come down swiftly with the slope of the ground in my favor. They will not throw themselves upon my back in their hundreds, but—"

"I know it," said Bagheera. "Would that Baloo were here, but

THE JUNGLE STORY

了。我们会向你讲述我们一切最优秀的地方。"莫格里没有反对,于是成百上千只猴子聚集在露台上,听他们自己的演说家们赞美着自己,每当一个演说家停下来歇口气的时候,他们就会齐声叫道:"这是真的,我们都这么说。"莫格里点点头,眨着眼睛,当他们问他问题的时候,他就回答"是的"。吵闹声吵得他头昏脑涨。"豺狗塔巴奇肯定咬过他们这些猴子,"他自言自语道,"现在他们都得了疯病。当然这就是狂犬病,疯病。他们从来不睡觉吗?现在有朵云飘过来要挡住月亮了。如果那朵云够大的话,我就可以趁黑跑掉了。但是我太累了。"

在城墙下面的废水沟里,他的两个好朋友也正盯着同一片云,因为巴格西拉和卡阿清楚地知道成群的猴子有多危险,他们不想冒险。猴子们只有在一百对一的时候才会开始打斗,而丛林里很少有人注意到这种数量上的差距。

"我到西面那堵墙边去,"卡阿低声说,"然后快速地冲下去,那里的斜坡对我有利。他们不会几百只扑到我背上,但是——"

"我知道,"巴格西拉说,"要是巴洛在这儿就好了,但是我们必须

---

objection *n.* 反对,异议   blink *v.* 眨眼   whisper *v.* 低声说

丛林的故事

we must do what we can. When that cloud covers the moon I shall
go to the terrace. They hold some sort of council there over the
boy."

"Good hunting," said Kaa grimly, and **glided** away to the west
wall. That happened to be the least ruined of any, and the big snake
was **delayed** awhile before he could find a way up the stones. The
cloud hid the moon, and as Mowgli wondered what would come next
he heard Bagheera's light feet on the terrace. The Black Panther had
raced up the slope almost without a sound and was striking—he
knew better than to waste time in biting—right and left among the
monkeys, who were seated round Mowgli in circles fifty and sixty
deep. There was a howl of **fright** and rage, and then as Bagheera
tripped on the rolling kicking bodies beneath him, a monkey
shouted: "There is only one here! Kill him! Kill." A scuffling mass
of monkeys, biting, scratching, tearing, and pulling, closed over
Bagheera, while five or six laid hold of Mowgli, dragged him up the
wall of the summerhouse and pushed him through the hole of the
broken dome. A man-trained boy would have been badly bruised, for
the fall was a good fifteen feet, but Mowgli fell as Baloo had taught
him to fall, and landed on his feet.

THE JUNGLE STORY

做我们能做的事情。等云遮住了月亮,我就跑到露台那去。他们正在开
会讨论那个男孩子的事情。"

　　"打猎顺利,"卡阿神情庄重地说完后,就滑向了西墙。那里的墙碰
恰巧是遭到破坏最少的,大蟒蛇在找到一条能爬上石头的路之前耽搁
了一会。云遮住了月亮,莫格里正在思量接着会发生什么事,这时他
听到了巴格西拉在露台上的轻轻的脚步声。黑豹几乎毫无声息地冲上
斜坡,在猴群中左扑右击——他知道,最好不要浪费时间去咬——猴
子们正围坐在莫格里旁边,有五六十圈之多。这时响起了一阵惊吓、愤
怒的嚎叫声。然后当巴格西拉被身下打滚乱蹬着腿的猴子绊倒时,一
只猴子大喊道:"只有他一个!杀了他!杀!"乱成一团的猴子咬着、抓
着、扯着、拉着巴格西拉,而五六只猴子紧紧地抓住莫格里,把他拖到
花园凉亭的顶上,然后从破屋顶的一个窟窿里推了下去。一个由人训
练的男孩可能会摔得鼻青脸肿,因为高度足有十五英尺。但是莫格里
是像巴洛教他的那样掉下去的,双脚着地。

---

glide *v.* 滑行　　delay *v.* 耽搁　　fright *n.* 惊吓　　trip *v.* 绊倒

"Stay there," shouted the monkeys, "till we have killed your friends, and later we will play with you—if the Poison-people leave you alive."

"We be of one blood, you and I," said Mowgli, quickly giving the snake's call. He could hear rustling and hissing in the rubbish all round him and gave the call a second time, to make sure.

"Even ssso! Down hoods all! " said half a dozen low voices (every ruin in India becomes sooner or later a **dwelling** place of snakes, and the old summerhouse was alive with cobras). "Stand still, little brother, for your feet may do us harm."

Mowgli stood as quietly as he could, peering through the open work and listening to the furious din of the fight round the Black Panther—the yells and chatterings and scufflings, and Bagheera's deep, hoarse cough as he backed and bucked and twisted and plunged under the **heaps** of his enemies. For the first time since he was born, Bagheera was fighting for his life.

"Baloo must be at hand; Bagheera would not have come alone," Mowgli thought. And then he called aloud: "To the tank, Bagheera. Roll to the water tanks. Roll and plunge! Get to the

THE JUNGLE STORY

"待在那儿，"猴子们喊道，"等我们杀了你的朋友后，再和你玩——如果那些毒蛇让你活着的话。"

"我们是同一血脉的，你和我，"莫格里马上用蛇的密语说。他能听到他周围垃圾堆里发出窸窸窣窣的声音，于是他又发出一声呼叫，来证实一下。

"就是这样！都放下头罩！"有六个低沉的声音说。(印度的每一个废墟都很快成为蛇居住的地方，而这个花园的凉亭就住满了眼镜蛇。)"站着别动，小兄弟，你的脚会伤害我们。"

莫格里尽量站着一动不动，他透过浮雕的镂空处往外看，听着黑豹周围激烈的打斗声、喊叫声、喋喋不休的吵闹声、混战声和巴格西拉从一堆敌人身下往后退、突然弯背跃起、扭动身子猛烈前冲时发出的低沉、嘶哑的咳声。这是他有生以来第一次为了生存而战斗。

"巴洛肯定就在附近，巴格西拉不会单身一个来的，"莫格里想。然后他大叫："巴格西拉，到水池那里！翻滚到水池那里！滚过去，然后猛

---

dwell *v.* 居住　　heap *n.* 堆

water! "

Bagheera heard, and the cry that told him Mowgli was safe gave him new courage. He worked his way **desperately**, inch by inch, straight for the reservoirs, halting in silence. Then from the ruined wall nearest the jungle rose up the rumbling war-shout of Baloo. The old Bear had done his best, but he could not come before. "Bagheera," he shouted, "I am here. I climb! I haste! Ahuwora! The stones slip under my feet! Wait my coming, O most **infamous** Bandar-log! " He panted up the terrace only to disappear to the head in a wave of monkeys, but he threw himself squarely on his haunches, and, spreading out his forepaws, hugged as many as he could hold, and then began to hit with a regular bat-bat-bat, like the flipping strokes of a paddle wheel. A crash and a splash told Mowgli that Bagheera had fought his way to the tank where the monkeys could not follow. The Panther lay gasping for breath, his head just out of the water, while the monkeys stood three deep on the red steps, dancing up and down with rage, ready to spring upon him from all sides if he came out to help Baloo. It was then that Bagheera lifted up his dripping chin, and in **despair**

THE JUNGLE STORY

冲！到水那里去！"

　　巴格西拉听到了,那声喊叫也告诉他莫格里安全无事,这给了他新的勇气。他拼命地、一寸一寸地笔直地向水池靠近,然后一声不响地停住了。接着从最靠近丛林那边的废弃城墙传来巴洛隆隆的战斗的吼叫声。老巴洛已经尽了最大努力了,但是不可能再早点到了。"巴格西拉,"他喊道,"我来了。我爬上来了！我马上来了！哇呼啦！石头从我脚下掉下去了！等我来,你们这些臭名昭著的猴子！"他喘着气爬上了露台,只是在猴群中露出了一个头,但他猛地用后腰腿笔直地站了起来,摊开前爪,能抓住几只就抓住几只,然后开始有规律地啪啪啪地拍打起来,就像船桨急速转动一样。哗啦一声,然后扑通一声,莫格里知道巴格西拉已经一路打到水池边,跳了下去,猴子们没办法跟着他。豹子躺在那里,喘着气,他只把头露在水面上,而猴子们在红色的台阶上站成三排,气得上窜下跳,如果他上来帮巴洛,他们就会从四面八方跳到他身上。那时,巴格西拉抬起他滴着水的头,绝望地发出蛇类密语寻

---

　　desperately adv. 不顾一切地,拼死地　　infamous a. 臭名昭著的　　despair n. 绝望

丛林的故事

gave the Snake's Call for protection—"We be of one blood, you and I"— for he believed that Kaa had turned tail at the last minute. Even Baloo, half smothered under the monkeys on the edge of the terrace, could not help chuckling as he heard the Black Panther asking for help.

Kaa had only just worked his way over the west wall, landing with a wrench that dislodged a coping stone into the ditch. He had no intention of losing any advantage of the ground, and coiled and uncoiled himself once or twice, to be sure that every foot of his long body was in working order. All that while the fight with Baloo went on, and the monkeys yelled in the tank round Bagheera, and Mang the Bat, flying to and fro, carried the news of the great battle over the jungle, till even Hathi the Wild Elephant trumpeted, and, far away, scattered bands of the Monkey-Folk woke and came leaping along the tree-roads to help their comrades in the Cold Lairs, and the noise of the fight roused all the day birds for miles round. Then Kaa came straight, quickly, and anxious to kill. The fighting strength of a python is in the driving blow of his head backed by all the strength and weight of his body. If you can imagine a lance, or a battering ram, or a hammer weighing nearly half a ton driven by a

THE JUNGLE STORY

求保护:"我们是同一血脉的,你和我"——因为他认为卡阿在最后时刻已经转身逃跑了。即使巴洛在露台边上被猴子们压得快窒息了,听到黑豹的呼救还是忍不住笑了。

卡阿才刚刚越过西墙,落地的时候猛地一扭把一块压顶石推到沟里去了。他不想失去位置上的优势,于是几次蜷起来又松开,以确保他长长的身体的每一个部位都能起作用。那时,巴洛的战斗还在继续,猴子们围着水池,冲着巴格西拉喊叫,蝙蝠曼尼来来回回地飞,把这个大战役的消息传遍整个丛林,直到野象海蒂也大声吼叫起来。远处,分散的猴群们被吵醒了,他们沿着树道一路跳过来,去寒穴帮助他们的同伴。战斗的吵闹声惊醒了方圆数里所有白天活动的鸟儿。然后卡阿径直地过来,急于想捕杀猎物。一条蟒蛇的战斗力在于他用全身的力量和体重使头部发出

141

cool, quiet mind living in the handle of it, you can roughly imagine what Kaa was like when he fought. A python four or five feet long can knock a man down if he hits him fairly in the chest, and Kaa was thirty feet long, as you know. His first **stroke** was delivered into the heart of the crowd round Baloo. It was sent home with shut mouth in silence, and there was no need of a second. The monkeys scattered with cries of—"Kaa! It is Kaa! Run! Run! "

Generations of monkeys had been scared into good behavior by the stories their elders told them of Kaa, the night thief, who could slip along the branches as quietly as moss grows, and steal away the strongest monkey that ever lived; of old Kaa, who could make himself look so like a dead branch or a rotten stump that the wisest were **deceived**, till the branch caught them. Kaa was everything that the monkeys feared in the jungle, for none of them knew the limits of his power, none of them could look him in the face, and none had ever come alive out of his hug. And so they ran, **stammering** with terror, to the walls and the roofs of the houses, and Baloo drew a deep breath of relief. His fur was much thicker than Bagheera's, but he had suffered sorely in the fight. Then Kaa opened his mouth for the first time and spoke one long hissing

THE JUNGLE STORY

一击。如果你可以想象一根长矛,或者一只连续猛击的公羊,或者一个头脑冷静的人手里拿着将近半吨重的锤子,你大概就可以想象卡阿战斗时是什么样子了。一条四五英尺长的蟒蛇如果正中一个人的胸部,就足以把他摔倒,而你要知道,卡阿有三十英尺长。他第一击打向巴洛周围猴群的中心——闭着嘴巴无声地打中了他们的要害,不需要再来第二次。猴子们大喊着逃散开去:"卡阿!是卡阿!跑啊!快跑!"

一代代猴子都被他们的长辈讲述的关于卡阿的故事吓得挺听话的。夜贼卡阿,会像苔藓生长那样,悄无声息地顺着树枝爬上树,偷走最强壮的猴子;卡阿,能使自己看上去像一根枯树枝或者一个烂树桩,即使是最聪明的猴子也会被骗,直到被那树枝抓住。猴子们在丛林里最怕的就是卡阿,因为他们没人知道他的力量到底有多么强大,没有人敢看他的脸,没有人被他抱住了还有生还的可能,所以他们吓得结结巴巴地喊着,跑到城墙和屋顶上。巴洛深深地松了口气。他的皮毛比巴格西拉的厚多了,但是他在战斗中也伤得不轻。这时,卡阿第一次张

---

stroke *n.* 打;击　　deceive *v.* 欺骗　　stammer *v.* 结结巴巴地说

word, and the far-away monkeys, hurrying to the defense of the Cold Lairs, stayed where they were, cowering, till the loaded branches bent and crackled under them. The monkeys on the walls and the empty houses stopped their cries, and in the stillness that fell upon the city Mowgli heard Bagheera shaking his wet sides as he came up from the tank. Then the clamor broke out again. The monkeys leaped higher up the walls. They clung around the necks of the big stone idols and shrieked as they skipped along the battlements, while Mowgli, dancing in the summerhouse, put his eye to the screenwork and hooted owl-fashion between his front teeth, to show his derision and contempt.

"Get the man-cub out of that trap; I can do no more," Bagheera gasped. "Let us take the man-cub and go. They may attack again."

"They will not move till I order them. Stay you sssso! " Kaa hissed, and the city was silent once more. "I could not come before, Brother, but I think I heard you call"—this was to Bagheera.

"I—I may have cried out in the battle," Bagheera answered. "Baloo, art you hurt?"

"I am not sure that they did not pull me into a hundred little

THE JUNGLE STORY

大了嘴巴,发出一声长长的嘶声,那些已经逃到远处准备跑回去躲在寒穴里的猴子们,吓得待在原地一动不动,哆嗦着,直到不堪重负的树枝在他们身下弯曲、断裂。城墙上和空房子里的猴子停止了喊叫,城市里一片寂静。莫格里听到巴格西拉从水池里上来,抖动着湿漉漉的身体。然后吵闹声又一次响起来了。猴子们从城墙上跳到高处,他们在沿着城墙蹦跳的时候,紧紧抱着巨大的石雕像的脖子,发出尖叫。而莫格里在花园凉亭里跳跃着,透过屏风看着外面,用门牙发出猫头鹰般的叫声,表示他的嘲笑和轻蔑。

"把人娃娃从陷阱里弄出来,我只能做这么多了。"巴格西拉喘着气说,"让我们带上人娃娃走吧。他们可能会再次进攻的。"

"我不发命令,他们不敢动的。待在原地!"卡阿咝咝地说,整个城市又再次安静了。"我没能再早点赶到,兄弟,不过我想我听到你的呼叫了。"——那是对巴格西拉说的。

"我——我可能是在战斗的时候叫的吧,"巴格西拉回答说,"巴洛,你受伤了吗?"

"我不确定,他们没把我撕成一百块吧,"巴洛庄重地说,边说边交

---

clamor *n.* 吵闹声 　　 derision *n.* 嘲弄,嘲笑 　　 contempt *n.* 轻蔑 　　 attack *v.* 攻击

bearlings," said Baloo, gravely shaking one leg after the other. "Wow! I am sore. Kaa, we owe you, I think, our lives—Bagheera and I."

"No matter. Where is the manling?"

"Here, in a trap. I cannot climb out," cried Mowgli. The **curve** of the broken dome was above his head.

"Take him away. He dances like Mao the Peacock. He will **crush** our young," said the cobras inside.

"Hah! " said Kaa with a chuckle, "he has friends everywhere, this manling. Stand back, manling. And hide you, O Poison People. I break down the wall."

Kaa looked carefully till he found a discolored crack in the marble tracery showing a weak spot, made two or three light taps with his head to get the distance, and then lifting up six feet of his body clear of the ground, sent home half a dozen full-power smashing blows, nose-first. The screen-work broke and fell away in a cloud of dust and rubbish, and Mowgli leaped through the opening and **flung** himself between Baloo and Bagheera—an arm around each big neck.

"Art you hurt?" said Baloo, hugging him softly.

替地抖动两条腿。"哇！我好生气。卡阿，我想我们——巴格西拉和我，多亏了你才没事。"

"没关系。人娃娃在哪里呢？"

"这里，陷阱里。我爬不出去，"莫格里喊道。他头的上方是坍塌的圆顶屋拱起的部分。

"带他走吧。他跳起来像孔雀玛奥一样。他会压坏我们的小蛇的。"里面的眼镜蛇说。

"哈阿！"卡阿笑着说，"这个人娃娃到处都有朋友。后退一些，人娃娃。还有你们，毒蛇们，找地方躲起来。我要把墙推倒了。"

卡阿仔细地观察了一番，发现大理石窗花格上有个褪色的裂缝，表明那个地方不牢固。他用头敲了两三下来测量一下距离，然后把他六英尺长的身体完全抬离了地面，鼻子在前，用尽全力，狠狠地撞了六下。屏风破了，在一阵灰尘和垃圾中消失了。莫格里从缺口处跳了出来，扑到巴洛和巴格西拉中间——一手搂着一个粗脖子。

"你受伤了吗？"巴洛轻轻地抱着他问。

---

curve *n*. 曲线,弧度　　crush *v*. 压破,压伤　　fling *v*. 使扑

"I am sore, hungry, and not a little bruised. But, oh, they have handled you grievously, my Brothers! Ye bleed."

"Others also," said Bagheera, licking his lips and looking at the monkey-dead on the terrace and round the tank.

"It is nothing, it is nothing, if you are safe, oh, my pride of all little frogs! " whimpered Baloo.

"Of that we shall judge later," said Bagheera, in a dry voice that Mowgli did not at all like. "But here is Kaa to whom we owe the battle and you owest your life. Thank him according to our customs, Mowgli."

Mowgli turned and saw the great Python's head swaying a foot above his own.

"So this is the manling," said Kaa. "Very soft is his skin, and he is not unlike the Bandar-log. Have a care, manling, that I do not mistake you for a monkey some twilight when I have newly changed my coat."

"We be one blood, you and I," Mowgli answered. "I take my life from you tonight. My kill shall be your kill if ever you are hungry, O Kaa."

"All thanks, Little Brother," said Kaa, though his eyes twinkled.

THE JUNGLE STORY

"我又气又饿,但是一点也没受伤。但是,哦,他们怎么对你们下手这么狠啊,我的兄弟们!你们在流血。"

"他们也是。"巴格西拉说,他舔了舔嘴唇,看着露台上、水池边横躺着的猴子尸体。

"这没什么,这没什么,只要你安全,哦,所有的小青蛙中你最让我骄傲!"巴洛哽咽着说。

"那事我们稍后再来评判,"巴格西拉用冷冰冰的声音说,那个声音莫格里一点也不喜欢,"但是这次战斗和你的性命都多亏了卡阿。根据我们的习俗,莫格里,你要好好谢谢他。"

莫格里转过身,看到在他头上方一英尺的地方,大蟒蛇正挥动着他的脑袋。

"原来这就是人娃娃。"卡阿说,"他的皮肤真嫩,和猴子们还真有点像。小心点,人娃娃,等我重新蜕皮以后的某个黄昏里,可别把你错当成猴子了。"

"我们是同一血脉的,你和我,"莫格里回答道,"今晚我的性命是你救的。以后只要你饿了,我的猎物就是你的猎物,哦,卡阿。"

"太感谢了,小兄弟,"卡阿说,虽然他的眼睛闪烁着,"这么勇敢的

---

bleed *v.* 流血　　dry *a.* 冷冰冰的　　custom *n.* 习惯,习俗

"And what may so bold a hunter kill? I ask that I may follow when next he goes abroad."

"I kill nothing,—I am too little,—but I drive goats toward such as can use them. When you are empty come to me and see if I speak the truth. I have some skill in these [he held out his hands], and if ever you are in a trap, I may pay the debt which I owe to you, to Bagheera, and to Baloo, here. Good hunting to you all, my masters."

"Well said," growled Baloo, for Mowgli had returned thanks very prettily. The Python dropped his head lightly for a minute on Mowgli's shoulder. "A brave heart and a **courteous** tongue," said he. "They shall carry you far through the jungle, manling. But now go hence quickly with your friends. Go and sleep, for the moon sets, and what follows it is not well that you shouldst see."

The moon was sinking behind the hills and the lines of **trembling** monkeys **huddled** together on the walls and battlements looked like ragged shaky fringes of things. Baloo went down to the tank for a drink and Bagheera began to put his fur in order, as Kaa glided out into the center of the terrace and brought his jaws together with a ringing snap that drew all the monkeys' eyes upon

THE JUNGLE STORY

猎人会猎取什么样的猎物呢？下次他去外面打猎的时候，让我跟着去吧。"

"我什么都不猎杀——我还太小，但是我会把山羊赶到我能利用他们的地方。等你无聊的时候过来找我，看看我说的是不是实话。我在这些事情上面有一些本领(他伸出了他的双手)。如果你掉入了陷阱，我会报答我欠你们的恩情，你，巴格西拉还有巴洛。祝大家打猎愉快，我的老师们。"

"说得很好，"巴洛欢叫着说，因为莫格里非常真诚地表达了谢意。蟒蛇把头轻轻地靠在莫格里的肩膀上，搁了一会。"一颗勇敢的心和礼貌的语言，"他说，"他们要把你抬到丛林深处，人娃娃。但是现在你和你的朋友们快点离开这里吧，去睡觉吧，月亮已经落下去了，你会发现接下来发生的不会是什么好事。"

月亮已经落到山后面去了。一排排颤抖的猴子在城墙和城墙垛上挤作一团，他们看上去就像参差不齐、摇摇晃晃的穗子。巴洛到下面水池里喝了点水，巴格西拉开始梳理自己的皮毛，这时卡阿滑到露台的中央。他把下巴啪地一下合上，把猴子们所有的目光都吸引到他这里。

---

courteous *a.* 礼貌的   tremble *v.* 发抖，哆嗦   huddle *v.* 挤作一团

him.

"The moon sets," he said. "Is there yet light enough to see?"

From the walls came a moan like the wind in the tree-tops—
"We see, O Kaa."

"Good. Begins now the dance—the Dance of the Hunger of
Kaa. Sit still and watch."

He turned twice or **thrice** in a big circle, weaving his head from
right to left. Then he began making loops and figures of eight with
his body, and soft, oozy triangles that melted into squares and five-
sided figures, and coiled mounds, never resting, never hurrying, and
never stopping his low humming song. It grew darker and darker,
till at last the dragging, shifting coils disappeared, but they could
hear the rustle of the scales.

Baloo and Bagheera stood still as stone, growling in their
throats, their neck hair bristling, and Mowgli watched and
wondered.

"Bandar-log," said the voice of Kaa at last, "can you stir foot or
hand without my order? Speak! "

"Without your order we cannot stir foot or hand, O Kaa! "

THE JUNGLE STORY

"月亮下山了,"他说,"还有亮光足够看得见吗?"

从城墙上传来呻吟声,就像树顶上的萧萧风声——"我们能看见,卡阿。"

"很好。现在开始跳舞了——猎手卡阿的舞蹈。静静地坐着看吧。"

他转了两三个大圈,左右摇晃着脑袋。然后他的身体摆成圈圈、八字型、软绵绵的三角形,三角形又变成四边形、五边形,他一刻不停地、不慌不忙地一圈一圈地往上堆,嘴里还一直低沉地哼着歌。天越来越黑了,直到最后,这慢慢拖动、变换的盘圈看不到了,但是他们能听到蜕皮的沙沙声。

巴洛和巴格西拉像石头一样站着一动不动,喉咙里发出咆哮声,他们脖子上的刚毛都竖了起来,莫格里诧异地看着这一切。

"猴子们,"终于传来卡阿的声音,"没有我的命令,你们能移动你们的手和脚吗?说!"

"没有你的命令,我们不能移动我们的手和脚,卡阿。"

"很好!都向我这边靠近一步。"

---

thrice *adv.* 三次

丛林的故事

"Good! Come all one pace nearer to me."

The lines of the monkeys swayed forward helplessly, and Baloo and Bagheera took one stiff step forward with them.

"Nearer! " hissed Kaa, and they all moved again.

Mowgli laid his hands on Baloo and Bagheera to get them away, and the two great beasts started as though they had been waked from a dream.

"Keep your hand on my shoulder," Bagheera whispered. "Keep it there, or I must go back—must go back to Kaa. Aah! "

"It is only old Kaa making circles on the dust," said Mowgli. "Let us go." And the three slipped off through a gap in the walls to the jungle.

"Whoof!" said Baloo, when he stood under the still trees again. "Never more will I make an ally of Kaa," and he shook himself all over.

"He knows more than we," said Bagheera, trembling. "In a little time, had I stayed, I should have walked down his throat."

"Many will walk by that road before the moon rises again,"said Baloo. "He will have good hunting—after his own fashion."

"But what was the meaning of it all?" said Mowgli, who did not

THE JUNGLE STORY

一排排的猴子无助地往前走了一步,巴洛和巴格西拉也跟着他们坚定地往前走了一步。

"再近点!"卡阿嗖嗖地说,他们又都走近了一步。

莫格里把手放在巴洛和巴格西拉身上,提醒他们该走了。这两只大野兽好像刚刚从梦中醒来一样,出发了。

"把你的手放在我的肩膀上,"巴格西拉小声说,"放在那里,否则我又要走回去了——又要走回到卡阿那里去了。啊!"

"那只是老卡阿在尘土里打圈圈,"莫格里说,"我们走吧。"他们三个从城墙的一个缺口悄悄地溜了出去,往丛林方向去了。

"哇呜!"当巴洛又站在静止的树下的时候说,"我再也不和卡阿结盟了,"他浑身上下抖动了起来。

"他比我们懂得多。" 巴格西拉颤抖着说,"我如果再呆一会儿的话,就要走到他的喉咙里去了。"

"在月亮重新升起以前会有很多猴子走上那条路的。"巴洛说,"他将会打猎顺利的——以他自己的方式。"

"但是这所有的一切有什么意义啊?"莫格里说,他对于蟒蛇的魅力了解不多,"我看到的只不过是一条大蛇傻傻地转着圈,一直到天

---

helplessly adv. 无助地   gap n. 缺口   ally n. 同盟,结盟   fashion n. 方式

155

know anything of a python's powers of **fascination**. "I saw no more than a big snake making foolish circles till the dark came. And his nose was all sore. Ho! Ho! "

"Mowgli," said Bagheera angrily, "his nose was sore on your **account**, as my ears and sides and paws, and Baloo's neck and shoulders are bitten on your account. Neither Baloo nor Bagheera will be able to hunt with pleasure for many days."

"It is nothing," said Baloo, "we have the man-cub again."

"True, but he has cost us heavily in time which might have been spent in good hunting, in wounds, in hair—I am half plucked along my back—and last of all, in honor. For, remember, Mowgli, I, who am the Black Panther, was forced to call upon Kaa for protection, and Baloo and I were both made stupid as little birds by the Hunger Dance. All this, man-cub, came of your playing with the Bandar-log."

"True, it is true," said Mowgli sorrowfully. "I am an evil man-cub, and my stomach is sad in me."

"Mf! What says the Law of the Jungle, Baloo?"

Baloo did not wish to bring Mowgli into any more trouble, but he could not **tamper** with the Law, so he **mumbled**: "Sorrow never

THE JUNGLE STORY

黑,而且他的鼻子都破了,嘀! 嘀! "

"莫格里,"巴格西拉生气地说,"他的鼻子破了是因为你,就像我的耳朵、身上、爪子还有巴洛的脖子、肩膀被咬了都是因为你。我们许多天都不能快乐地打猎了。"

"这没什么,"巴洛说,"我们又找回了人娃娃。"

"不错,但是他浪费了我们这么多原本可以用来好好打猎的时间,害我们受了伤,掉了毛——我背上的毛都快被拔掉了一半,还有自尊。因为,你要记住,莫格里,我,黑豹,不得不向卡阿寻求保护,看到他的捕食舞蹈,巴洛和我都像小鸟一样成了傻子。所有的这一切,人娃娃,都是因为你和猴子们玩引起的。"

"真的,这是真的。"莫格里痛苦地说,"我是可恶的人娃娃,我感到很愧疚。"

"唔! 丛林法则是怎么说的,巴洛? "

巴洛不想再给莫格里任何惩罚,但是他不能篡改丛林法则,所以他只能含糊地说,"懊悔永远不能延缓惩罚。但是你别忘了,巴格西拉,他还小。"

---

fascination *n.* 魅力　　account *n.* 原因，理由　　tamper *v.* 篡改　　mumble *v.* 含糊地说
sorrow *n.* 懊悔

stays punishment. But remember, Bagheera, he is very little."

"I will remember. But he has done **mischief**, and blows must be dealt now. Mowgli, have you anything to say?"

"Nothing. I did wrong. Baloo and you are wounded. It is just."

Bagheera gave him half a dozen love-taps from a panther's point of view (they would hardly have waked one of his own cubs), but for a seven-year-old boy they **amounted** to as severe a beating as you could wish to avoid. When it was all over Mowgli **sneezed**, and picked himself up without a word.

"Now," said Bagheera, "jump on my back, little brother, and we will go home."

One of the beauties of Jungle Law is that punishment settles all scores. There is no nagging afterward.

Mowgli laid his head down on Bagheera's back and slept so deeply that he never waked when he was put down in the home-cave.

THE JUNGLE STORY

"我知道,但是他闯了祸,现在必须得挨打。莫格里,你有什么要说的吗?"

"没有,我是做错了。巴洛和你都受伤了。挨打是我应得的。"

巴格西拉爱惜地打了他六下,从一只豹子的角度来看,这几下很轻,轻得都不会把他自己的小豹子拍醒。但是对于一个七岁的男孩来说,这几下是你很想躲开的一顿痛打。等巴格西拉打完了,莫格里打了个喷嚏,一言不发地站了起来。

"现在,"巴格西拉说,"跳到我的背上,小兄弟,我们回家了。"

丛林法则的一个好处就是惩罚解决了所有的宿怨,以后不会再纠缠不清。

莫格里把头靠在巴格西拉的背上睡着了,被带回到狼穴的时候,他也没有醒。

---

mischief *n.* 调皮,捣蛋　　amount *v.* 相当于　　sneeze *v.* 打喷嚏

丛林的故事

Chapter 4 Road-Song of the Bandar-Log

Here we go in a flung festoon,

Half-way up to the jealous moon!

Don't you envy our pranceful bands?

Don't you wish you had extra hands?

Wouldn't you like if your tails were—so—

Curved in the shape of a Cupid's bow?

Now you're angry, but—never mind,

Brother, your tail hangs down behind!

Here we sit in a branchy row,

Thinking of beautiful things we know;

Dreaming of deeds that we mean to do,

All complete, in a minute or two—

THE JUNGLE STORY

第四章　猴子进行曲

我们像挥动的花彩那样排着队，
在去令人羡慕的月亮途中！
你不羡慕我们这群昂首阔步的队伍吗？
你不希望自己再多些手吗？
你不希望你的尾巴能像——我们这样——
像丘比特的弯弓一样吗？
现在你很生气，但是——没关系，
兄弟，你的尾巴挂在身后！

我们像树枝那样在这里坐成一排，
想着我们所知道的令人愉快的事情；
梦想着我们打算要去做的事情，
过一两分钟以后所有的事情都会完成——

---

half-way *adv.* 在中途

丛林的故事

Something noble and wise and good,
Done by merely wishing we could.
We've forgotten, but—never mind,
Brother, your tail hangs down behind!

All the talk we ever have heard
 Uttered by bat or beast or bird—
Hide or fin or scale or feather—
Jabber it quickly and all together!
Excellent!   Wonderful!   Once again!

Now we are talking just like men!
Let's pretend we are ... never mind,
Brother, your tail hangs down behind!
This is the way of the Monkey-kind.

THE JUNGLE STORY

一些高尚、聪明而优秀的事情，
仅仅因为我们想去完成而完成了。
我们已经忘记了，但是——没关系，
兄弟，你的尾巴挂在身后！

所有我们听到的，
不管是蝙蝠、野兽还是鸟儿说的话——
不管是毛皮、鳍、鳞片还是羽毛——
快点一起说！
太好了！太棒了！再来一次！

现在我们像人类一样说话了！
让我们假装我们是——没关系，
兄弟，你的尾巴挂在身后！
这是猴子的方式。

---

utter *v.* 说,讲

丛林的故事

Then join our leaping lines that scumfish through the pines,

That rocket by where, light and high, the wild grape swings.

By the rubbish in our wake, and the noble noise we make,

Be sure, be sure, we're going to do some splendid things!

THE JUNGLE STORY

那么加入到我们在松树上扭打跳跃的行列里来，
加入到我们在轻飘飘、高高的野葡萄中急速前进的队伍里来。
以我们睡醒时所在的垃圾堆和我们发出的吵闹声起誓，
我们一定要，一定要去做些出色的事情！

中英对照

J.K.罗琳的读书单

丛林故事

THE JUNGLE STORY

［英］吉卜林◎著

辛　静◎译

中

《哈里·波特》作者J.K.罗琳

最喜爱的英美经典文学名著

中国书籍出版社

图书在版编目（CIP）数据

丛林故事／（英）吉卜林著；辛静译 . —北京：中国
书籍出版社，2007.1
（J. K. 罗琳的读书单）
书名原文：The Jungle Story
ISBN 978 - 7 - 5068 - 1721 - 9

Ⅰ. 丛 ... 　Ⅱ. ①吉 ... ②辛 ... 　Ⅲ. ①英语—汉语—
对照读物②童话—作品集—英国—近代
Ⅳ. H319.4：I

中国版本图书馆 CIP 数据核字（2006）第 159971 号

责任编辑／毕　磊　李立云
责任印制／熊　力　武雅彬
封面设计／汇智泉文化设计公司
出版发行／中国书籍出版社
　　　　　地　　　址：北京市丰台区三路居路 97 号（邮编：100073）
　　　　　电　　　话：(010)52257142(总编室)　(010)52257154(发行部)
　　　　　电子邮箱：chinabp@ vip. sina. com
经　　销／全国新华书店
印　　刷／三河市杨庄镇明华印装厂
开　　本／690 毫米×960 毫米　1/16
印　　张／31
字　　数／238 千字
版　　次／2013 年第 1 月第 2 版，2013 第 2 次印刷
定　　价／61.80 元（上、中、下）

版权所有　翻印必究

目录

丛林的故事

Chapter 5 "Tiger! Tiger!"

What of the hunting, hunter bold?
Brother, the watch was long and cold.
What of the quarry you went to kill?
Brother, he crops in the jungle still.
Where is the power that made your pride?
Brother, it ebbs from my flank and side.
Where is the haste that you hurry by?
Brother, I go to my lair—to die.

Now we must go back to the first tale. When Mowgli left the wolf's cave after the fight with the pack at the Council Rock, he went down to the plowed lands where the villagers lived, but he would not stop there because it was too near to the jungle, and he knew that he had made at least one bad enemy at the Council. So he hurried on, keeping to the **rough** road that ran down the valley, and followed it at a steady jog-trot for nearly twenty miles, till he came to a country that he did not know. The valley opened out into

THE JUNGLE STORY

第五章 "老虎！老虎！"

打猎如何啊，勇敢的猎手？

兄弟，守候猎物，既长久又寒冷。

你去捕杀的猎物是什么？

兄弟，他还躲在丛林里。

曾经令你骄傲的力量去哪儿了？

兄弟，它已从我的胁腹和肋肉间消失了。

你急匆匆地去哪里？

兄弟，我去我的兽穴——去死。

现在我们必须回到第一个故事。莫格里在会议岩上和狼群打过一场后，他离开了狼穴，下山往村民居住的耕地里去。但他没有停下来，因为离丛林还是太近，他知道他在会议上至少树立了一个死对头。于是，他继续前进，沿着顺山谷而下的崎岖的大路，缓缓地走了大约二十公里，直到一个他不认识的乡村。山谷变得豁然开朗，眼前出现了一大

---

rough *a.* 崎岖的，不平的

a great plain **dotted** over with rocks and cut up by ravines. At one end stood a little village, and at the other the thick jungle came down in a **sweep** to the grazing-grounds, and stopped there as though it had been cut off with a hoe. All over the plain, cattle and buffaloes were grazing, and when the little boys in **charge** of the herds saw Mowgli they shouted and ran away, and the yellow pariah dogs that hang about every Indian village barked. Mowgli walked on, for he was feeling hungry, and when he came to the village gate he saw the big thorn-bush that was drawn up before the gate at twilight, pushed to one side.

"Umph! " he said, for he had come across more than one such **barricade** in his night rambles after things to eat. "So men are afraid of the people of the jungle here also." He sat down by the gate, and when a man came out he stood up, opened his mouth, and pointed down it to show that he wanted food. The man stared, and ran back up the one street of the village shouting for the priest, who was a big, fat man dressed in white, with a red and yellow mark on his forehead. The priest came to the gate, and with him at least a hundred people, who stared and talked and shouted and pointed at

THE JUNGLE STORY

片平原,上面布满了星星点点的岩石,一道道的沟壑把平原分成一块块的。在平原的尽头,是个小村庄,另一头是茂密的丛林,连着大片的牧地。牧地和丛林的界限分明,好似用锄头割开的一样。平原上,耕牛和水牛在吃着草,放牛的娃娃见到莫格里都大叫着逃走了。那些经常在印度村里徘徊的黄毛野狗也狂吠起来。莫格里继续往前走着,因为他觉得饿了。当他走到村口的时候,他看见傍晚用来挡住路口的荆棘丛已经被挪到一边了。

"哼!"他说,因为他晚上出来打猎觅食时,好几次都遇到过这样的路障。"看来人也是怕丛林里的动物的。"他在路口坐了下来。当看到有个人走了过来,他就站起来,指着自己张大的嘴巴,意思是他想要吃东西。这个人呆呆地看着他,然后跑回到村里的一条路上,大声叫来了牧师,一个穿着白色衣服、高高胖胖的人,前额上还涂着红黄色的记号。牧师走到路口,至少还有一百多人跟着他,他们目不转睛地盯着

---

dot *v.* 星罗棋布于　　sweep *n.* 连绵的一片　　charge *n.* 负责　　barricade *n.* 路障,街垒

171

丛林的故事

Mowgli.

"They have no manners, these Men Folk," said Mowgli to himself. "Only the gray ape would behave as they do." So he threw back his long hair and frowned at the crowd.

"What is there to be afraid of?" said the priest. "Look at the marks on his arms and legs. They are the bites of wolves. He is but a wolf-child run away from the jungle."

Of course, in playing together, the cubs had often nipped Mowgli harder than they intended, and there were white scars all over his arms and legs. But he would have been the last person in the world to call these bites, for he knew what real biting meant.

"Arre! Arre! " said two or three women together. "To be bitten by wolves, poor child! He is a handsome boy. He has eyes like red fire. By my honor, Messua, he is not unlike your boy that was taken by the tiger."

"Let me look," said a woman with heavy copper rings on her wrists and ankles, and she peered at Mowgli under the palm of her hand. "Indeed he is not. He is thinner, but he has the very look of my boy."

他,大声地议论着,叫嚷着,对着莫格里指指点点。

"他们一点礼貌都没有,这些被称为人的家伙。"莫格里自言自语道, "只有灰猿才会这么做。"他把长发往后一甩,皱着眉看着大伙。

"这有什么好害怕的?"牧师说。"看看他手臂上、腿上的疤。都是被狼咬的。他只是个从丛林里跑出来的狼孩罢了。"

当然,一起玩的时候,狼崽们常常会啃得重了一点,所以他的腿上、手臂上都是苍白的疤痕。但是无论如何这都不能称为咬,因为他知道真正的咬是什么样的。

"啊呀!啊呀!"两三个妇女一起叫了起来。"他被狼咬了,可怜的孩子!他真是个漂亮的孩子。他的眼睛像红红的火焰。我敢发誓,梅苏亚,他真像你那个被老虎叼走的男孩。"

"让我瞧瞧,"一个手腕上、脚腕上带着沉甸甸的铜镯子的女人说道,她用手掌挡着眼睛,盯着莫格里看了半天。"还真有点像。他比较瘦一点,但神情还真像。"

丛林的故事

The priest was a clever man, and he knew that Messua was wife to the richest villager in the place. So he looked up at the sky for a minute and said solemnly: "What the jungle has taken the jungle has **restored**. Take the boy into your house, my sister, and forget not to honor the priest who sees so far into the lives of men."

"By the Bull that bought me," said Mowgli to himself, "but all this talking is like another looking-over by the pack! Well, if I am a man, a man I must become."

The crowd parted as the woman **beckoned** Mowgli to her hut, where there was a red lacquered bedstead, a great earthen grain chest with funny raised patterns on it, half a dozen copper cooking pots, an image of a Hindu god in a little alcove, and on the wall a real looking glass, such as they sell at the country fairs.

She gave him a long drink of milk and some bread, and then she laid her hand on his head and looked into his eyes; for she thought perhaps that he might be her real son come back from the jungle where the tiger had taken him. So she said, "Nathoo, O Nathoo! " Mowgli did not show that he knew the name. "Dost you not remember the day when I gave you the new shoes?" She touched his foot, and it was almost as hard as horn. "No," she said

174

THE JUNGLE STORY

　　牧师是个聪明人,他知道梅苏亚是这里最富有的村民的妻子。于是,他抬起头看着天空好一会儿,然后庄重地说:"丛林从你这里夺走的已经归还给你了。把男孩带回家吧,我的姐妹,别忘了向能看透人类命运的牧师表示你的敬意。"

　　"我以赎买我的那头公牛起誓,"莫格里自言自语地说,"但这些谈话就好比是另外一个被狼群接纳的审查仪式一样!好吧,如果我是个人,那么我就必须变成人。"

　　妇女招手让莫格里去她的小屋,人群也就散开了。屋里放着一张刷了红漆的床架,一只陶制的存放粮食的大箱子,上面有许多滑稽的凸起的花纹。六只铜锅、一尊印度神像安放在一个小小的壁龛里。墙上挂着一块真正的镜子,就像农村集市上卖的那种。

　　她给了他一大杯牛奶和一些面包,然后她把手放在他的头上,凝望着他的眼睛,因为她在想,也许真的是他的儿子,被老虎叼进丛林里,现在又回来了。于是她说:"纳索,噢纳索!"莫格里看上去没听过这个名字。"你还记得我给你穿上新鞋的那天吗?"她抚摸着他的脚,那脚坚硬得像鹿角。"不,"她痛苦地说,"这双脚从来没有穿过鞋子,

---

restore v. 归还　　beckon v. (用点头、招手等方式)召唤

sorrowfully, "those feet have never worn shoes, but you are very like my Nathoo, and you shall be my son."

Mowgli was uneasy, because he had never been under a roof before. But as he looked at the thatch, he saw that he could tear it out any time if he wanted to get away, and that the window had no fastenings. "What is the good of a man," he said to himself at last, "if he does not understand man's talk? Now I am as silly and dumb as a man would be with us in the jungle. I must speak their talk."

It was not for fun that he had learned while he was with the wolves to imitate the challenge of bucks in the jungle and the grunt of the little wild pig. So, as soon as Messua pronounced a word Mowgli would imitate it almost perfectly, and before dark he had learned the names of many things in the hut.

There was a difficulty at bedtime, because Mowgli would not sleep under anything that looked so like a panther trap as that hut, and when they shut the door he went through the window. "Give him his will," said Messua's husband. "Remember he can never till now have slept on a bed. If he is indeed sent in the place of our son he will not run away."

So Mowgli stretched himself in some long, clean grass at the

THE JUNGLE STORY

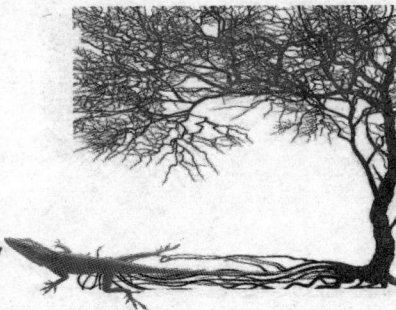

但是你真的很像我的纳索,你就当我的儿子吧。"

莫格里觉得很不自在,因为他从来没在屋顶下呆过。但当他抬头看到茅草屋的屋顶时,他知道,任何时候只要他想离开,他就可以把它撕开,而且窗户上也都没有窗拴。"如果听不懂别人在说什么,"他自言自语地说,"做人有什么好的?现在我像个傻瓜和哑巴,就像人来到丛林里生活一样。我必须学会他们说的话。"

以前在狼群里的时候,他也模仿过丛林里公鹿的挑战声和小野猪的呼噜声,那都不过是为了好玩。所以每当梅苏亚说出一个字,莫格里几乎可以一点不差地学着说。在天黑以前,他已经学会了屋里许多东西的名称。

睡觉的时候,麻烦就来了。因为莫格里不肯睡在那个像猎豹的陷阱似的小屋,当他们关上门的时候,他从窗口跳了出去。"随他去吧,"梅苏亚的丈夫说道。"别忘了他还从来没有在床上睡过觉。如果他真的是被派来代替我们的儿子的,他就一定不会逃走。"

所以莫格里就在耕地边上一片长长的、干净的草地上躺了下来。

---

challenge *n.* 挑战

edge of the field, but before he had closed his eyes a soft gray nose poked him under the chin.

"Phew! " said Gray Brother (he was the eldest of Mother Wolf's cubs). "This is a poor reward for following you twenty miles. You smellest of wood smoke and cattle—altogether like a man already. Wake, Little Brother; I bring news."

"Are all well in the jungle?" said Mowgli, hugging him.

"All except the wolves that were burned with the Red Flower. Now, listen. Shere Khan has gone away to hunt far off till his coat grows again, for he is badly singed. When he returns he swears that he will lay your bones in the Waingunga."

"There are two words to that. I also have made a little promise. But news is always good. I am tired tonight,—very tired with new things, Gray Brother,—but bring me the news always."

"You will not forget that you are a wolf? Men will not make you forget?" said Gray Brother anxiously.

"Never. I will always remember that I love you and all in our cave. But also I will always remember that I have been cast out of the pack."

THE JUNGLE STORY

但还没等他闭上眼睛，一只软软的灰鼻子就开始戳他的下巴。

"呦，"灰兄弟说(他是狼妈妈的崽子中最年长的一个)，"追踪了你二十英里，就得到这样的回报啊。你身上都是篝火和耕牛的气味——你已经像个人了。醒醒，小兄弟，我带来了消息。"

"丛林里都还好吧？"莫格里抱了抱他说道。

"都好，除了被红花烫伤的那些狼。现在，听着，萨克汗跑到很远的地方去狩猎了，一直要等到他的毛皮重新长出来再回来，因为他被烧得很厉害。他发誓说等他回来，要把你的骨头埋在维冈加。"

"那就走着瞧了。我也许下了一个小小的诺言。但是，有消息总是好的。今晚，我很累了——学新东西学得太累了，灰兄弟，记住要常常给我带消息来啊。"

"你不会忘了你是狼吧？那些人会不会让你忘了这一点？"灰兄弟急切地问道。

"永远不会。我会永远记得我爱你和我们山洞里所有的狼，但是我也会永远记得我被赶出了狼群。"

---

cast *v.* 扔，丢弃

丛林的故事

"And that you mayest be cast out of another pack. Men are only men, little brother, and their talk is like the talk of frogs in a pond. When I come down here again, I will wait for you in the bamboos at the edge of the grazing-ground."

For three months after that night Mowgli hardly ever left the village gate, he was so busy learning the ways and customs of men. First he had to wear a cloth round him, which **annoyed** him horribly; and then he had to learn about money, which he did not in the least understand, and about plowing, of which he did not see the use. Then the little children in the village made him very angry. Luckily, the Law of the Jungle had taught him to keep his temper, for in the jungle life and food depend on keeping your **temper**; but when they made fun of him because he would not play games or fly kites, or because he **mispronounced** some word, only the knowledge that it was unsportsmanlike to kill little naked cubs kept him from picking them up and breaking them in two.

He did not know his own strength in the least. In the jungle he knew he was weak **compared** with the beasts, but in the village people said that he was as strong as a bull.

And Mowgli had not the faintest idea of the difference that

THE JUNGLE STORY

"那么你也会被赶出另外一个群体。人就是人,小兄弟,他们说话就像池塘里的青蛙叽哩哇啦。等我再下山来的时候,我会在牧地旁边的竹林里等你。"

在那天晚上以后的三个月里,莫格里几乎没有走出过村子,他忙着学习人类的生活方式和生活习惯。首先,他得在身上缠一块布,这使他非常懊恼;其次,他得学习钱的事情,这他一点儿都不懂;他还得学习耕种,虽然他一点也不明白这有什么用。村里的小娃娃总惹他非常生气。幸好,丛林法则教会了他控制自己的脾气,因为丛林里的生活和猎食都要靠冷静,但是每当他们因为他不会玩游戏或者不会放风筝,或是因为他某些字发错音而嘲笑他的时候,仅仅是因为他知道杀死这些光着身子的小娃娃是不公正的,才使他没有伸手抓起他们,把他们撕成两半。

他丝毫不了解自己的力量。在丛林里,他知道和其他的野兽相比,他是弱的,但是村里的人都说他力气大得像公牛。

莫格里也毫不了解人与人之间的等级差别。有一次他看到卖陶器

---

annoy v. 使烦恼;使恼怒　　temper n. 情绪,脾气　　mispronounce v. 发错音
compare v. 比较

caste makes between man and man. When the potter's donkey slipped in the clay pit, Mowgli hauled it out by the tail, and helped to stack the pots for their journey to the market at Khanhiwara. That was very shocking, too, for the potter is a low-caste man, and his donkey is worse. When the priest scolded him, Mowgli threatened to put him on the donkey too, and the priest told Messua's husband that Mowgli had better be set to work as soon as possible; and the village head-man told Mowgli that he would have to go out with the buffaloes next day, and herd them while they grazed. No one was more pleased than Mowgli; and that night, because he had been appointed a servant of the village, as it were, he went off to a circle that met every evening on a masonry platform under a great fig-tree. It was the village club, and the head-man and the watchman and the barber, who knew all the gossip of the village, and old Buldeo, the village hunter, who had a Tower musket, met and smoked. The monkeys sat and talked in the upper branches, and there was a hole under the platform where a cobra lived, and he had his little platter of milk every night because he was sacred; and the old men sat around the tree and talked, and pulled at the big huqas (the water-pipes) till far into the night. They told

THE JUNGLE STORY

的小贩的驴滑到了土坑里,莫格里拽着它的尾巴把它拖了起来。他还帮小贩堆好陶罐,好拉到肯西瓦拉的市场上去卖。这事让人们大为震惊,因为卖陶器的小贩是个下层人,他的驴子就更加低贱了。当牧师责怪莫格里的时候,莫格里威胁说要把他也放到驴背上。牧师告诉梅苏亚的丈夫,最好尽快地打发莫格里去干活,村里的头头告诉莫格里,第二天他得赶着水牛出去放牧。莫格里高兴极了。那天晚上,因为他已经被指派去做村里的雇工,他就去参加村里的聚会了。每天晚上,人们在一棵巨大的无花果树下围坐在一块石台边上。这是村里的俱乐部,村里的头头、巡夜人和剃头师傅(他们知道村里的所有的小道消息)还有拥有一枝塔尔牌步枪的老猎人布尔迪奥,他们在这里聚会、抽烟。一群猴子在高高的枝头上唧唧咕咕地说个不停,石台底下有个小洞,住着一条蛇,因为被认为是神蛇,所以人们每天会给他送上一小盘牛奶。老

---

haul *v.* 用力拖　　scold *v.* 责骂　　appoint *v.* 任命,委任

wonderful tales of gods and men and ghosts; and Buldeo told even more wonderful ones of the ways of beasts in the jungle, till the eyes of the children sitting outside the circle bulged out of their heads. Most of the tales were about animals, for the jungle was always at their door. The deer and the wild pig grubbed up their crops, and now and again the tiger carried off a man at twilight, within sight of the village gates.

Mowgli, who naturally knew something about what they were talking of, had to cover his face not to show that he was laughing, while Buldeo, the Tower musket across his knees, climbed on from one wonderful story to another, and Mowgli's shoulders shook.

Buldeo was explaining how the tiger that had carried away Messua's son was a ghost-tiger, and his body was **inhabited** by the ghost of a wicked, old money-lender, who had died some years ago. "And I know that this is true," he said, "because Purun Dass always limped from the blow that he got in a riot when his account books were burned, and the tiger that I speak of he limps, too, for the tracks of his pads are unequal."

"True, true, that must be the truth," said the gray-beards, nodding together.

THE JUNGLE STORY

人们围坐在树下，聊着天，抽着巨大的水烟袋，一直到深夜。他们常讲一些关于神、人和鬼的故事；布尔迪奥还常讲一些关于丛林里野兽的生活方式的故事，听得坐在圈子外面的孩子们的眼睛都快要鼓出了脑袋。大部分的故事都是关于动物的，因为丛林就在他们家门口。鹿和野猪偷吃他们的庄稼，老虎常常在黄昏的时候，在离村口不远的地方叼走一个人。

莫格里当然知道一些他们谈论的东西，他只好遮着脸，不让他们看见他在笑。而布尔迪奥，膝盖上搁着他那把塔尔步枪，一个接一个讲着故事，莫格里的肩膀晃个不停。

这会儿布尔迪奥正在解释说，那个曾经叼走梅苏亚儿子的老虎是个鬼虎。他曾被一个几年前去世的、邪恶的放债人的鬼魂附身。"我知道这是真的，"他说，"因为在一次暴动中，普让·达斯的账本被烧，人也被打瘸了。我说的那只老虎也是瘸的，因为它的爪印有深有浅。"

"真的，真的，那一定是真的。"灰胡子的老人们一起点着头。

---

inhabit *v.* 居住于　　riot *n.* 暴动，骚乱

"Are all these tales such cobwebs and moon talk?" said Mowgli. "That tiger limps because he was born lame, as everyone knows. To talk of the soul of a money-lender in a beast that never had the courage of a jackal is child's talk."

Buldeo was speechless with surprise for a moment, and the head-man stared.

"Oho! It is the jungle brat, is it?" said Buldeo. "If you are so wise, better bring his hide to Khanhiwara, for the Government has set a hundred rupees on his life. Better still, talk not when your elders speak."

Mowgli rose to go. "All the evening I have lain here listening," he called back over his shoulder, "and, except once or twice, Buldeo has not said one word of truth concerning the jungle, which is at his very doors. How, then, shall I believe the tales of ghosts and gods and goblins which he says he has seen?"

"It is full time that boy went to herding," said the head-man, while Buldeo puffed and snorted at Mowgli's **impertinence**.

The custom of most Indian villages is for a few boys to take the cattle and buffaloes out to graze in the early morning, and bring them back at night. The very cattle that would **trample** a white man

186

THE JUNGLE STORY

"所有的故事都是异想天开、瞎编乱造的吗？"莫格里说，"那个老虎是瘸的，因为他生下来就是瘸的，这大家都知道。说放债人附魂到那个比豺狼胆子还小的野兽身上，完全是想象出来的。"

"啊哈！那是丛林里回来的小鬼，是吗？"布尔迪奥说，"如果你那么聪明，最好把它的皮毛带到肯西瓦拉，因为政府正在悬赏一百卢布要他的命。不然，长辈说话，最好别插嘴。"

莫格里站起来要走了。"整个晚上我都躺在这儿听，"他回头说道，"布尔迪奥说的关于丛林的事情，除了一两句以外，其他都不是真的。可丛林就在他家门口呀。那么，我要怎么相信他说他见过的关于鬼、上帝和妖精的故事呢？"

"这孩子确实该去放牛了。"村头说。布尔迪奥被莫格里的顶撞气得大口地抽着烟，鼻子里发出哼哼的声音。

大多数印度村庄的习惯是在清晨的时候，由几个孩子赶着牛群和水牛出去放牧，晚上再把它们赶回来。这群可以把一个白人活活踩死的牛，却任由够不着他们鼻子的孩子们打骂。只要孩子们跟着牛群，他

---

impertinence *n.* 不礼貌,鲁莽   trample *v.* 踩,践踏

丛林的故事

to death allow themselves to be banged and **bullied** and shouted at by children that hardly come up to their noses. So long as the boys keep with the herds they are safe, for not even the tiger will charge a mob of cattle. But if they **straggle** to pick flowers or hunt lizards, they are sometimes carried off. Mowgli went through the village street in the dawn, sitting on the back of Rama, the great herd bull. The slaty-blue buffaloes, with their long, backward-sweeping horns and **savage** eyes, rose out their byres, one by one, and followed him, and Mowgli made it very clear to the children with him that he was the master. He beat the buffaloes with a long, polished bamboo, and told Kamya, one of the boys, to graze the cattle by themselves, while he went on with the buffaloes, and to be very careful not to **stray** away from the herd.

An Indian grazing ground is all rocks and scrub and tussocks and little ravines, among which the herds **scatter** and disappear. The buffaloes generally keep to the pools and **muddy** places, where they lie wallowing or basking in the warm mud for hours. Mowgli drove them on to the edge of the plain where the Waingunga came out of the jungle; then he dropped from Rama's neck, **trotted** off to a bamboo clump, and found Gray Brother. "Ah," said Gray Brother,

188

THE JUNGLE STORY

们就很安全,因为即使是老虎也不敢冲向一群牛。但是如果落在后面去采花或是捉蜥蜴,有时就会被叼走了。破晓时分,莫格里骑在领头牛罗玛的身上,穿过村里的大街。那些深蓝灰色的水牛,长着向后弯曲的牛角、野性的眼睛,一头一头地从牛棚出来,跟着他。莫格里明确地告诉孩子们:他是头领。他用一根长长的光滑的竹竿敲打着水牛。他告诉

其中一个叫卡亚的小男孩,让他们自己去放牧牛群,而他继续赶着水牛,叮嘱他们小心点,不要离开牛群。

印度的牧地到处都是岩石、低矮丛林、杂草丛和小河谷,牛群一到里面就分散了,消失得无影无踪。水牛总是待在池塘和泥泞的地方,他们在暖暖的烂泥中往往一躺就是几个小时,打打滚,晒晒太阳。莫格里赶着牛一直走到平原边上,维冈加河就是从这里流出丛林的;然后他从罗玛的脖子上跳下,一路小跑来到一片竹林,找到了灰兄弟。"啊,"灰兄弟说,"我在这里等了

---

bully v. 推,强迫   straggle v. 迷路,掉队   savage a. 野性的   stray v. 迷路,离群
scatter v. 分散   muddy a. 泥泞的   trot v. 小跑,快步走

丛林的故事

"I have waited here very many days. What is the meaning of this cattle-herding work?"

"It is an order," said Mowgli. "I am a village herd for a while. What news of Shere Khan?"

"He has come back to this country, and has waited here a long time for you. Now he has gone off again, for the game is scarce. But he means to kill you."

"Very good," said Mowgli. "So long as he is away do you or one of the four brothers sit on that rock, so that I can see you as I come out of the village. When he comes back wait for me in the ravine by the dhak tree in the center of the plain. We need not walk into Shere Khan's mouth."

Then Mowgli picked out a shady place, and lay down and slept while the buffaloes grazed round him.

Herding in India is one of the laziest things in the world. The cattle move and crunch, and lie down, and move on again, and they do not even low. They only grunt, and the buffaloes very seldom say anything, but get down into the muddy pools one after another, and work their way into the mud till only their noses and staring china-blue eyes show above the surface, and then they lie like logs. The

你很多天了。这个放牛的工作有什么意思啊？"

"这是命令，"莫格里说，"我现在暂时给村里放牛。有萨克汗的消息吗？"

"他已经回到这儿来了，而且在这儿等了你很长时间了。现在这里猎物太少，他又走了。但他打算要杀了你。"

"很好，"莫格里说，"只要他没回来，你或者四个狼兄弟当中的一个就坐在那块岩石上，让我一出村子就可以看到。等他回来了，就在平原中间达克树下的河谷里等我。我们可不要走到萨克汗嘴巴里去。"

然后莫格里找了一块树荫，躺下来睡着了，水牛在他身边吃着草。

在印度放牛是世界上最懒惰的事情之一。牛群走动着，嘎吱嘎吱地吃着草，然后躺下来休息一会，接着又往前走，他们甚至都不哞哞地叫。他们只是哼哼，水牛也很少说什么，只是一个接一个地走到泥潭里去，慢慢地把身子沉下去，直到只有鼻子和瞪大的青瓷色的眼睛露出水面，然后他们躺在那里一动不动。太阳晒在岩石上，使之在热浪中跳

丛林的故事

sun makes the rocks dance in the heat, and the herd children hear
one kite (never any more) whistling almost out of sight **overhead**,
and they know that if they died, or a cow died, that kite would
sweep down, and the next kite miles away would see him drop and
follow, and the next, and the next, and almost before they were
dead there would be a score of hungry kites come out of nowhere.
Then they sleep and wake and sleep again, and weave little baskets
of dried grass and put grasshoppers in them; or catch two praying
mantises and make them fight; or string a necklace of red and black
jungle nuts; or watch a lizard basking on a rock, or a snake hunting
a frog near the wallows. Then they sing long, long songs with odd
native quavers at the end of them, and the day seems longer than
most people's whole lives, and perhaps they make a mud castle with
mud **figures** of men and horses and buffaloes, and put reeds into the
men's hands, and pretend that they are kings and the figures are
their armies, or that they are gods to be **worshiped**. Then evening
comes and the children call, and the buffaloes lumber up out of the
sticky mud with noises like gunshots going off one after the other,
and they all string across the gray plain back to the **twinkling** village
lights.

THE JUNGLE STORY

起了舞,放牛娃们听见有一只鸢(永远只有一只)在头顶上看不见的地方啸叫。他们知道如果他们死了,或是有一头母牛死了,那只鸢就会俯冲下来, 数里以外的鸢看到他冲下来也会紧随其后,一只接一只,几乎在他们断气之前, 会有二十多只饿鸢不知道从哪里冒出来。接着放牛娃们睡了又醒,醒了又睡,用干草编制小篮子,把蚱蜢放到里面;或是捉两只螳螂,让他们打架;或是用红色、黑色的干果编成一条项链;或是看蜥蜴在岩石上晒太阳, 在泥沼旁看蛇吞噬青蛙。然后他们唱起了长长的歌,还带着当地人奇怪的颤音。这一天似乎比很多人的一生还要漫长, 也许他们会堆一个烂泥城堡,用泥捏出人、马和水牛,然后在泥人的手中放上芦苇,假装他们是国王,泥人就是他们的军队,或者假装他们是被敬仰的神。傍晚来了,孩子们大声地叫喊着,水牛从泥泞的地里笨拙地爬出来,发出一声接一声如枪声一般的声音。他们排成一列,穿过灰色的平原,回到灯火闪亮的村庄。

---

overhead *adv.* 在头顶上　　　figure *n.* 外形,轮廓,形象　　　worship *v.* 崇拜,尊敬
twinkling *a.* 闪烁的

丛林的故事

Day after day Mowgli would lead the buffaloes out to their wallows, and day after day he would see Gray Brother's back a mile and a half away across the plain (so he knew that Shere Khan had not come back), and day after day he would lie on the grass listening to the noises round him, and dreaming of old days in the jungle. If Shere Khan had made a false step with his lame paw up in the jungles by the Waingunga, Mowgli would have heard him in those long, still mornings.

At last a day came when he did not see Gray Brother at the signal place, and he laughed and headed the buffaloes for the ravine by the dhk tree, which was all covered with golden-red flowers. There sat Gray Brother, every bristle on his back lifted.

"He has hidden for a month to throw you off your guard. He crossed the ranges last night with Tabaqui, hot-foot on your trail," said the Wolf, panting.

Mowgli frowned. "I am not afraid of Shere Khan, but Tabaqui is very cunning."

"Have no fear," said Gray Brother, licking his lips a little. "I met Tabaqui in the dawn. Now he is telling all his wisdom to the kites, but he told me everything before I broke his back. Shere

THE JUNGLE STORY

日复一日,莫格里带着水牛们到泥地里,每天他都能看见灰兄弟在穿过平原一公里半的地方坐着的背影(他知道萨克汗还没有回来),他就可以每天躺在草地上听着周围的声音,梦想着过去在丛林里的日子。在那些长长的安静的早晨,如果萨克汗在维冈加河边的丛林里用他的瘸爪迈出错误的一步,莫格里也会看见的。

终于有一天,他没有在约好的地方看见灰兄弟,他哈哈大笑,领着水牛来到达克树下的河谷边。树上开满了金红色的花。狼兄弟坐在那里,背上的每一根刚毛都竖在那里。

"他躲了一个月就是为了让你放松警惕。昨天晚上,他和塔巴奇翻过山,在追踪你的足迹。"狼兄弟喘着气说。

莫格里皱着眉说,"我不怕萨克汗,但是塔巴奇很狡猾。"

"不用怕,"狼兄弟边说边舔了舔自己的嘴巴。"我破晓时分碰到塔巴奇了。现在他正在向鸢卖弄他的聪明呢,但是在我打断他的背脊骨之前,他把一切都告诉我了。萨克汗的计划是今天晚上在村口等

---

signal *n.* 信号,暗号   guard *n.* 警惕

195

Khan's plan is to wait for you at the village gate this evening—for you and for no one else. He is lying up now, in the big dry ravine of the Waingunga."

"Has he eaten today, or does he hunt empty?" said Mowgli, for the answer meant life and death to him.

"He killed at dawn,—a pig,—and he has drunk too. Remember, Shere Khan could never fast, even for the sake of revenge."

"Oh! Fool, fool! What a cub's cub it is! Eaten and drunk too, and he thinks that I shall wait till he has slept! Now, where does he lie up? If there were but ten of us we might pull him down as he lies. These buffaloes will not charge unless they wind him, and I cannot speak their language. Can we get behind his track so that they may smell it?"

"He swam far down the Waingunga to cut that off," said Gray Brother.

"Tabaqui told him that, I know. He would never have thought of it alone." Mowgli stood with his finger in his mouth, thinking. "The big ravine of the Waingunga. That opens out on the plain not half a mile from here. I can take the herd round through the jungle to the head of the ravine and then sweep down —but he would

196

THE JUNGLE STORY

你——只等你,不等别人。他现在正在维冈加那条干枯的大河谷里躺着呢。"

"他今天吃过东西了吗,还是空着肚子出来打猎的?"莫格里问,这个答案对他来说生死攸关。

"早上他杀了一头猪,他也喝过水了。记住,萨克汗从来不会禁食,即使是为了报仇。"

"哦,傻瓜,傻瓜!真是狗崽子!吃过东西也喝过水了。他以为我会等他睡醒!现在,他躺在哪里呢?如果我们有十个,我们就可以在他睡的地方制服他。可这些水牛只有嗅到他的气味才会冲上去,我又不会说他们的语言。我们能不能绕到他的背后,让水牛能嗅出他的味道呢?"

"他跳下维冈加河游了很长一段路,好不留下自己的踪迹。"灰兄弟说。

"我知道,肯定是塔巴奇教他的。他自己决不可能会想出来。"莫格里站在那里,把手指放在嘴边,思索着。"维冈加河的大河谷,它通向离这里不到半公里的平原。我可以带着我的牛群绕过丛林,到大河谷

---

fast *v.* 禁食,节制饮食   revenge *n.* 报仇;报复   wind *v.* 嗅出(猎物)的气味

slink out at the foot. We must **block** that end. Gray Brother, can you cut the herd in two for me?"

"Not I, perhaps—but I have brought a wise helper." Gray Brother trotted off and dropped into a hole. Then there lifted up a huge gray head that Mowgli knew well, and the hot air was filled with the most **desolate** cry of all the jungle—the hunting howl of a wolf at midday.

"Akela! Akela! " said Mowgli, clapping his hands. "I might have known that you wouldst not forget me. We have a big work in hand. Cut the herd in two, Akela. Keep the cows and calves together, and the bulls and the plow buffaloes by themselves."

The two wolves ran, ladies'-chain fashion, in and out of the herd, which snorted and threw up its head, and separated into two clumps. In one, the cow-buffaloes stood with their calves in the center, and glared and pawed, ready, if a wolf would only stay still, to charge down and trample the life out of him. In the other, the bulls and the young bulls snorted and stamped, but though they looked more imposing they were much less dangerous, for they had no calves to protect. No six men could have divided the herd so neatly.

THE JUNGLE STORY

的入口,然后横扫下来,但是他会从另一端鬼鬼祟祟地溜走。我们必须堵住那一头。灰兄弟,你能帮我把牛群一分为二吗?"

"我可能不行,但我带了一个聪明的帮手来。"灰兄弟快步走过去,跳进了一个洞里。然后从那里伸出了一个莫格里十分熟悉的大大的灰脑袋。炎热的空气里响起了一声丛林里最凄凉的叫声——一头在正午猎食的狼的叫声。

"阿克拉!阿克拉!"莫格里拍着手叫道,"我就知道你不会忘了我。我们手头有个很重要的事情。阿卡拉,把牛群分成两半。母牛和小牛一堆,公牛和耕地的水牛一堆。"

两只狼在牛群里穿进穿出,像跳女子连手式舞似的,牛群喷着鼻息,抬起头,很快被分成了两堆。一堆是母牛,她们把小牛围在了中间。她们瞪着眼睛,脚爪蹭着地面,如果有一头狼稍稍站住一会,她们就准备立刻冲上去把他踩死。另一堆是成年的公牛和年轻的公牛。他们喷着鼻息,跺着脚,虽然令他们看上去更加吓人,但实际上并没有这么危险,因为他们没有小牛要保护。就算有六个成年男子也不能这么干净利落地把牛群分开。

---

block *v.* 阻塞,堵塞　　desolate *a.* 凄凉的

丛林的故事

"What orders! " panted Akela. "They are trying to join again."

Mowgli slipped on to Rama's back. "Drive the bulls away to the left, Akela. Gray Brother, when we are gone, hold the cows together, and drive them into the foot of the ravine."

"How far?" said Gray Brother, panting and snapping.

"Till the sides are higher than Shere Khan can jump," shouted Mowgli. "Keep them there till we come down." The bulls swept off as Akela bayed, and Gray Brother stopped in front of the cows. They charged down on him, and he ran just before them to the foot of the ravine, as Akela drove the bulls far to the left.

"Well done! Another charge and they are fairly started. Careful, now—careful, Akela. A snap too much and the bulls will charge. Hujah! This is wilder work than driving black-buck. Didst you think these creatures could move so swiftly?" Mowgli called.

"I have—have hunted these too in my time," gasped Akela in the dust. "Shall I turn them into the jungle?"

"Ay! Turn. Swiftly turn them! Rama is mad with rage. Oh, if I could only tell him what I need of him to-day."

The bulls were turned, to the right this time, and crashed into

THE JUNGLE STORY

"还有什么指示！"阿克拉喘着气说。"他们又要跑到一块了。"

莫格里爬上罗玛的背。"把公牛赶到左边,阿克拉。灰兄弟,等我们走了,把母牛赶到一块,把她们赶到河谷里去。"

"赶到多远？"灰兄弟喘着气急促地问。

"一直到两边河岸高得萨克汗跳不上去为止。"莫格里喊道,"让她们待在那儿直到我们下来。"随着阿克拉的叫喊声,公牛飞奔开去。灰兄弟站在母牛前挡着她们。她们向着他冲过去,他就在前头跑,一直把她们引到河谷里,而此时阿克拉正赶着公牛往左边越赶越远。

"做得很好！再冲一次他们就真的跑起来了。小心点,——现在要小心点了,阿克拉。再猛扑过去,公牛就要向你冲过来了。唉呦！这可比赶黑公鹿要有意思多了。你有没想到过这些动物能跑这么快？"莫格里叫道。

"我以前也——也捕猎过这些动物。"阿克拉在尘埃中喘着气说,"要把他们赶到丛林里去吗？"

"啊！赶吧,快点赶他们！罗玛已经气疯了。哦,要是我能告诉他我今天需要他帮什么忙该多好啊！"

这次公牛被赶到了右边,他们冲进了高高的灌木丛里。在半公里

---

mad *a.* 发疯的　rage *n.* 狂怒

the standing thicket. The other herd children, watching with the cattle half a mile away, hurried to the village as fast as their legs could carry them, crying that the buffaloes had gone mad and run away.

But Mowgli's plan was simple enough. All he wanted to do was to make a big circle uphill and get at the head of the ravine, and then take the bulls down it and catch Shere Khan between the bulls and the cows; for he knew that after a meal and a full drink Shere Khan would not be in any condition to fight or to **clamber** up the sides of the ravine. He was **soothing** the buffaloes now by voice, and Akela had dropped far to the **rear**, only whimpering once or twice to hurry the rear-guard. It was a long, long circle, for they did not wish to get too near the ravine and give Shere Khan warning. At last Mowgli rounded up the **bewildered** herd at the head of the ravine on a grassy patch that sloped steeply down to the ravine itself. From that height you could see across the tops of the trees down to the plain below; but what Mowgli looked at was the sides of the ravine, and he saw with a great deal of satisfaction that they ran nearly straight up and down, while the vines and creepers that hung over them would give no **foothold** to a tiger who wanted to

202

外带着耕牛的其他的放牛娃们看到了这一切,拼命地跑回村里,嘴里喊着,说水牛都发了疯跑掉了。

不过,莫格里的计划其实相当简单。他想做的只是在山上绕个圈,绕到河谷的出口,然后带着公牛下来,把萨克汗困在公牛和母牛之间,因为他知道吃饱了喝足了的萨克汗是无法战斗的,也爬不上河谷的两岸。他用声音稍稍地安慰了一下水牛,此时阿克拉已经远远地落在了后面,偶尔喊两声催促落在后面的水牛。他们绕了很大很大一个圈,因为他们不想离河谷太近,让萨克汗有所警觉。最后,莫格里把迷失了方向的牛群带到了河谷的出口, 来到一片急转直下斜插入河谷的草地。从那个高度上,你可以越过树林顶端看到下面的平原,但莫格里关注的是河谷的两岸,他满意地看到两岸非常陡峭,长满了藤蔓和爬山虎,

---

clamber v. 攀登　　soothe v. 抚慰,使平静　　rear n. 后部,后面　　bewildered a. 糊涂的,迷惑的　　foothold n. 立足点

get out.

"Let them breathe, Akela," he said, holding up his hand. "They have not winded him yet. Let them breathe. I must tell Shere Khan who comes. We have him in the trap."

He put his hands to his mouth and shouted down the ravine—it was almost like shouting down a tunnel—and the echoes jumped from rock to rock.

After a long time there came back the drawling, sleepy snarl of a full-fed tiger just wakened.

"Who calls?" said Shere Khan, and a splendid peacock fluttered up out of the ravine screeching.

"I, Mowgli. Cattle thief, it is time to come to the Council Rock! Down—hurry them down, Akela! Down, Rama, down! "

The herd paused for an instant at the edge of the slope, but Akela gave tongue in the full hunting-yell, and they pitched over one after the other, just as steamers shoot rapids, the sand and stones spurting up round them. Once started, there was no chance of stopping, and before they were fairly in the bed of the ravine Rama winded Shere Khan and bellowed.

"Ha! Ha! " said Mowgli, on his back. "Now you knowest! "

THE JUNGLE STORY

一只想逃出去的老虎在上面是找不到一个立足点的。

"让他们喘口气,阿克拉,"他抬起手说。"他们还没嗅到他的气味呢。我必须告诉萨克汗谁来了。我们已经让他落在陷阱里了。"

他把双手放在嘴里,冲着下面的河谷大喊——这就像对着地道喊一样——回声从一块岩石弹到另一块岩石。

过了很长时间,传来一头吃饱了、刚刚睡醒的老虎慢吞吞、充满睡意的吼叫声。

"是谁在叫啊?"萨克汗说,一只漂亮的孔雀吓得从河谷里拍翅飞出。

"是我,莫格里。偷牛的贼,是时候让你到会议岩去了!下去,赶他们下去,阿克拉!下去,罗玛,下去!"

牛群在斜坡边上停顿了一会,但是阿克拉喊出了狩猎的吼叫,他们就一个接一个地向前冲了,就像轮船冲破急流,沙石在周围喷溅,一旦跑起来了,他们就不可能停下了。他们还没跑到河谷的河床那里,罗玛就闻到了萨克汗的气息,吼叫起来。

"哈!哈!"莫格里骑在他的背上,"现在你知道了吧!"黑色的牛角,

---

echo *n.* 回声   instant *n.* 刹那,瞬息   steamer *n.* 轮船   rapid *n.* 急流   spurt *v.* 喷射,喷出

205

and the torrent of black horns, foaming muzzles, and staring eyes whirled down the ravine just as boulders go down in floodtime; the weaker buffaloes being shouldered out to the sides of the ravine where they tore through the creepers. They knew what the business was before them—the terrible charge of the buffalo herd against which no tiger can hope to stand. Shere Khan heard the thunder of their hoofs, picked himself up, and lumbered down the ravine, looking from side to side for some way of escape, but the walls of the ravine were straight and he had to hold on, heavy with his dinner and his drink, willing to do anything rather than fight. The herd **splashed** through the pool he had just left, bellowing till the narrow cut rang. Mowgli heard an answering bellow from the foot of the ravine, saw Shere Khan turn (the tiger knew if the worst came to the worst it was better to meet the bulls than the cows with their calves), and then Rama **tripped**, stumbled, and went on again over something soft, and, with the bulls at his **heels**, crashed full into the other herd, while the weaker buffaloes were lifted clean off their feet by the shock of the meeting. That charge carried both herds out into the plain, goring and stamping and snorting. Mowgli watched his time, and slipped off Rama's neck, laying about him

THE JUNGLE STORY

冒着泡泡的牛鼻子,瞪起的眼睛,像山洪爆发时砾石滚滚地冲下河谷。较弱的水牛被挤到河谷两边,他们拼命地扯着两边的爬山虎。他们知道眼前要做什么——面对水牛群的疯狂进攻,没有一只老虎能够抵挡得住。萨克汗听到他们雷鸣般的蹄声,就站起来,缓慢地往河谷下方走去,边走边东张西望地寻找逃跑的地方,但是河谷两岸都太陡了,他只好继续往前走,肚子装满了吃的喝的,他可一点都不想战斗。牛群冲过了他刚走过的池塘,激起许多水花。

他们吼叫着,回声在狭小的河谷里回响。莫格里听到河谷另一端传来回应的吼叫;看到萨克汗转身了(萨克汗知道,如果最坏的事情发生,面对公牛总比面对带着小牛的母牛要好),然后罗玛被绊了一下,跌跌撞撞地踩在什么软绵绵的东西上过去了,其他公牛跟在他后面,冲进了另外一群牛中。那些较弱的水牛被撞得飞离了地面。这次冲撞让两群牛都冲进了平原,他们互相用角抵着,用蹄子踏着,喘着鼻息。莫格

---

splash *v.* 溅,泼   trip *v.* 绊;绊倒   heel *n.* 脚后跟

right and left with his stick.

"Quick, Akela! Break them up. Scatter them, or they will be fighting one another. Drive them away, Akela. Hai, Rama! Hai, hai, hai! my children. Softly now, softly! It is all over."

Akela and Gray Brother ran to and fro nipping the buffaloes' legs, and though the herd wheeled once to charge up the ravine again, Mowgli managed to turn Rama, and the others followed him to the wallows.

Shere Khan needed no more trampling. He was dead, and the kites were coming for him already.

"Brothers, that was a dog's death," said Mowgli, feeling for the knife he always carried in a sheath round his neck now that he lived with men. "But he would never have shown fight. His hide will look well on the Council Rock. We must get to work swiftly."

A boy trained among men would never have dreamed of skinning a ten-foot tiger alone, but Mowgli knew better than anyone else how an animal's skin is fitted on, and how it can be taken off. But it was hard work, and Mowgli slashed and tore and grunted for an hour, while the wolves lolled out their tongues, or came forward and tugged as he ordered them. Presently a hand fell on his

THE JUNGLE STORY

里看准了时机,从罗玛脖子上滑下来,用棍子在他周围乱打。

"快点,阿克拉!把他们分开。把他们散开,否则他们就要互相打起来了。把他们赶开,阿克拉。嘿,罗玛!嘿,嘿,嘿!我的孩子们。平静点,现在,平静点!一切都结束了。"

阿克拉和灰兄弟前前后后地跑着,咬水牛的脚。虽然牛群转身想再次冲进山谷里,莫格里设法让罗玛掉转了头,其他牛也就跟着他走到泥沼里。

萨克汗不需要牛群再去践踏了。他已经死了,鸢们早已经飞下来啄食他的肉了。

"兄弟,他死得像只狗。"莫格里说,一边摸着他的刀。自从他和人类生活在一起后,这刀就一直挂在脖子上的刀鞘里。"但是他就是不想战斗。他的皮毛放在会议岩上一定会很不错的。我们得快点动手了。"

一个在人类的教养下长大的孩子,做梦都不会想到独自一人去剥掉一头十英尺长的老虎皮,但是莫格里比任何人都清楚地知道动物的皮是怎么长的,又是怎么剥下来的。但这是一项艰苦的工作,莫格里用刀又砍又扯,嘴里还哼哼着,忙活了一个钟头,而两只狼在一旁伸着舌

---

swiftly *adv.* 迅速地   presently *adv.* 一会儿,不久

丛林的故事

shoulder, and looking up he saw Buldeo with the Tower musket. The children had told the village about the buffalo stampede, and Buldeo went out angrily, only too anxious to correct Mowgli for not taking better care of the herd. The wolves dropped out of sight as soon as they saw the man coming.

"What is this folly?" said Buldeo angrily. "To think that you can skin a tiger! Where did the buffaloes kill him? It is the Lame Tiger too, and there is a hundred rupees on his head. Well, well, we will **overlook** your letting the herd run off, and perhaps I will give you one of the rupees of the **reward** when I have taken the skin to Khanhiwara." He fumbled in his waist cloth for flint and steel, and **stooped** down to singe Shere Khan's whiskers. Most native hunters always singe a tiger's whiskers to prevent his ghost from **haunting** them.

"Hum! " said Mowgli, half to himself as he ripped back the skin of a forepaw. "So you will take the hide to Khanhiwara for the reward, and perhaps give me one rupee? Now it is in my mind that I need the skin for my own use. Heh! Old man, take away that fire! "

THE JUNGLE STORY

头,或是当莫格里命令他们的时候就走上前去帮他用力地拖。不久,有只手搭在他的肩膀上,他抬起头看到布尔迪奥拿着他那把塔尔牌步枪。放牛娃们告诉村里人,水牛都惊跑了。布尔迪奥就怒气冲冲地跑出来,急着想教训莫格里没有照顾好牛群。一看到有人来了,两头狼就跑得无影无踪了。

"这是什么蠢事?"布尔迪奥生气地说。"你以为你能剥下一张老虎皮!水牛是在哪里踩死他的?原来还是那只瘸腿虎啊,他头上还悬赏了一百卢比呢。好吧,好吧,我们就不怪你放跑了牛群的事情了,让我把虎皮拿到肯西瓦拉去,也许我会给你一个卢比的赏钱呢。"他从腰上围着的布里摸出了打火石和火镰,弯下腰去烧萨克汗的胡须。当地的许多猎人总是烧掉老虎的胡须,以免老虎的鬼魂缠着他们。

"哼!"莫格里似乎是对自己说,边说边扯下老虎前爪的毛皮。"那么你是要带着毛皮去肯西瓦拉领赏喽,也许还会给我一个卢比?可是我自己心里另有打算,这毛皮我自己有用。喂,老头,把火拿开!"

---

overlook v. 忽略,忽视　　reward n. 奖赏,赏金　　stoop v. 俯身,弯腰　　haunt v. (鬼魂)常出没

"What talk is this to the chief hunter of the village? Thy luck and the stupidity of your buffaloes have helped you to this kill. The tiger has just fed, or he would have gone twenty miles by this time. You can not even skin him properly, little beggar brat, and forsooth I, Buldeo, must be told not to singe his whiskers. Mowgli, I will not give you one anna of the reward, but only a very big beating. Leave the carcass! "

"By the Bull that bought me," said Mowgli, who was trying to get at the shoulder, "must I stay **babbling** to an old ape all noon? Here, Akela, this man **plagues** me."

Buldeo, who was still stooping over Shere Khan's head, found himself sprawling on the grass, with a gray wolf standing over him, while Mowgli went on skinning as though he were alone in all India.

"Ye-es," he said, between his teeth. "Thou art altogether right, Buldeo. Thou will never give me one anna of the reward. There is an old war between this lame tiger and myself—a very old war, and—I have won."

To do Buldeo **justice**, if he had been ten years younger he would have taken his chance with Akela had he met the wolf in the woods, but a wolf who obeyed the orders of this boy who had

212

THE JUNGLE STORY

"你这是和村里的猎人首领在说话吗？是你的运气加上水牛的蠢劲才帮你杀了这老虎。这老虎刚吃饱，否则现在他早已逃到二十里外了。你连剥皮也剥不好，小叫化子！你真不让我烧他的胡须呀，莫格里，那我可就连一个安那的赏钱都不会给你了，还要好好揍你一顿。离尸体远点！"

"我以赎买我的那头公牛发誓，"莫格里说，他正剥到肩膀的地方，"我必须整个中午听着老猴子烦个没完吗？这儿，阿克拉，这人烦死我了。"

布尔迪奥正弯腰对着萨克汗的脑袋，突然发现自己仰天倒在草地上，一头灰色的狼站在他旁边，而莫格里继续剥着皮，似乎整个印度都只有他一个人。

"好吧，"他低声说，"你都是对的，布尔迪奥。你连一个安那的赏钱也不会给我。这是我和这个瘸腿虎之间很久以前的恩怨了——很久以前，现在我赢了。"

说句公道话，如果布尔迪奥年轻十岁的话，在森林里遇到了阿克拉，也许还能碰碰运气。但一头听从一个男孩命令的狼，而且这个男孩和一只吃人的老虎有过私人恩怨，这头狼就不是普通的动物了。布尔

---

babble *v.* 喋喋不休   **plague** *v.* 使苦恼，烦扰   **justice** *n.* 公正，正义，公平

213

private wars with man-eating tigers was not a common animal. It was sorcery, magic of the worst kind, thought Buldeo, and he wondered whether the amulet round his neck would protect him. He lay as still as still, expecting every minute to see Mowgli turn into a tiger too.

"Maharaj! Great King," he said at last in a husky whisper.

"Yes," said Mowgli, without turning his head, chuckling a little.

"I am an old man. I did not know that you was anything more than a herdsboy. May I rise up and go away, or will your servant tear me to pieces?"

"Go, and peace go with you. Only, another time do not meddle with my game. Let him go, Akela."

Buldeo hobbled away to the village as fast as he could, looking back over his shoulder in case Mowgli should change into something terrible. When he got to the village he told a tale of magic and enchantment and sorcery that made the priest look very grave.

Mowgli went on with his work, but it was nearly twilight before he and the wolves had drawn the great gay skin clear of the body.

"Now we must hide this and take the buffaloes home! Help me to herd them, Akela."

214

THE JUNGLE STORY

迪奥认为这是妖术,最厉害的妖术,他想知道他脖子上的护身符是不是能够保护他。他躺在那儿一动不动,随时准备看见莫格里也变成一只老虎。

"王公!伟大的国王,"终于他用嘶哑的嗓子低声喊道。

"嗯,"莫格里头也没回地应着,暗自发笑。

"我是个老人家。我不知道你不是个普通的放牛娃。我可以站起来离开吗?或者你要让你的仆人把我扯成碎片?"

"走吧,一路走好。但是,下次别再干涉我的猎物。让他走吧,阿克拉。"

布尔迪奥拼命地一瘸一拐跑回村里,不时地回头看看,怕莫格里变成什么可怕的东西。等他回到村里的时候,他讲了一个关于魔法、妖术和巫术的故事,听得牧师的神情变得非常庄重。

莫格里继续做着他的事情,直到黄昏时分,他和两头狼才把巨大的华丽的老虎皮整张地剥了下来。

"现在我们得把这个藏起来,把水牛们带回家。帮我把水牛赶到一块儿,阿克拉。"

---

chuckle *v.* 暗笑   meddle v. 干涉

215

The herd rounded up in the misty twilight, and when they got near the village Mowgli saw lights, and heard the conches and bells in the temple blowing and banging. Half the village seemed to be waiting for him by the gate. "That is because I have killed Shere Khan," he said to himself. But a shower of stones whistled about his ears, and the villagers shouted: "Sorcerer! Wolf's brat! Jungle demon! Go away! Get hence quickly or the priest will turn you into a wolf again. Shoot, Buldeo, shoot! "

The old Tower musket went off with a bang, and a young buffalo bellowed in pain.

"More sorcery! " shouted the villagers. "He can turn bullets. Buldeo, that was your buffalo."

"Now what is this?" said Mowgli, bewildered, as the stones flew thicker.

"They are not unlike the pack, these brothers of your," said Akela, sitting down composedly. "It is in my head that, if bullets mean anything, they would cast you out."

"Wolf! Wolf's cub! Go away! " shouted the priest, waving a sprig of the sacred tulsi plant.

THE JUNGLE STORY

牛群在起了薄雾的暮色中聚到了一起，当他们走近村子的时候，莫格里看到了火光，听到了海螺吹响的声音，庙宇里响起了钟声。似乎将近一半的村民在村口等着他。"那是因为我杀了萨克汗。"他对自己说。但石头如阵雨般在他耳边呼啸而过，村民们大声喊道："巫师！狼崽子！丛林里的魔鬼！滚吧！快点滚，否则牧师要再次把你变回狼。开枪，布尔迪奥，开枪！"

那旧的塔尔步枪砰地一声响了，一头年轻的水牛发出痛苦的吼叫。

"那也是巫术！"村民们喊道，"他可以使子弹转向，布尔迪奥，那是你的水牛。"

"这是怎么了呀？"莫格里困惑地说，石头却越扔越多了。

"你的这些兄弟和狼群没什么两样，"阿克拉镇静地坐下来说。"在我看来，如果说子弹能说明什么的话，他们是要把你赶出去。"

"狼！狼崽子！滚吧！"牧师手里挥着一枝神圣的塔尔西树枝，大声地喊道。

---

blow v. 吹响　　shower n. 一阵　　composedly *adv.* 镇静地

丛林的故事

"Again? Last time it was because I was a man. This time it is because I am a wolf. Let us go, Akela."

A woman—it was Messua—ran across to the herd, and cried: "Oh, my son, my son! They say you are a sorcerer who can turn himself into a beast at will. I do not believe, but go away or they will kill you. Buldeo says you are a wizard, but I know you have **avenged** Nathoo's death."

"Come back, Messua!" shouted the crowd. "Come back, or we will stone you."

Mowgli laughed a little short ugly laugh, for a stone had hit him in the mouth. "Run back, Messua. This is one of the foolish tales they tell under the big tree at dusk. I have at least paid for your son's life. **Farewell**; and run quickly, for I shall send the herd in more swiftly than their brickbats. I am no wizard, Messua. Farewell!"

"Now, once more, Akela," he cried. "Bring the herd in."

The buffaloes were anxious enough to get to the village. They hardly needed Akela's yell, but charged through the gate like a **whirlwind**, scattering the crowd right and left.

"Keep count!" shouted Mowgli **scornfully**. "It may be that I have stolen one of them. Keep count, for I will do your herding no

THE JUNGLE STORY

"又一次叫我滚？上次是因为我是一个人，而这一次，因为我是一头狼。我们走吧，阿克拉。"

一个妇女——那是梅苏亚——从人群里跑出来，喊道："噢，我的儿子，我的儿子！他们说你是巫师，能随意把自己变成野兽。我不相信，但是你走吧，要不然他们会杀了你。布尔迪奥说你是个巫师，但是我知道，你为纳索的死报了仇。"

"回来，梅苏亚！"人群喊道，"回来，否则我们朝你扔石头了。"

莫格里冷笑了一声，一块石头刚好打在他的嘴巴上。"跑回去吧，梅苏亚。这是他们黄昏时在大树下编出来的一个愚蠢的故事。至少，我已经为你儿子的性命报了仇。再见了，快点跑回去，因为我要把牛群赶过去了，那比他们扔的砖块要快得多了。我不是巫师，梅苏亚。再见了！"

"现在，再来一次，阿克拉，"他喊道，"把牛群赶进去。"

水牛们早就急着要回到村子里去了，不等阿克拉吼叫，他们就像旋风般冲进村口，把人群冲得七零八落。

"好好数清楚！"莫格里轻蔑地喊道，"也许我偷了一头呢。数清楚了，

---

avenge v. 替……报仇　　farewell int. 再见　　whirlwind n. 旋风　　scornfully adv. 轻蔑地

219

more. Fare you well, children of men, and thank Messua that I do not come in with my wolves and hunt you up and down your street."

He turned on his heel and walked away with the Lone Wolf, and as he looked up at the stars he felt happy. "No more sleeping in traps for me, Akela. Let us get Shere Khan's skin and go away. No, we will not hurt the village, for Messua was kind to me."

When the moon rose over the plain, making it look all milky, the horrified villagers saw Mowgli, with two wolves at his heels and a bundle on his head, trotting across at the steady wolf's trot that eats up the long miles like fire. Then they banged the temple bells and blew the conches louder than ever. And Messua cried, and Buldeo embroidered the story of his adventures in the jungle, till he ended by saying that Akela stood up on his hind legs and talked like a man.

The moon was just going down when Mowgli and the two wolves came to the hill of the Council Rock, and they stopped at Mother Wolf's cave.

"They have cast me out from the Man-Pack, Mother," shouted Mowgli, "but I come with the hide of Shere Khan to keep my word."

THE JUNGLE STORY

我再也不会给你们放牛了。再见吧,人的孩子们,你们要感谢梅苏亚,因为她,我才没有带着我的狼在你们的街上到处捕猎你们。"

他转过身,和独身老狼一起走了。当他抬头看着星星时,他觉得心情非常愉快。"我不用再睡在陷阱里了,阿克拉。我们去取萨克汗的虎皮,然后离开这儿。不,我们不要伤害这个村子,因为梅苏亚对我很好。"

月亮从平原上升起,使一切看上去都是乳白色的一片,受了惊吓的村民看到莫格里身后跟着两头狼,头上顶着一个包裹,以狼平稳的小跑速度跑着,像一阵火烧过那样,很快地跑过了很长一段距离。于是他们把庙里的钟敲得更响了,把海螺吹得更响了。梅苏亚在那儿哭,而布尔迪奥编制着他在丛林冒险的故事,编到最后竟然说阿克拉用后脚站立,像人一样说话了。

月亮慢慢地沉了下去,莫格里和两头狼来到会议岩的山上,他们先在狼妈妈的洞口前停下了。

"他们把我从人群中赶出来了,妈妈,"莫格里喊道,"但是我带来了萨克汗的皮,实现了我的诺言。"

---

horrified *adj.* 感到震惊的,恐怖的　　embroider *v.* 给(故事等)添油加醋

丛林的故事

Mother Wolf walked stiffly from the cave with the cubs behind her, and her eyes glowed as she saw the skin.

"I told him on that day, when he crammed his head and shoulders into this cave, hunting for your life, Little Frog—I told him that the hunter would be the hunted. It is well done."

"Little Brother, it is well done," said a deep voice in the thicket. "We were lonely in the jungle without you," and Bagheera came running to Mowgli's bare feet. They clambered up the Council Rock together, and Mowgli spread the skin out on the flat stone where Akela used to sit, and pegged it down with four slivers of bamboo, and Akela lay down upon it, and called the old call to the Council, "Look—look well, O Wolves," exactly as he had called when Mowgli was first brought there.

Ever since Akela had been deposed, the pack had been without a leader, hunting and fighting at their own pleasure. But they answered the call from habit; and some of them were lame from the traps they had fallen into, and some limped from shot wounds, and some were mangy from eating bad food, and many were missing. But they came to the Council Rock, all that were left of them, and saw Shere Khan's striped hide on the rock, and the huge claws

THE JUNGLE STORY

　　狼妈妈从洞里艰难地走出来,狼崽子们跟在身后,她看到虎皮时,眼睛一亮。

　　"那天他把脑袋肩膀塞进这个洞里,要猎取你这个小青蛙的性命的时候,我就告诉过他,捕猎别人的总有一天要被人捕猎。做得很好!"

　　"小兄弟,做得很好,"灌木丛里传来一个低沉的声音,"没有你我们在丛林里很寂寞。"巴格西拉跑到光着脚的莫格里跟前。他们一起爬上了岩石,莫格里在阿克拉曾经坐过的那块平石上摊开虎皮,用四片竹子钉牢。阿克拉在上面躺下来,用以前召唤开大会的声音说,"看看吧——好好看看,大伙儿!"就像莫格里第一次被带到这里的时候一样。

　　自从阿克拉被赶下台之后,狼群就没有了首领,他们随心所欲地打猎和打架。但是出于习惯,他们回答了那声召唤。他们中有些狼因为掉进了陷阱而瘸了,有些中了枪受了伤,走起路来一瘸一拐的,还有些吃了不干净的东西长了疥癣,还有许多失踪了。但是剩下的狼都来了,他们来到会议岩,看到岩石上萨克汗的花斑皮毛,巨大的爪子在空荡

---

stiffly *adv.* 僵硬地　　depose *v.* 免职;罢官　　striped *a.* 有条纹的

223

dangling at the end of the empty dangling feet. It was then that Mowgli made up a song that came up into his throat all by itself, and he shouted it aloud, leaping up and down on the **rattling** skin, and beating time with his heels till he had no more breath left, while Gray Brother and Akela howled between the verses.

"Look well, O Wolves. Have I kept my word?" said Mowgli. And the wolves bayed "Yes," and one tattered wolf howled:

"Lead us again, O Akela. Lead us again, O Man-cub, for we be sick of this lawlessness, and we would be the free people once more."

"**Nay**," purred Bagheera, "that may not be. When you are full-fed, the madness may come upon you again. Not for nothing are you called the Free People. Ye fought for freedom, and it is yours. Eat it, O Wolves."

"Man-Pack and Wolf-Pack have cast me out," said Mowgli. "Now I will hunt alone in the jungle."

"And we will hunt with you," said the four cubs.

So Mowgli went away and hunted with the four cubs in the jungle from that day on. But he was not always alone, because, years afterward, he became a man and married.

But that is a story for grown-ups.

THE JUNGLE STORY

荡的虎脚上悬荡。这时候,莫格里编了一首歌,从他的喉咙里唱了出来。他大声地唱着,在发出格格响的毛皮上跳上跳下,用脚后跟打着拍子,直到喘不过气为止。灰兄弟和阿克拉不时地在他的独唱中也吼上几声。

"好好看看,狼们。我是否遵守了诺言?"莫格里说。所有的狼齐声叫嚷:"是!"其中一头毛发凌乱的狼嚎叫着:

"再领导我们吧,哦,阿克拉。再次领导我们,哦,人娃娃,因为我们已经厌倦了没有法律的生活。我们要再次成为自由的狼民。"

"不,"巴格西拉说,"不行。等你们吃饱了,疯劲又要上来了。把你们叫做自由的狼民不是没有原因的。你们为自由而战斗过了,现在自由是你们的了。享受它吧,狼们。"

"人群和狼群都我把赶出去了。"莫格里说,"现在我要独自在丛林里狩猎了。"

"我们和你一起狩猎。"四只狼崽说。

于是从那一天起,莫格里离开了那里,和四只狼崽在丛林里狩猎。但是他不是一直孤独,因为数年以后,他长大成人,还结了婚。

但那是一个讲给成年人听的故事了。

---

dangle v. 悬荡　　rattle v. 发出格格声　　nay adv. (古)否,不

225

丛林的故事

Chapter 6　Mowgli's Song

That he sang at the council rock when he danced on Shere Khan's hide

The Song of Mowgli—I, Mowgli, am singing.
Let the jungle listen to the things I have done.

Shere Khan said he would kill—would kill!
At the gates in the twilight he would kill Mowgli, the Frog!

He ate and he drank. Drink deep, Shere Khan, for when will you drink again?
Sleep and dream of the kill.

I am alone on the grazing-grounds. Gray Brother, come to me!
Come to me, Lone Wolf, for there is big game afoot!

Bring up the great bull buffaloes, the blue-skinned herd bulls
with the angry eyes. Drive them to and fro as I order.

THE JUNGLE STORY

第六章　莫格里之歌

在会议岩上,莫格尔在萨克汗的皮毛上跳舞时唱的歌

莫格里之歌——我,莫格里,在唱歌。
让丛林听听我所做的事情。

萨克汗说他要杀我——要杀我!
黄昏时在村口边他要杀了莫格里,这个青蛙!

他吃饱了喝足了! 担心何时能再有水喝,萨克汗,他喝了个够。
然后躺下睡觉,做着杀了我的美梦。

我独自一人在牧地上。灰兄弟来找我了!
独身老狼来找我了,因为有个大猎物在活动!

带上睁着怒目的大水牛,蓝色皮毛的大公牛,
把他们来来回回地赶到我指定的地方。

---

afoot *adv.* 活动着的

丛林的故事

Sleepest you still, Shere Khan? Wake, oh, wake!
Here come I, and the bulls are behind.

Rama, the King of the Buffaloes, stamped with his foot.
Waters of the Waingunga, whither went Shere Khan?

He is not Ikki to dig holes, nor Mao, the Peacock, that he
should fly.
He is not Mang the Bat, to **hang** in the branches.
Little bamboos that **creak** together, tell me where he ran?

Ow! He is there. Ahoo! He is there.
Under the feet of Rama lies the Lame One!
Up, Shere Khan!

Up and kill! Here is meat; break the necks of the bulls!

Hsh! He is asleep. We will not wake him, for his strength is

THE JUNGLE STORY

还在睡觉吧,萨克汗? 醒来吧,哦,醒来吧!
我来了,身后跟着公牛。

罗玛,水牛之王,用他的双脚践踏着。
维冈加的河水啊,萨克汗去了哪里?

他不是伊基会挖洞,不像孔雀玛奥会飞翔。
他也不是蝙蝠曼尼,能倒挂在树枝上。
沙沙作响的竹子啊,告诉我萨克汗跑去了哪里?

噢,他在那里。啊嗨! 他在那里。
罗玛的脚下躺着那瘸腿的!
起来,萨克汗!

起来杀啊! 这可是大餐啊! 咬断公牛的脖子!

嘘! 他在睡觉。我们不要吵醒他,他的力气可大了。

---

hang *v.* 悬挂,低垂　　creak *v.* 吱吱作响

229

very great.

The kites have come down to see it.

The black ants have come up to know it.

There is a great assembly in his honor.

Alala! I have no cloth to wrap me.

The kites will see that I am naked.

I am **ashamed** to meet all these people.

Lend me your coat, Shere Khan.

Lend me your gay striped coat that I may go to the Council
Rock.

By the Bull that bought me I made a promise—a little promise.

Only your coat is lacking before I keep my word.

With the knife, with the knife that men use, with the knife of
the hunter,

I will stoop down or my gift.

THE JUNGLE STORY

鸢鹰已经飞下来看了，
黑蚂蚁也都过来瞧个究竟了，
为了他，这里有个盛大的集会。

啊呀呀！我没有衣服穿，
鸢鹰会看到赤裸着的我。
我不好意思见所有的动物。
把你的毛皮借给我，萨克汗。
把你的华丽的花毛皮借给我，好让我带回会议岩。

我以赎买我的那头公牛发誓——许下了一个小小的誓言。
现在离完成我的誓言只差这个毛皮了。

用刀，人类用的刀，猎人用的刀，
我弯下腰来取我的礼物。

---

ashamed *a.* 羞愧的

丛林的故事

Waters of the Waingunga, Shere Khan gives me his coat for the love that he bears me.

Pull, Gray Brother!   Pull, Akela!

Heavy is the hide of Shere Khan.

The Man Pack are angry. They throw stones and talk child's talk.

My mouth is **bleeding**. Let me run away.

Through the night, through the hot night, run swiftly with me, my brothers.

We will leave the lights of the village and go to the low moon.

Waters of the Waingunga, the Man-Pack have cast me out.

I did them no harm, but they were afraid of me. Why?

Wolf Pack, you have cast me out too.

The jungle is shut to me and the village gates are shut. Why?

As Mang flies between the beasts and birds,

THE JUNGLE STORY

维冈加的河水啊,萨克汗因为他对我的爱,把他的皮毛给了我。
拉呀,灰兄弟! 拉呀,阿克拉!
萨克汗的虎皮还真重!

人群愤怒了。他们扔着石头,说话像孩子。
我的嘴角在流血。让我逃走吧。

在黑夜里,在炎热的黑夜里,我和我的兄弟们跑得飞快。
我们把村里的火光抛在了身后,朝着垂挂在半空的月亮跑去。

维冈加的河水啊,人们把我赶了出来。
我没做什么伤害他们的事情,但是他们都怕我。这是为什么?

狼群啊,你们也把我赶出来了。
丛林对我关上了大门,村子对我关上了大门。这是为什么?

就像曼尼在野兽和鸟类之间飞舞,

---

bleed *v.* 出血,流血

丛林的故事

so fly I between the village and the jungle. Why?

I dance on the hide of Shere Khan, but my heart is very heavy.
My mouth is cut and wounded with the stones from the village,
but my heart is very light, because I have come back to the
jungle. Why?

These two things fight together in me as the snakes fight in the
spring.
The water comes out of my eyes; yet I laugh while it falls. Why?

I am two Mowglis, but the hide of Shere Khan is under my feet.

All the jungle knows that I have killed Shere Khan. Look—look
well, O Wolves!

Ahae! My heart is heavy with the things that I do not
understand.

THE JUNGLE STORY

所以我也将在村子和丛林之间徘徊。这是为什么？

我在萨克汗的皮毛上跳舞,但是我的心情是沉重的。
我的嘴角被村民扔的石头打到了,受伤了,
但是我的心情很愉快,因为我又回到丛林里来了。这是为什么？

这两件事情在我心里激烈地冲突着,就像蛇在春天里打架。
我的眼睛里流出了泪水；当我笑的时候它留了下来,这是为什么？

我很矛盾,但是萨克汗的毛皮在我的脚下。

丛林里所有的动物都知道我杀了萨克汗。看——看
哦,狼们！

唉！这些令我无法理解的事情使我的心情无比沉闷。

Chapter 7 The White Seal

Oh! hush you, my baby, the night is behind us,

And black are the waters that sparkled so green.

The moon, o'er the combers, looks downward to find us,

At rest in the hollows that rustle between.

Where billow meets billow, then soft be your pillow,

Ah, weary wee flipperling, curl at your ease!

The storm shall not wake you, nor shark overtake you,

Asleep in the arms of the slow-swinging seas!

Seal Lullaby

All these things happened several years ago at a place called
Novastoshnah, or North East Point, on the Island of St. Paul, away
and away in the Bering Sea. Limmershin, the Winter Wren, told me
the tale when he was blown on to the rigging of a steamer going to
Japan, and I took him down into my cabin and warmed and fed him

THE JUNGLE STORY

第七章 白海豹

哦！嘘，轻点，我的宝贝，黑夜在我们身后，
黑色的海水闪烁着绿色的光芒。
月亮，在海浪上方，俯视着我们，
看着我们在起伏的海浪中休憩。
浪头一个接着一个，那是你柔软的枕头，
啊，长鳍的小家伙，自在地蜷着身子！
风暴不会把你吵醒，鲨鱼也不会将你追赶，
在轻轻荡漾的海水的怀抱里睡吧！

——海豹摇篮曲

这些事情都是几年前发生在一个叫诺瓦斯图夏纳的地方，或者称它为东北岬，它位于远离伯林海的圣保罗岛上。这个故事是冬鹩鹩林默辛告诉我的。有一次他被风吹到开往日本的轮船的缆绳上，我把他带到船舱里，给他暖暖身子，喂养了他好多天，直到他康复能够再飞

---

sparkle v. 闪耀   pillow n. 枕头   overtake v. 追上，赶上   lullaby n. 摇篮曲

for a couple of days till he was fit to fly back to St. Paul's again. Limmershin is a very quaint little bird, but he knows how to tell the truth.

Nobody comes to Novastoshnah except on business, and the only people who have regular business there are the seals. They come in the summer months by hundreds and hundreds of thousands out of the cold gray sea. For Novastoshnah Beach has the finest **accommodation** for seals of any place in all the world.

Sea Catch knew that, and every spring would swim from whatever place he happened to be in—would swim like a torpedo-boat straight for Novastoshnah and spend a month fighting with his companions for a good place on the rocks, as close to the sea as possible. Sea Catch was fifteen years old, a huge gray fur seal with almost a mane on his shoulders, and long, wicked dog teeth. When he heaved himself up on his front flippers he stood more than four feet clear of the ground, and his weight, if anyone had been bold enough to weigh him, was nearly seven hundred pounds. He was **scarred** all over with the marks of savage fights, but he was always ready for just one fight more. He would put his head on one side,

THE JUNGLE STORY

回到圣保罗岛上。林默辛是一只很古怪的鸟儿,但是他知道怎么说实话。

没有人会到诺瓦斯图夏纳来,除非来办事,而经常来这里办事的是那些海豹。夏天的时候,几十万只海豹从冰冷、灰暗的海洋来到这里,因为诺瓦斯图夏纳海滩是世界上最适合海豹居住的地方。

西卡其知道这一点。每年春天——不论他在哪里——他都会从那里像鱼雷快艇一样,笔直游向诺瓦斯图夏纳,在那里花上一个月的时间和同伴打架,争夺岩石上的好地盘,越靠近海的越好。西卡其十五岁了,是一头巨大的灰色海豹,肩膀上长着浓密的鬃毛,还长着长长的、凶狠的犬牙。当他用前鳍把自己身子抬起的时候,他站在那里离地面足有四英尺。他的体重,如果真有人敢称一下的话,几乎达到了七百磅。他全身都是野蛮打架时留下的疤痕,但是他总是随时为下一次打架做好准备。他会故意把头倒向一边,装作好像很害怕不敢正视他的敌人的样子;然后他会像闪电一样冲出去,当他的大牙齿紧紧咬住另

---

accommodation n. 住处　　scar v. 使留下伤痕

丛林的故事

as though he were afraid to look his enemy in the face; then he would shoot it out like lightning, and when the big teeth were firmly fixed on the other seal's neck, the other seal might get away if he could, but Sea Catch would not help him.

Yet Sea Catch never chased a beaten seal, for that was against the Rules of the Beach. He only wanted room by the sea for his nursery. But as there were forty or fifty thousand other seals hunting for the same thing each spring, the whistling, bellowing, roaring, and blowing on the beach was something frightful.

From a little hill called Hutchinson's Hill, you could look over three and a half miles of ground covered with fighting seals; and the surf was dotted all over with the heads of seals hurrying to land and begin their share of the fighting. They fought in the breakers, they fought in the sand, and they fought on the smooth-worn basalt rocks of the nurseries, for they were just as stupid and unaccommodating as men. Their wives never came to the island until late in May or early in June, for they did not care to be torn to pieces; and the young two-, three-, and four-year-old seals who had not begun **housekeeping** went **inland** about half a mile through the ranks of the fighters and played about on the sand dunes in droves

240

THE JUNGLE STORY

外一头海豹的脖子时,这头海豹拼命地想逃跑,但是西卡其是不会让他逃走的。

但是西卡其从来不追逐一头被打败的海豹,因为那是违反海滩法则的。他只是想在海边为小海豹找个地方住。但是因为每年春天都有大约四五万只海豹来这里找窝,海滩上到处是可怕的啸叫声、咆哮声、怒吼声、打架声。

从那座叫做哈奇森的小山上,你可以看到方圆三英里半的地方到处都是在打架的海豹。海浪里海豹的头星星点点,他们正在匆匆忙忙地赶往海滩,加入到打架的行列里。他们在浪花里打架,在沙地里打架,在磨光的用来做小海豹窝的玄武岩上打架,因为他们和男人一样愚蠢好斗。他们的妻子要到五月底或者六月初才到岛上来,因为她们不想被扯成碎片。那些年轻的还没开始操持家务的海豹——两三岁、三四岁的海豹——穿过打架的豹子中间,往里走大约半英里,然后成群结队地在沙丘上玩耍,把地上长的所有绿色的东西都蹭光了。他们

---

housekeeping n. 操持家务　　inland n. 内陆

and legions, and rubbed off every single green thing that grew. They were called the holluschickie—the bachelors—and there were perhaps two or three hundred thousand of them at Novastoshnah alone.

Sea Catch had just finished his forty-fifth fight one spring when Matkah, his soft, sleek, gentle-eyed wife, came up out of the sea, and he caught her by the scruff of the neck and dumped her down on his **reservation**, saying gruffly: "Late as usual. Where have you been?"

It was not the fashion for Sea Catch to eat anything during the four months he stayed on the beaches, and so his temper was generally bad. Matkah knew better than to answer back. She looked round and cooed: "How **thoughtful** of you. You've taken the old place again."

"I should think I had," said Sea Catch. "Look at me! "

He was scratched and bleeding in twenty places; one eye was almost out, and his sides were torn to **ribbons**.

"Oh, you men, you men! " Matkah said, fanning herself with her hind flipper. "Why can't you be sensible and settle your places quietly? You look as though you had been fighting with the Killer

THE JUNGLE STORY

被称为霍卢斯奇科——单身汉的意思——光是在诺瓦斯图夏纳也许就有二三十万只。

　　一年春天,西卡其刚打完第四十五场架,他皮毛光滑油亮、眼神温柔的妻子马特卡从海里爬上来,他抓住她颈背上的皮把她拎起来放在他抢到的位置上,生硬地说:"又这么晚。你去哪里了?"

　　在待在海滩上的四个月里,西卡其通常是不吃东西的,所以他的脾气往往变得很坏。马特卡当然知道最好不要顶撞他。她转过身,轻轻地说:"你想得真周到啊!你又占了老地方。"

　　"我当然应该找老地方,"西卡其说,"你看看我!"

　　他被抓得伤痕累累,有二十处地方在流血;一只眼睛都快掉出来了,身上被扯出一丝丝的伤痕。

　　"哦,你们这些男人啊,你们这些男人!"马特卡说,她用后鳍给自己扇着风。"你们就不能理智一点,和平地解决地盘的问题吗?你看上

---

reservation n. 保留,预留　　　thoughtful a. 体贴的,考虑周到的　　　ribbon n. 丝带

243

Whale."

"I haven't been doing anything but fight since the middle of May. The beach is disgracefully crowded this season. I've met at least a hundred seals from Lukannon Beach, house hunting. Why can't people stay where they belong?"

"I've often thought we should be much happier if we hauled out at Otter Island instead of this crowded place," said Matkah.

"Bah! Only the holluschickie go to Otter Island. If we went there they would say we were afraid. We must **preserve** appearances, my dear."

Sea Catch sunk his head proudly between his fat shoulders and pretended to go to sleep for a few minutes, but all the time he was keeping a sharp **lookout** for a fight. Now that all the seals and their wives were on the land, you could hear their clamor miles out to sea above the loudest gales. At the lowest counting there were over a million seals on the beach—old seals, mother seals, tiny babies, and holluschickie, fighting, scuffling, bleating, crawling, and playing together—going down to the sea and coming up from it in gangs and regiments, lying over every foot of ground as far as the eye could reach, and skirmishing about in **brigades** through the fog. It is

THE JUNGLE STORY

去好像和虎鲸打过架一样。"

"我从五月中旬开始除了打架什么也没做。这个季节海滩上挤得太不像话了。我至少碰到了一百多只从洛卡农海滩来这里找窝的海豹,为什么人们就不能待在他们自己的地方呢?"

"我常常想,如果我们不到这个拥挤的地方,而是到海獭岛去,我们会更快乐的。"马特卡说。

"呸!只有霍卢斯奇科才去海獭岛。如果我们也去那里,他们会以为我们害怕了。我们必须保持颜面,亲爱的。"

西卡其骄傲地把头埋在他肥胖的肩膀中间,一动不动地待了几分钟假装睡了,但是他一直警惕地看着四周,准备打架。现在所有海豹和他们的妻子都在沙滩上了,在离海边几公里的地方你都可以听见他们的吵闹声,这声音盖过了最猛烈的狂风。在这个海滩上少说也有一百万只海豹——老海豹、海豹妈妈、小海豹和霍卢斯奇科,他们打架混战、咩咩地叫、爬来爬去、一起玩耍——成群结队地游到海里,又浮出海面,满眼望去,海滩上躺满了海豹;在雾气中,他们一队队地出去打

---

preserve v. 保护,维持　lookout n. 监视,注意　brigade n. 队

nearly always foggy at Novastoshnah, except when the sun comes out and makes everything look all pearly and rainbow-colored for a little while.

Kotick, Matkah's baby, was born in the middle of that confusion, and he was all head and shoulders, with pale, watery blue eyes, as tiny seals must be, but there was something about his coat that made his mother look at him very closely.

"Sea Catch," she said, at last, "our baby's going to be white! "

"Empty clam-shells and dry seaweed! " snorted Sea Catch. "There never has been such a thing in the world as a white seal."

"I can't help that," said Matkah; "there's going to be now." And she sang the low, crooning seal song that all the mother seals sing to their babies:

You mustn't swim till you're six weeks old,

Or your head will be sunk by your heels;

And summer gales and Killer Whales,

Are bad for baby seals.

Are bad for baby seals, dear rat,

As bad as bad can be; But splash and grow strong,

And you can't be wrong.

架。在诺瓦斯图夏纳几乎一直都是雾蒙蒙的,只有当太阳出来的时候,一切看上去才是珍珠般明亮和五彩缤纷的。

马特卡的孩子科迪克就是在那种混乱状态中出生的,像一般的小海豹那样,他的脑袋和肩膀特别大,有着一双苍白的水灵灵的蓝眼睛。但是他的皮毛使得他的妈妈不禁要仔细地看看。

"西卡其,"她终于说道,"我们的孩子将来会长成白色的!"

"瞎说!"西卡其哼着鼻子说,"世界上从来就没有白色的海豹。"

"我也没办法,"马特卡说,"但是以后就有了。"然后她开始低声地轻唱起所有的海豹妈妈都会唱给她们的孩子听的歌:

没到六个月大以前,你都不能去游泳,
否则你会头朝下鳍朝天沉到水里;
夏天的风暴和虎鲸,
会伤害我们的小海豹们。
会伤害我们的小海豹们,亲爱的小老鼠,
他们坏透顶了;但是戏水吧,
快快长大吧,你会一帆风顺的,

---

confusion n. 混乱;混乱状态

丛林的故事

Child of the Open Sea!

Of course the little fellow did not understand the words at first. He paddled and scrambled about by his mother's side, and learned to scuffle out of the way when his father was fighting with another seal, and the two rolled and roared up and down the slippery rocks. Matkah used to go to sea to get things to eat, and the baby was fed only once in two days, but then he ate all he could and throve upon it.

The first thing he did was to crawl inland, and there he met tens of thousands of babies of his own age, and they played together like puppies, went to sleep on the clean sand, and played again. The old people in the nurseries took no notice of them, and the holluschickie kept to their own grounds, and the babies had a beautiful playtime.

When Matkah came back from her deep-sea fishing she would go straight to their playground and call as a sheep calls for a lamb, and wait until she heard Kotick bleat. Then she would take the straightest of straight lines in his direction, striking out with her fore flippers and knocking the youngsters head over heels right and left. There were always a few hundred mothers hunting for their children

248

THE JUNGLE STORY

大海的孩子！

当然小家伙开始听不懂这些话。他在妈妈身边划着水，爬来爬去，他懂得了在他爸爸和其他海豹打架、吼叫，在光滑的岩石上滚上滚下的时候，躲到一边。马特卡常常到海里去找吃的，小家伙只要两天喂一次就够了，但是每次他都吃得饱饱的，茁壮地成长起来了。

他学会的第一件事情就是往内陆爬去，在那里他遇到了成千上万和他一样年纪的小海豹，他们像小狗一样一起玩耍，在干净的沙地上睡觉，醒来又一起玩耍。待在窝里的老海豹们不理会他们，霍卢斯奇科也总待在他们自己的地盘上，所以小海豹们玩得可高兴了。

当马特卡从深海捕鱼回来，她总径直走向他们玩耍的地方，然后像母羊呼喊小羊羔那样喊着他的名字，直到他听见科迪克咩咩地叫着回答她。然后她笔直地朝他的方向走去，用前鳍开辟道路，把小海豹们左右推开，撞倒在地。总是有几百只海豹妈妈在玩耍的地方找她们的

---

paddle v. 划水   scramble v. 爬行   thrive v. 茁壮成长

249

丛林的故事

through the playgrounds, and the babies were kept lively. But, as Matkah told Kotick, "So long as you don't lie in muddy water and get mange, or rub the hard sand into a cut or scratch, and so long as you never go swimming when there is a heavy sea, nothing will hurt you here."

Little seals can no more swim than little children, but they are unhappy till they learn. The first time that Kotick went down to the sea a wave carried him out beyond his depth, and his big head sank and his little hind flippers flew up exactly as his mother had told him in the song, and if the next wave had not thrown him back again he would have **drowned**.

After that, he learned to lie in a beach pool and let the wash of the waves just cover him and lift him up while he paddled, but he always kept his eye open for big waves that might hurt. He was two weeks learning to use his flippers; and all that while he floundered in and out of the water, and coughed and grunted and crawled up the beach and took **catnaps** on the sand, and went back again, until at last he found that he truly belonged to the water.

Then you can imagine the times that he had with his

THE JUNGLE STORY

孩子,所以小海豹们总是不得安宁。但是,正如马特卡告诉科迪克的那样,"只要你不在泥水里玩耍,不染上疥癣;也不把硬沙子揉进抓破的伤口里;也不在阴沉的大海里游泳,这里就没什么能伤害你。"

小海豹和小孩子一样不会游泳,但是他们在学会游泳之前总觉得心里痒痒的。科迪克第一次下海的时候,一个浪头把他冲到站不住的地方,他的大脑袋沉了下去,小小的后鳍就像他妈妈在歌里告诉他的那样翘了起来。如果第二个浪头没有把他冲回到岸边的话,他可能已经淹死了。

在那之后,他学会了躺在沙滩上的水坑里,让浪头把他淹没,他划动着鳍,让自己浮起来,但是他总是小心地留意着可能会伤害他的大波浪。他用两个礼拜学会了使用他的鳍。在那段时间里,他跟跟跄跄地在水里浮上浮下,有时被水呛得直咳嗽,哼哼着,有时爬上沙滩,在沙滩上打个瞌睡,然后又回到水里,直到最终他才发现自己是属于水中的。

接着,你可以想象他和他的同伴们一起度过的快乐时光。他们像

---

drown v. 使淹死   catnap n. 瞌睡

251

companions, **ducking** under the rollers; or coming in on top of a comber and landing with a **swash** and a **splutter** as the big wave went **whirling** far up the beach; or standing up on his tail and scratching his head as the old people did; or playing "I'm the King of the Castle" on slippery, weedy rocks that just stuck out of the wash. Now and then he would see a thin fin, like a big shark's fin, drifting along close to shore, and he knew that that was the Killer Whale, the Grampus, who eats young seals when he can get them; and Kotick would head for the beach like an arrow, and the fin would jig off slowly, as if it were looking for nothing at all.

Late in October the seals began to leave St. Paul's for the deep sea, by families and tribes, and there was no more fighting over the nurseries, and the holluschickie played anywhere they liked. "Next year," said Matkah to Kotick, "you will be a holluschickie; but this year you must learn how to catch fish."

They set out together across the Pacific, and Matkah showed Kotick how to sleep on his back with his flippers tucked down by his side and his little nose just out of the water. No **cradle** is so comfortable as the long, rocking swell of the Pacific. When Kotick felt his skin tingle all over, Matkah told him he was learning the

252

THE JUNGLE STORY

鸭子一样突然一头扎进浪头里;或者踏着卷浪,随着卷浪扑向海滩,猛得一下子落在沙滩上,水花四溅;或者像老海豹那样,用尾巴站立,抓抓自己的脑袋;或者在海滩上凸出的、长满野草的光滑岩石上玩"我是城堡国王"的游戏。他常常会在水面上看到一个薄薄的鳍,像大鲨鱼一样的鳍,向海边越漂越近,他知道那是虎鲸格兰普斯,要是他抓到小海豹的话,就会把他们吃了。这时,科迪克会像一枝箭一样向海滩冲去,而那个鳍就慢慢地游开了,装作他没在找什么东西。

到了十月,海豹们开始一家家地,或者一个部落一个部落地离开圣保罗岛游去深海,这时他们不会再为了抢窝而打架了,霍卢斯奇科们也可以自由地玩耍了。"明年,"马特卡对科迪克说,"你就是一只霍卢斯奇科了;但是今年你必须学会怎么捕鱼。"

他们一起出发横渡太平洋,马特卡教他怎样仰面躺在海面上,把鳍贴着身子收起来,只让他的小鼻子露在水面上。没有什么样的摇篮能像太平洋上摇晃的长波浪那样舒服了。当科迪克感到全身的皮肤有些刺痛时,马特卡告诉他他正在学习感受"海水的味道",那种刺痛

---

duck v. (鸭子似地) 突然扎入水中   swash n. 冲击;拍打   splutter n. 喷溅   whirl v. 使旋转;使急转   cradle n. 摇篮

253

"feel of the water," and that tingly, prickly feelings meant bad weather coming, and he must swim hard and get away.

"In a little time," she said, "you'll know where to swim to, but just now we'll follow Sea Pig, the Porpoise, for he is very wise." A school of porpoises were ducking and tearing through the water, and little Kotick followed them as fast as he could. "How do you know where to go to?" he panted. The leader of the school rolled his white eye and ducked under. "My tail tingles, youngster," he said. "That means there's a gale behind me. Come along! When you're south of the Sticky Water [he meant the Equator] and your tail tingles, that means there's a gale in front of you and you must head north. Come along! The water feels bad here."

This was one of very many things that Kotick learned, and he was always learning. Matkah taught him to follow the cod and the halibut along the under-sea banks and wrench the rockling out of his hole among the weeds; how to skirt the wrecks lying a hundred fathoms below water and dart like a rifle bullet in at one porthole and out at another as the fishes ran; how to dance on the top of the waves when the lightning was racing all over the sky, and wave his flipper politely to the stumpy-tailed Albatross and the Man-of-war

254

THE JUNGLE STORY

的感觉意味着坏天气就要来临,他必须努力地游,离开那里。

　　"很快,"她说,"你就会知道该往哪儿游,但是现在我们就跟着海豚希皮格吧,因为他非常聪明。"一群海豚在水里扎着猛子,飞快得游着,小科迪克拼命地跟着他们。"你们怎么知道该往哪里游呢?"他喘着气问。海豚的首领转动着他的白眼睛,一头扎进水里。"我的尾巴有点刺痛,年轻人,"他说,"那就是说在我身后有一场风暴。赶快!当你在'粘乎乎的海'南面的时候(他是指赤道),你的尾巴感到刺痛,那就是说在你面前有一场风暴,所以你必须往北面去。赶快!我觉得这里的海水不太对劲。"

　　这是科迪克所学的许多事情当中的一小件,而他总是在不断地学习。马特卡教他沿着海底的沙洲追踪鳕鱼和大比目鱼,从海草丛中的洞穴里挖出三须鳕来;如何避开水下一百英寻深的地方的失事船只残骸,在鱼群中像一颗步枪子弹那样从一扇舷窗穿进,从另外一扇穿出;当天空电闪雷鸣的时候,如何在浪尖上跳舞,有礼貌地向顺风而行的短尾巴信天翁和军舰鹰挥挥他的鳍;他还学会了如何像海豚那样,把

---

　　school n. 鱼群;同类水生动物群　　skirt v. 避开　　dart v. 飞奔

255

Hawk as they went down the wind; how to jump three or four feet clear of the water like a dolphin, flippers close to the side and tail curved; to leave the flying fish alone because they are all bony; to take the shoulder-piece out of a cod at full speed ten fathoms deep, and never to stop and look at a boat or a ship, but particularly a row-boat. At the end of six months what Kotick did not know about deep-sea fishing was not worth the knowing. And all that time he never set flipper on dry ground.

One day, however, as he was lying half asleep in the warm water somewhere off the Island of Juan Fernandez, he felt faint and lazy all over, just as human people do when the spring is in their legs, and he remembered the good firm beaches of Novastoshnah seven thousand miles away, the games his companions played, the smell of the seaweed, the seal roar, and the fighting. That very minute he turned north, swimming steadily, and as he went on he met scores of his mates, all bound for the same place, and they said: "Greeting, Kotick! This year we are all holluschickie, and we can dance the Fire-dance in the breakers off Lukannon and play on the new grass. But where did you get that coat?"

Kotick's fur was almost pure white now, and though he felt very

鳍贴着身子收起,卷起尾巴,跳出水面三四英尺高;她教他不要去理会那些飞鱼,因为他们瘦骨嶙峋;他学会了在十英寻深的地方,全速前进时一口咬下鳕鱼肩头的肉,他还知道永远不要停下来看一艘小船或者是海船,特别是划艇。在六个月以后,科迪克还不知道的那些关于深海捕鱼的知识就是那些不值得学的东西了。在那段时间里,他的鳍都没有碰过干燥的土地。

然而有一天,他正半梦半醒地躺在离裘·弗南德斯岛不远的温暖的海水里,突然觉得全身软弱无力、懒洋洋地,就像人们感觉到春天要来了一样,他想起了七千英里外诺瓦斯图夏纳又好又结实的沙滩,想起了他和同伴们一起玩的游戏,想起了海草的味道、海豹的怒吼和斗殴。就在那时,他一转身,朝着北面坚定地游去。一路上,他碰到了几十只同伴,都朝同一个地方奔去,他们说:"你好啊,科迪克!今年我们是霍卢斯奇科了,我们可以在洛卡农那的浪花上跳火焰舞了,可以在新长出的草地上玩耍了。但是你从哪里弄来的这身皮毛?"

科迪克的皮毛现在几乎是纯白的了,虽然他对此十分自豪,但他

---

faint a. 软弱无力的

257

proud of it, he only said, "Swim quickly! My bones are aching for the land." And so they all came to the beaches where they had been born, and heard the old seals, their fathers, fighting in the rolling mist.

That night Kotick danced the Fire-dance with the **yearling** seals. The sea is full of fire on summer nights all the way down from Novastoshnah to Lukannon, and each seal leaves a wake like burning oil behind him and a flaming flash when he jumps, and the waves break in great phosphorescent streaks and swirls. Then they went inland to the holluschickie grounds and rolled up and down in the new wild wheat and told stories of what they had done while they had been at sea. They talked about the Pacific as boys would talk about a wood that they had been nutting in, and if anyone had understood them he could have gone away and made such a **chart** of that ocean as never was. The three- and four-year-old holluschickie **romped** down from Hutchinson's Hill crying: "Out of the way, youngsters! The sea is deep and you don't know all that's in it yet. Wait till you've rounded the Horn. Hi, you yearling, where did you get that white coat?"

"I didn't get it," said Kotick. "It grew." And just as he was going

THE JUNGLE STORY

只是回答说："快点游！我的骨头想陆地都想得疼了。"于是他们一起到了他们出生的海滩上，听到了老海豹，他们的父亲们在飘忽的雾气中争斗着。

那天晚上，科迪克和一岁的海豹们跳起了火焰舞。夏天的晚上，从诺瓦斯图夏纳到洛卡农的海上到处充满了火焰，每一头海豹身后都留下了一条痕迹，就像燃烧着的油。当他们跳起来的时候，身后留下一道闪光，波浪化成了一条条闪闪的条纹和漩涡。接着他们跑到内陆，霍卢斯奇科的地盘上，在新长出的野小麦地里滚来滚去，互相讲述着他们在海上的故事。他们谈起太平洋就像一群男孩子在谈论他们采坚果的小树林，如果有人能听懂他们的话，他回去一定可以画出一幅前所未有的海洋图。一群三、四岁的霍卢斯奇科从哈奇森的小山上嘻嘻哈哈地蹦下来，喊着："让开，小家伙们！海里可深了，里面你们不知道的东西还多着呢。等你们绕过了合恩角再说吧。嘿！一岁的小家伙，你从哪里弄来的这身白皮毛？"

"我没从哪里弄来，"科迪克说，"是它自己长出来的。"他正要把说话

---

yearling a. 一岁的；   chart n. 海图   romp v. 嬉闹玩耍

259

to roll the speaker over, a couple of black-haired men with flat red faces came from behind a sand dune, and Kotick, who had never seen a man before, coughed and lowered his head. The holluschickie just **bundled** off a few yards and sat staring stupidly. The men were no less than Kerick Booterin, the chief of the seal-hunters on the island, and Patalamon, his son. They came from the little village not half a mile from the sea nurseries, and they were deciding what seals they would drive up to the killing pens—for the seals were driven just like sheep—to be turned into seal-skin jackets later on.

"Ho! " said Patalamon. "Look! There's a white seal! "

Kerick Booterin turned nearly white under his oil and smoke, for he was an Aleut, and Aleuts are not clean people. Then he began to mutter a prayer. "Don't touch him, Patalamon. There has never been a white seal since—since I was born. Perhaps it is old Zaharrof's ghost. He was lost last year in the big gale."

"I'm not going near him," said Patalamon. "He's unlucky. Do you really think he is old Zaharrof come back? I owe him for some gulls' eggs."

"Don't look at him," said Kerick. "Head off that drove of four-

THE JUNGLE STORY

的这个海豹掀翻,两个黑头发,长着扁平的红脸颊的人从沙丘后面走出来。科迪克以前从来没见过人,他咳嗽起来,低下了头。那些霍卢斯奇科慌忙逃开几码远,傻坐在那里看着。那两个不是别人,是捕猎海豹的首领科力克•布特林和他的儿子帕达拉蒙。他们是从一个离小海豹窝不到半英里的村子里来的。他们正在考虑把哪些海豹赶到屠宰场去——因为海豹和羊一样,是赶着走的——稍后会把他们变成海豹皮外套。

"嚯!"帕达拉蒙说,"看!那里有只白海豹!"

科力克•布特林尽管脸上蒙着油烟,还是脸色一下子变得苍白,他是阿留申人,阿留申人都不怎么干净。然后他开始低声祈祷。"别碰他,帕达拉蒙。从——从我出生到现在,都没看到过一只白色的海豹。也许这是老扎哈罗夫的鬼魂。他去年在大风暴里失踪了。"

"我不会走过去的。"帕达拉蒙说。"他很不吉利的。你真的认为他是老扎哈罗夫回来了?我还欠他几只海鸥蛋呢。"

"别看他,"科力克说,"去赶那些四岁大的吧。工人们今天应该剥

---

bundle v. 匆忙离开

261

year-olds. The men ought to skin two hundred to-day, but it's the beginning of the season and they are new to the work. A hundred will do. Quick! "

Patalamon **rattled** a pair of seal's shoulder bones in front of a herd of holluschickie and they stopped dead, puffing and blowing. Then he stepped near and the seals began to move, and Kerick headed them inland, and they never tried to get back to their companions. Hundreds and hundreds of thousands of seals watched them being driven, but they went on playing just the same. Kotick was the only one who asked questions, and none of his companions could tell him anything, except that the men always drove seals in that way for six weeks or two months of every year.

"I am going to follow," he said, and his eyes nearly **popped** out of his head as he **shuffled** along in the wake of the herd.

"The white seal is coming after us," cried Patalamon. "That's the first time a seal has ever come to the killing-grounds alone."

"Hsh! Don't look behind you," said Kerick. "It is Zaharrof's ghost! I must speak to the priest about this."

The distance to the killing-grounds was only half a mile, but it took an hour to cover, because if the seals went too fast Kerick

THE JUNGLE STORY

二百只海豹皮,但是这一季刚刚开始,他们又都是新手,一百只就够了。快点!"

帕达拉蒙拿着一副海豹的肩胛骨在一群霍卢斯奇科面前敲得格格响,他们都呆在那里一动不动了,呼呼地喘着气。等他走近一点,海豹们便开始移动了,科力克就赶着他们往内陆走了,他们也没想过要回到他们的同伴那里。几十万只海豹就看着他们被赶走,但是他们继续像往常一样玩耍着。科迪克是惟——个提出疑问的海豹,但是没有一个同伴能回答他,只是说每年的六个星期或者两个月里,人们总是这样驱赶海豹的。

"我要跟着他们,"他说,当他拖着步子跟在海豹群后面的时候,他的眼睛都要从脑袋上瞪出来了。

"那只白海豹跟着我们,"帕达拉蒙叫道,"这是第一次看到有只海豹独自走向屠宰场。"

"嘘!别回头看,"科力克说,"那是扎哈罗夫的鬼魂!我得和牧师谈谈这事。"

从这里到屠宰场的距离只有半里路,但是得走上一个小时,因为

---

rattle v. 发出咯咯声　　pop v. (眼睛) 瞪出;突出　　shuffle v. 拖着(脚)走

263

丛林的故事

knew that they would get heated and then their fur would come off in patches when they were skinned. So they went on very slowly, past Sea Lion's Neck, past Webster House, till they came to the Salt House just beyond the sight of the seals on the beach. Kotick followed, panting and wondering. He thought that he was at the world's end, but the roar of the seal nurseries behind him sounded as loud as the roar of a train in a tunnel. Then Kerick sat down on the moss and pulled out a heavy pewter watch and let the drove cool off for thirty minutes, and Kotick could hear the fog-dew dripping off the brim of his cap. Then ten or twelve men, each with an iron-bound club three or four feet long, came up, and Kerick pointed out one or two of the drove that were bitten by their companions or too hot, and the men kicked those aside with their heavy boots made of the skin of a walrus's throat, and then Kerick said, "Let go! " and then the men clubbed the seals on the head as fast as they could.

Ten minutes later little Kotick did not recognize his friends any more, for their skins were ripped off from the nose to the hind flippers, whipped off and thrown down on the ground in a pile. That was enough for Kotick. He turned and galloped (a seal can

THE JUNGLE STORY

科力克知道,如果海豹走得太快,他们会变得很热,然后剥皮的时候,他们的毛皮会一块块地掉下来。所以他们走得很慢,经过了海狮颈,走过了韦波斯特家,他们一直走到海滩上的海豹们看不到的撒尔特家。科迪克跟在后面,喘着粗气,诧异极了。他以为他走到世界尽头了,但是身后的小海豹窝传来的吼叫声像火车穿过隧道那样震耳欲聋。然后,科力克在苔藓上坐了下来,拿出一块沉甸甸的青灰色的表,让海豹群凉快了半个小时。科迪克听到露水从他的帽檐上流下来的声音。接着,有十个、还是十二个男人走了过来,每人手上拿着一根三四英寸长的包着铁皮的棍子。科力克把海豹群里一两只被同伴咬伤的海豹和仍然太热的海豹指给他们看,他们抬起海象颈皮做的厚靴子把这些海豹踢到一边,然后科力克说,"动手吧!"那些人就用棍子狠狠地敲着海豹们的脑袋。

　　十分钟以后,小科迪克再也认不出他的朋友们了,因为他们的毛皮从鼻子一直到后鳍都被撕开,扯下来扔在地上堆成了一堆。科迪克再也看不下去了。他转过身,飞奔起来(一头海豹能飞奔一小会儿),

---

　　rip v. 撕,扯　　gallop v. 飞奔

gallop very swiftly for a short time) back to the sea; his little new mustache bristling with horror. At Sea Lion's Neck, where the great sea lions sit on the edge of the surf, he flung himself flipper-overhead into the cool water and rocked there, gasping miserably. "What's here?" said a sea lion gruffly, for as a rule the sea lions keep themselves to themselves.

"Scoochnie! Ochen scoochnie! " ("I'm **lonesome**, very lonesome! ") said Kotick. "They're killing all the holluschickie on all the beaches! "

The Sea Lion turned his head **inshore**. "**Nonsense!** " he said. "Your friends are making as much noise as ever. You must have seen old Kerick polishing off a drove. He's done that for thirty years."

"It's horrible," said Kotick, backing water as a wave went over him, and steadying himself with a screw stroke of his flippers that brought him all standing within three inches of a **jagged** edge of rock.

"Well done for a yearling! " said the Sea Lion, who could **appreciate** good swimming. "I suppose it is rather awful from your way of looking at it, but if you seals will come here year after year,

THE JUNGLE STORY

往海边跑去,他新长出来的小胡子吓得都竖了起来。他跑到海狮颈,鳍朝上,一头扎进清凉的海水里,在水里颤抖着,痛苦地喘着气。大海狮们正坐在那里的海浪边上。"这是什么?"一只海狮生硬地问,因为通常海狮不和别人打交道。

"斯库奇尼!欧辰·斯库奇尼!"("我很寂寞,非常寂寞!")科迪克说,"他们把沙滩上所有的霍卢斯奇科都杀死了!"

大海狮把头转向海岸边。"胡说八道!"他说,"你的朋友们还是像往常一样那么喧闹呢。你肯定是看到老科力克杀死了一群海豹。他这么做都已经三十年了。"

"太可怕了,"科迪克说道,这时一个浪头打过来,他用鳍把水推开,接着双鳍一转,在离参差不齐的岩石边三英寸的地方站稳了。

"干得很好!一岁的小海豹!"海狮说,他很欣赏他高超的游泳技术。"我想从你的角度来看,这很可怕,但是如果你们海豹年年都到这里来,人类当然都会知道了,除非你能找到一个人类从来没有去过的

---

lonesome a. 寂寞的　　inshore adv. 向海岸地;靠近岸边的　　nonsense n. 胡说

jagged a. 参差不齐的　　appreciate v. 欣赏

of course the men get to know of it, and unless you can find an island where no men ever come you will always be driven."

"Isn't there any such island?" began Kotick.

"I've followed the poltoos [the halibut] for twenty years, and I can't say I've found it yet. But look here—you seem to have a fondness for talking to your betters—suppose you go to Walrus Islet and talk to Sea Vitch. He may know something. Don't flounce off like that. It's a six-mile swim, and if I were you I should haul out and take a nap first, little one."

Kotick thought that that was good advice, so he swam round to his own beach, hauled out, and slept for half an hour, twitching all over, as seals will. Then he headed straight for Walrus Islet, a little low sheet of rocky island almost **due** northeast from Novastoshnah, all ledges and rock and gulls' nests, where the walrus **herded** by themselves.

He landed close to old Sea Vitch—the big, ugly, bloated, pimpled, fat-necked, long-tusked walrus of the North Pacific, who has no **manners** except when he is asleep—as he was then, with his hind flippers half in and half out of the surf.

"Wake up! " barked Kotick, for the gulls were making a great noise.

小岛,否则人们总是会来驱赶你们的。"

"有这样的小岛吗?"科迪克问道。

"我跟着波尔冬(大比目鱼)有二十年了,还从来没有找到过这样的一个地方。但是你看——你似乎挺喜欢和比你身份高的人说话——你可以去海象岛,找西维奇谈谈。他可能知道些什么。别马上就出发,得游上六英里呢。如果我是你的话,我就先上岸睡一会,小家伙。"

科迪克认为那是个好建议,于是他游回到自己的海滩上,爬上岸,睡了半小时,像所有的海豹那样,他睡着的时候全身抽搐着。醒来后,他就径直朝海象岛游去,海象岛是一座位于诺瓦斯图夏纳正东北方的低矮多岩石的小岛。岛上都是岩层、岩石和海鸥巢,海象在那里成群地生活。

他在靠老西维奇很近的地方上了岸,西维奇是一头北太平洋的又大又丑的海象。他身材臃肿,身上长满了脓包,长着肥肥的脖子和长长的象牙。他对别人毫无礼貌,除非他睡着了——那时候,他正在睡觉,他的后鳍一半露在水面上,一半在水下。

"醒醒!"科迪克大声地喊道,因为海鸥正发出很响的噪音。

---

due adv. 正(南、北等)　　herd v. 使集在一起　　manner n. (pl.) 礼貌

"Hah! Ho! Hmph! What's that?" said Sea Vitch, and he struck the next walrus a blow with his tusks and waked him up, and the next struck the next, and so on till they were all awake and staring in every direction but the right one.

"Hi! It's me," said Kotick, bobbing in the surf and looking like a little white slug.

"Well! May I be—skinned! " said Sea Vitch, and they all looked at Kotick as you can fancy a club full of drowsy old gentlemen would look at a little boy. Kotick did not care to hear any more about skinning just then; he had seen enough of it. So he called out: "Isn't there any place for seals to go where men don't ever come?"

"Go and find out," said Sea Vitch, shutting his eyes. "Run away. We're busy here."

Kotick made his dolphin-jump in the air and shouted as loud as he could: "Clam-eater! Clam-eater! " He knew that Sea Vitch never caught a fish in his life but always rooted for clams and seaweed; though he pretended to be a very terrible person. Naturally the Chickies and the Gooverooskies and the Epatkas—the Burgomaster Gulls and the Kittiwakes and the Puffins, who are always looking for

270

THE JUNGLE STORY

"哈！嗬！哼！谁啊？"西维奇说，他用他的象牙拱了一下旁边的海象，把他弄醒，旁边的海象又把下一头海象叫醒，就这样，直到所有的海象都被吵醒了，他们东张西望，就是不往该看的那个方向看。

"嗨！是我！"科迪克喊道，他在浪花中上蹿下跳，看上去就像一条小小的白色鼻涕虫。

"哎呀！天哪——剥了我的皮吧！"西维奇说。所有的海象都看着科迪克，你可以想象一下，这就像在一个俱乐部里一群昏昏欲睡的老绅士看到一个小男孩时的情景。科迪克那时不愿再听到任何有关剥皮的事情，他已经看够了。所以他喊道："有没有什么人类从来没去过的地方可以让海豹去？"

"你自己去找啊，"西维奇说完又闭上了眼睛，"走开，我们这里忙着呢。"

科迪克像海豚一样凌空跳起，大声地喊道："吃蛤蜊的家伙！吃蛤蜊的家伙！"他知道西维奇在他这一生中从未捕过一条鱼，总是用鼻子拱土找蛤蜊和海草吃；尽管他总是假装很吓人的样子。当然，那些总是在寻找机会能够粗鲁一下的奇基、古维卢斯基和伊佩特卡——领头

---

drowsy a. 昏昏欲睡的

丛林的故事

a chance to be rude, took up the cry, and—so Limmershin told me—
for nearly five minutes you could not have heard a gun fired on
Walrus Islet. All the population was yelling and screaming "Clam-
eater! Stareek [old man]! " while Sea Vitch rolled from side to side
grunting and coughing.

"Now will you tell?" said Kotick, all out of breath.

"Go and ask Sea Cow," said Sea Vitch. "If he is living still, he'll
be able to tell you."

"How shall I know Sea Cow when I meet him?" said Kotick,
sheering off.

"He's the only thing in the sea uglier than Sea Vitch,"
screamed a Burgomaster gull, wheeling under Sea Vitch's nose.
"Uglier, and with worse manners! Stareek! "

Kotick swam back to Novastoshnah, leaving the gulls to scream.
There he found that no one sympathized with him in his little
attempt to discover a quiet place for the seals. They told him that
men had always driven the holluschickie—it was part of the day's
work—and that if he did not like to see ugly things he should not
have gone to the killing grounds. But none of the other seals had
seen the killing, and that made the difference between him and his

THE JUNGLE STORY

鸥、三趾鸥和角嘴海雀马上就响应了，然后——林默辛是这样告诉我的——在接下来的五分钟里，即使有炮弹打到海象岛上也听不见了。所有的岛上的居民都在喊着："吃蛤蜊的家伙！斯达力克（老家伙）！"西维奇把身子翻来翻去，嘴里一边咕哝着，一边咳嗽着。

"现在你能说了吧？"科迪克说道，他已经喘不过气来了。

"去问海牛吧，"西维奇说，"如果他还活着，他能够告诉你你想知道的。"

"我碰到他的时候，怎么知道他是海牛呢？"科迪克转过身子问。

"他是这海里惟一比西维奇还要丑陋的东西，"一只领头鸥尖叫道，他在西维奇的鼻子下盘旋，"更丑陋，而且更加没有礼貌！斯达力克！"

科迪克往诺瓦斯图夏纳游回去，留下这群海鸥在那儿尖叫。回到岛上，他发现尽管他尽了自己小小的努力为海豹们去寻找一块宁静的地方，这里却没有一只海豹同情他。他们告诉他人类一直都在驱赶霍卢斯奇科——那是他们每天工作的一部分——还告诉他，如果他不想看到这些丑陋的事情，他就不应该去屠宰场。但是并没有其他海豹看

---

sympathize v. 同情

friends. Besides, Kotick was a white seal.

"What you must do," said old Sea Catch, after he had heard his son's **adventures**, "is to grow up and be a big seal like your father, and have a nursery on the beach, and then they will leave you alone. In another five years you ought to be able to fight for yourself." Even gentle Matkah, his mother, said: "You will never be able to stop the killing. Go and play in the sea, Kotick." And Kotick went off and danced the Fire-dance with a very heavy little heart.

That autumn he left the beach as soon as he could, and set off alone because of a notion in his bullet-head. He was going to find Sea Cow, if there was such a person in the sea, and he was going to find a quiet island with good firm beaches for seals to live on, where men could not get at them. So he **explored** and explored by himself from the North to the South Pacific, swimming as much as three hundred miles in a day and a night. He met with more adventures than can be told, and narrowly escaped being caught by the Basking Shark, and the Spotted Shark, and the Hammerhead, and he met all the **untrustworyour** ruffians that loaf up and down the seas, and the heavy polite fish, and the **scarlet** spotted scallops that are moored in one place for hundreds of years, and grow very

THE JUNGLE STORY

见过屠杀,这也是他和他的朋友们对这件事有不同的看法的原因。而且,科迪克是只白色的海豹。

"你必须做的事情是,"老西卡其在听完儿子的冒险经历后说,"快点长大,长成和你爸爸一样的大海豹,在海滩上有个小海豹的窝,然后他们就不会来理睬你了。再过五年,你应该可以自己战斗了。"即使是温柔的马特卡,他的妈妈也说,"你永远也不能阻止杀戮。去海里玩吧,科迪克。"科迪克游开了,带着一颗小小的但是沉重的心跳着火焰舞。

那年秋天,他早早地离开了海滩,独自出发了,因为他圆圆的脑袋里有了一个想法。他要去寻找海牛,如果海里真有这样一个人的话,他还要去找一个安静的小岛,上面有坚实的沙滩,海豹可以在上面生活,而人类也捉不到他们。于是他独自从北往南沿着太平洋一路寻找,最多的时候一天一夜游了三百英里。他经历了数不清的冒险,差点被络鲨、斑点鲨和锤头双髻鲨抓住,他遇到了所有在海里游来荡去的不值得信赖的流氓,遇到了身体笨重的但是彬彬有礼的鱼和红色的斑点扇贝。那些扇贝几百年来都住在同一个地方,为此他们还非常骄傲,但是

---

adventure n. 冒险   explore v. 勘探,勘查   untrustworyour a. 不可靠的,不能信任的
scarlet a. 鲜红的

275

proud of it; but he never met Sea Cow, and he never found an island that he could fancy.

If the beach was good and hard, with a slope behind it for seals to play on, there was always the smoke of a whaler on the horizon, boiling down blubber, and Kotick knew what that meant. Or else he could see that seals had once visited the island and been killed off, and Kotick knew that where men had come once they would come again.

He picked up with an old stumpy-tailed albatross, who told him that Kerguelen Island was the very place for peace and quiet, and when Kotick went down there he was all but smashed to pieces against some wicked black cliffs in a heavy sleet-storm with lightning and thunder. Yet as he pulled out against the gale he could see that even there had once been a seal nursery. And it was so in all the other islands that he visited.

Limmershin gave a long list of them, for he said that Kotick spent five seasons exploring, with a four months' rest each year at Novastoshnah, when the holluschickie used to make fun of him and his imaginary islands. He went to the Gallapagos, a horrid dry place on the Equator, where he was nearly baked to death; he went to

THE JUNGLE STORY

他从未碰到过海牛,也从来没有找到一座他想象中的小岛。

有时他找到一个沙滩又好又结实的小岛,后面还有一个斜坡可以供海豹们玩耍,他总是会在地平线那里看到一艘冒着烟的捕鲸船,煮着鲸油,科迪克知道那意味着什么。有时他发现海豹们曾经来过某个小岛,但是都被屠宰了,科迪克知道人类来过一次的地方一定会再来。

他结识了一只短尾巴的老信天翁,信天翁告诉他科格斯兰岛是个十分宁静和平的小岛,但是当科迪克到那儿的时候,遇上了电闪雷鸣的雨夹雪,他在黑乎乎的险恶的悬崖上差点被击得粉身碎骨。然而当他顶着风暴出发的时候,他发现那里曾经也有过小海豹窝。他去过的所有其他小岛都是这样的情况。

林默辛列举了很长一串海岛的名称,因为他知道科迪克花了五个季节的时间在寻找,每年在诺瓦斯图夏纳海滩上休息四个月,那时霍卢斯奇科们总是会嘲笑他和他理想中的海岛。他去过加拉帕戈群岛,那是在赤道附近的一个崎岖不平、很干燥的群岛。在那里,他差点被烤死;他去过乔治亚群岛、奥克尼岛、艾莫鲁尔德岛、小南丁格尔岛、高夫

---

horizon n. 地平线　　sleet n. 雨夹雪

丛林的故事

the Georgia Islands, the Orkneys, Emerald Island, Little Nightingale Island, Gough's Island, Bouvet's Island, the Crossets, and even to a little **speck** of an island south of the Cape of Good Hope. But everywhere the people of the Sea told him the same things. Seals had come to those islands once upon a time, but men had killed them all off. Even when he swam thousands of miles out of the Pacific and got to a place called Cape Corrientes (that was when he was coming back from Gough's Island), he found a few hundred mangy seals on a rock and they told him that men came there too.

That nearly broke his heart, and he headed round the Horn back to his own beaches; and on his way north he hauled out on an island full of green trees, where he found an old, old seal who was dying, and Kotick caught fish for him and told him all his **sorrows**. "Now," said Kotick, "I am going back to Novastoshnah, and if I am driven to the killing-pens with the holluschickie I shall not care."

The old seal said, "Try once more. I am the last of the Lost Rookery of Masafuera, and in the days when men killed us by the hundred thousand there was a story on the beaches that some day a white seal would come out of the North and lead the seal people to a quiet place. I am old, and I shall never live to see that day, but

THE JUNGLE STORY

岛、布维岛、克罗赛特群岛,甚至是好望角以南的一个丁点大的岛。但
是不管他到那里,海里的居民都告诉他同样的话。海豹曾经来过那些
岛,但是人类把他们都杀光了。即便是他游出太平洋几万英里远,到了
一个叫科里恩特角的地方(那是在他从高夫岛往回游的路上发现的),
他看到在岩石上有几百只长了疥癣的海豹,他们告诉他人类也去过那
里了。

　　那真的让他很伤心,于是他绕过合恩角朝自己的海滩游了回去。
在他往北面回去的路上,他爬上一座长满绿树的小岛休息,在那儿他
碰到了一只非常非常年迈、已经奄奄一息的海豹。科迪克抓了些鱼给
他,还把自己的伤心事告诉了他。"现在,"科迪克说,"我准备回诺瓦斯
图夏纳了,如果我和其他霍卢斯奇科一起被赶到屠宰场去了,我也不
在乎了。"

　　老海豹说:"再试一试吧。我是已经灭绝的玛撒夫厄拉海豹家族的
最后一个成员。在我们几十万头的海豹被人类杀害的岁月里,海滩上
流传着这样一个故事。它说有一天,会有一只白海豹从北方来,带领海
豹们找到一个宁静的地方。我已经老了,我不可能活着看到那一天了,

___

speck n. 一点点　　sorrow n. 伤心事

279

others will. Try once more."

And Kotick curled up his mustache (it was a beauty) and said, "I am the only white seal that has ever been born on the beaches, and I am the only seal, black or white, who ever thought of looking for new islands."

This cheered him immensely; and when he came back to Novastoshnah that summer, Matkah, his mother, begged him to marry and settle down, for he was no longer a holluschick but a full-grown sea-catch, with a curly white mane on his shoulders, as heavy, as big, and as fierce as his father. "Give me another season," he said. "Remember, Mother, it is always the seventh wave that goes farthest up the beach."

Curiously enough, there was another seal who thought that she would put off marrying till the next year, and Kotick danced the Fire-dance with her all down Lukannon Beach the night before he set off on his last exploration. This time he went westward, because he had fallen on the trail of a great shoal of halibut, and he needed at least one hundred pounds of fish a day to keep him in good condition. He chased them till he was tired, and then he curled himself up and went to sleep on the hollows of the ground swell that

但是其他海豹可以。再试一次吧。”

科迪克卷起了自己的胡须(胡须很漂亮),说道,“我是有史以来海滩上出生的惟一的一头白海豹,不管是黑的还是白的海豹,我也是惟一想寻找新海岛的海豹。”

这件事情大大地鼓舞了他。那年夏天他返回诺瓦斯图夏纳的时候,他的妈妈马特卡要求他结婚,安顿下来,因为他不再是霍卢斯奇科了,他已经是一头成年海豹了,他的肩膀上长着卷曲的白色鬃毛,像他的父亲一样高大、健壮、勇猛。“再给我一个季节的时间,”他说,“记住,妈妈,第七个浪头离海边最远。”

说来也奇怪,另外也有一只海豹认为她可以等到下一年再结婚。在他出发去进行最后一次探险的前一个晚上,科迪克和她在洛卡农海滩上跳了一夜的火焰舞。这一次,他往西面去了,因为他跟在一大群大比目鱼后面,而他每天至少要吃一百磅鱼才能使他保持良好的身体状态。他一直追踪他们直到疲倦了,于是,他把身子蜷起来,躺在冲向科皮尔岛的波浪中睡着了。他十分了解那里的海滩,所以到了半夜的时候,他

---

cheer v. 使振奋　　immsensely adv. 大大地;无限地　fierce adj. 凶猛的,好斗的
curiously adv. 不可思议地　　　exploration n. 探究,探索;勘探

sets in to Copper Island. He knew the coast perfectly well, so about midnight, when he felt himself gently **bumped** on a weed-bed, he said, "Hm, tide's running strong tonight," and turning over under water opened his eyes slowly and stretched. Then he jumped like a cat, for he saw huge things nosing about in the shoal water and browsing on the heavy **fringes** of the weeds.

"By the Great Combers of Magellan! " he said, **beneath** his mustache. "Who in the Deep Sea are these people?"

They were like no walrus, sea lion, seal, bear, whale, shark, fish, squid, or scallop that Kotick had ever seen before. They were between twenty and thirty feet long, and they had no hind flippers, but a shovel-like tail that looked as if it had been whittled out of wet leather. Their heads were the most foolish-looking things you ever saw, and they balanced on the ends of their tails in deep water when they weren't grazing, **bowing solemnly** to each other and waving their front flippers as a fat man waves his arm.

"Ahem! " said Kotick. "Good sport, gentlemen?" The big things answered by bowing and waving their flippers like the Frog Footman. When they began feeding again Kotick saw that their upper lip was split into two pieces that they could twitch apart about

THE JUNGLE STORY

觉得自己轻柔地撞在海草丛上了,他说,"唔,今晚的潮水真厉害啊。"他在水下翻了个身,慢慢地睁开眼睛,伸了个懒腰。然后突然猫一样纵了起来,因为他看到水中有些硕大无比的家伙在东嗅西闻,咀嚼着茂密的海草丛边上的草。

"以麦盖伦的巨浪起誓,"他在胡须底下悄声说,"那些家伙到底是深海里的什么种族啊?"

他们不像科迪克以前见过的海象、海狮、海豹,也不像熊、鲸、鲨、鱼、鱿鱼或者扇贝。他们大约有二十到三十英尺长,没有后鳍,但是有一条像是用潮湿的皮革切割出来的铁锹状的尾巴。他们的脑袋是你所见过的最傻头傻脑的东西。当他们不吃草的时候,他们在深水里用尾巴末端支撑起身体,互相庄重地鞠着躬,挥动着他们的前鳍,就像一个胖男人挥动着他的手臂。

"呃哼!"科迪克说,"打猎顺利吗,先生们?"那些大家伙像青蛙仆人那样用鞠躬和挥动前鳍来回答他。当他们又开始吃东西的时候,科迪克看到他们的上嘴唇是裂成两半的,他们可以把嘴张开一英尺宽,

---

bump v. 撞击   fringe n. 边缘;外围   beneath prep. 在……下方   bow v. 鞠躬
solemnly adv. 庄严地;严肃地

a foot and bring together again with a whole bushel of seaweed between the splits. They tucked the stuff into their mouths and chumped solemnly.

"Messy style of feeding, that," said Kotick. They bowed again, and Kotick began to lose his temper. "Very good," he said. "If you do happen to have an extra joint in your front flipper you needn't show off so. I see you bow gracefully, but I should like to know your names." The split lips moved and twitched; and the glassy green eyes stared, but they did not speak.

"Well! " said Kotick. "You're the only people I've ever met uglier than Sea Vitch—and with worse manners."

Then he remembered in a flash what the Burgomaster gull had screamed to him when he was a little yearling at Walrus Islet, and he tumbled backward in the water, for he knew that he had found Sea Cow at last.

The sea cows went on schlooping and grazing and chumping in the weed, and Kotick asked them questions in every language that he had picked up in his travels; and the Sea People talk nearly as many languages as human beings. But the sea cows did not answer because Sea Cow cannot talk. He has only six bones in his neck

THE JUNGLE STORY

在裂口里塞进整整一普式耳的海草,然后再把嘴合上。他们把食物全都塞进嘴里,然后认真满足地咀嚼着。

"那样吃法真是邋遢,"科迪克说道。他们又开始鞠起了躬,科迪克开始失去耐心了。"很好,"他说,"即便是你们的前鳍比别人多出一节,也不用那样炫耀吧。我看你们鞠躬很优雅,但是我很想知道你们的名字。"裂开的嘴唇蠕动着,一张一合的,但是他们没有说话。

"好吧!"科迪克说,"你们是我见过的惟一比西维奇还要丑陋的动物——而且更加没有礼貌。"

突然,他想起了在他一岁的时候,在海象岛上领头鸥对他尖叫的那些话。他跌跌撞撞地回到海里,因为他知道他终于找到了海牛。

海牛们继续在海草丛里撕扯、吞食、咀嚼着,科迪克用他在历险途中学会的每一种语言向他们提问;海里的动物使用的语言种类几乎和人类一样多。但是海牛们没有回答,因为海牛不会说话。他们的颈部本来应该有七根骨头,但实际上只有六根,据说在海里,他们甚至不能和

---

bushel n. 普式耳(容量单位)　　split n. 裂口,裂缝　　gracefully adv. 优美地,优雅地

where he ought to have seven, and they say under the sea that that prevents him from speaking even to his companions. But, as you know, he has an extra joint in his foreflipper, and by waving it up and down and about he makes what answers to a sort of clumsy telegraphic code.

By daylight Kotick's mane was standing on end and his temper was gone where the dead crabs go. Then the Sea Cow began to travel northward very slowly, stopping to hold **absurd** bowing **councils** from time to time, and Kotick followed them, saying to himself, "People who are such idiots as these are would have been killed long ago if they hadn't found out some safe island. And what is good enough for the Sea Cow is good enough for the Sea Catch. All the same, I wish they'd hurry."

It was weary work for Kotick. The herd never went more than forty or fifty miles a day, and stopped to feed at night, and kept close to the shore all the time; while Kotick swam round them, and over them, and under them, but he could not hurry them up one-half mile. As they went farther north they held a bowing council every few hours, and Kotick nearly bit off his mustache with **impatience** till he saw that they were following up a warm **current** of

THE JUNGLE STORY

同伴进行交流。但是,你知道,他们的前鳍比别人长出一节,他们把前鳍上下左右地挥动,这也算是以一种笨拙的电报式代码回答吧。

到天亮的时候,科迪克的鬃毛都竖了起来,他的耐心也早跑到死螃蟹去的地方了。这时,海牛开始慢慢地往北走了,还不时地停下来笑容可掬地鞠着躬互相商量着。科迪克跟着他们,自言自语道,"像他们这些笨蛋如果不是发现了某个安全的海岛,早就该被杀光了。对海牛来说够好的地方,对海豹来说一定也够好了。不过,我希望他们最好快点走。"

跟着海牛对科迪克来说可是个令人厌倦的事情。海牛一天最多走四五十英里,晚上还要停下来吃东西,他们一直沿着靠近海岸的地方行走;不管科迪克是绕着他们游,还是游到他们上头,或者是他们身下,都不能让他们走快半英里。他们往北面越走越远,每过几个小时就会鞠着躬互相商量一番。科迪克不耐烦得差点要把自己的胡子咬掉

---

absurd adj. 可笑的　　council n. 会议　　impatience n. 不耐烦　　current n. 潮流、洋流

water, and then he respected them more.

One night they sank through the shiny water—sank like stones—and for the first time since he had known them began to swim quickly. Kotick followed, and the pace astonished him, for he never dreamed that Sea Cow was anything of a swimmer. They headed for a cliff by the shore—a cliff that ran down into deep water, and plunged into a dark hole at the foot of it, twenty fathoms under the sea. It was a long, long swim, and Kotick badly wanted fresh air before he was out of the dark tunnel they led him through.

"My wig! " he said, when he rose, gasping and puffing, into open water at the farther end. "It was a long dive, but it was worth it."

The sea cows had separated and were browsing lazily along the edges of the finest beaches that Kotick had ever seen. There were long stretches of smooth-worn rock running for miles, exactly fitted to make seal-nurseries, and there were play-grounds of hard sand sloping inland behind them, and there were rollers for seals to dance in, and long grass to roll in, and sand dunes to climb up and down, and, best of all, Kotick knew by the feel of the water, which never deceives a true sea catch, that no men had ever come there.

THE JUNGLE STORY

了,可后来他发现他们跟随着一股暖流在走,于是对他们多了些敬重。

一天,他们从闪着光的海水里沉了下去——像石头一样沉了下去——自从他认识这些海牛以来,他们第一次迅速地游起来。科迪克赶紧跟上,海牛的速度让他感到吃惊,因为他从来没想到海牛会是游泳健将。他们朝着海边的一个悬崖游去——这一悬崖的底部一直在海水的深处——他们钻进了悬崖底部的一个距离海面约二十英寻的黑洞里。他们游了很长的一段距离,科迪克跟着他们,在钻出那条黑暗的坑道之前,就很想呼吸新鲜的空气了。

"我的天哪!"他钻出坑道另一头的水面,站起身来,呼呼地喘着粗气。"这次潜水真够长的,不过还真值得。"

海牛们已经散开了,在科迪克所见过的最棒的沙滩边上懒散地吃着草。连绵不绝几英里都是光滑的岩石,正好适合做小海豹窝,岩石后面是一片可以用来做游乐场的坚实沙地,倾斜着伸向内陆。海边有滚滚卷浪,可以让海豹们在里面跳舞,也有长长的草地,可以让海豹在里面打滚,还有可以让海豹爬上爬下的沙丘。最重要的是,科迪克凭他对

---

astonish v. 使惊讶　　dive n. 潜水　　deceive v. 欺骗;蒙蔽

丛林的故事

The first thing he did was to assure himself that the fishing was good, and then he swam along the beaches and counted up the delightful low sandy islands half hidden in the beautiful rolling fog. Away to the northward, out to sea, ran a line of bars and shoals and rocks that would never let a ship come within six miles of the beach, and between the islands and the mainland was a stretch of deep water that ran up to the perpendicular cliffs, and somewhere below the cliffs was the mouth of the tunnel.

"It's Novastoshnah over again, but ten times better," said Kotick. "Sea Cow must be wiser than I thought. Men can't come down the cliffs, even if there were any men; and the shoals to seaward would knock a ship to splinters. If any place in the sea is safe, this is it."

He began to think of the seal he had left behind him, but though he was in a hurry to go back to Novastoshnah, he thoroughly explored the new country, so that he would be able to answer all questions.

Then he dived and made sure of the mouth of the tunnel, and raced through to the southward. No one but a sea cow or a seal would have dreamed of there being such a place, and when he

THE JUNGLE STORY

海水的感觉,这瞒不了一头真正的海豹,他知道从来没有人类来过这里。

他做的第一件事情就是确定这里可以捕到大量的鱼,然后他沿着海滩一路游去,数着美丽的薄雾里若隐若现的一座座低矮的沙岛。北面出海的地方是一排沙洲、浅滩和暗礁,这让任何船只都不能靠近海滩六英里之内。在小岛群和大陆之间是一片深水,一直延伸到陡峭的悬崖边,而悬崖下的某个地方就是坑道的出口。

"这儿就是另外一个诺瓦斯图夏纳,但是比那儿又好上十倍,"科迪克说,"海牛比我想象的要聪明得多了。人类不能从悬崖上下来,即使那里有人类的话;而临海的那些浅滩也能把船都撞得粉碎。如果海里有什么地方是安全的,那么就是这里了。"

他开始想念那些留在家里的海豹们了,但是虽然他急着返回诺瓦斯图夏纳,他还是彻底地勘探了一下这个新天地,这样回去他就可以回答所有的问题了。

接着他潜到海里,找到了坑道出口的位置,然后快速地穿过坑道往南游去。除了海牛或是一头海豹,没有人会想到还会有这样的地方

---

assure v. 使确信　　mainland n. 大陆　　perpendicular a. 垂直的
thoroughly adv. 彻底地,完全地

looked back at the cliffs even Kotick could hardly believe that he had been under them.

He was six days going home, though he was not swimming slowly; and when he hauled out just above Sea Lion's Neck the first person he met was the seal who had been waiting for him, and she saw by the look in his eyes that he had found his island at last.

But the holluschickie and Sea Catch, his father, and all the other seals laughed at him when he told them what he had discovered, and a young seal about his own age said, "This is all very well, Kotick, but you can't come from no one knows where and order us off like this. Remember we've been fighting for our nurseries, and that's a thing you never did. You preferred prowling about in the sea."

The other seals laughed at this, and the young seal began twisting his head from side to side. He had just married that year, and was making a great fuss about it.

"I've no nursery to fight for," said Kotick. "I only want to show you all a place where you will be safe. What's the use of fighting?"

"Oh, if you're trying to back out, of course I've no more to say," said the young seal with an ugly chuckle.

THE JUNGLE STORY

存在。当他回头看着悬崖的时候,即使是科迪克也不敢相信他曾经在那下面。

他花了整整六天的时间才回到家,尽管他游得并不慢。当他从海狮颈爬出水面的时候,看到的第一个人就是一直在等他的那头海豹,她从他的眼神里看出来他终于找到了他的海岛。

但是当他把他的发现告诉霍卢斯奇科、他爸爸西卡其和其他所有的海豹时,他们都嘲笑他。一头和他年纪相仿的年轻海豹说:"你说得都不错,科迪克,可是你不能从一个没人知道的地方跑到这儿来,这样子命令我们离开。你别忘了我们一直在为小海豹窝战斗,那可是你从来没做过的事情。你更喜欢在海里四处徘徊。"

其他海豹都笑了起来,那头年轻的海豹开始左右摇晃起脑袋。他那一年刚刚结婚,因而对这件事格外关注。

"我没有小海豹窝需要我战斗,"科迪克说,"我只是想把你们带到一个安全的地方。打架有什么用?"

"哦,如果你打算退出的话,我当然就没什么好说的了。"年轻的海豹冷笑着说。

---

prowl v. 徘徊,四处觅食　　fuss n. 大惊小怪

"Will you come with me if I win?" said Kotick. And a green light came into his eye, for he was very angry at having to fight at all.

"Very good," said the young seal carelessly. "If you win, I'll come."

He had no time to change his mind, for Kotick's head was out and his teeth sunk in the blubber of the young seal's neck. Then he threw himself back on his haunches and hauled his enemy down the beach, shook him, and knocked him over. Then Kotick roared to the seals: "I've done my best for you these five seasons past. I've found you the island where you'll be safe, but unless your heads are dragged off your silly necks you won't believe. I'm going to teach you now. Look out for yourselves! "

Limmershin told me that never in his life—and Limmershin sees ten thousand big seals fighting every year—never in all his little life did he see anything like Kotick's **charge** into the nurseries. He flung himself at the biggest sea catch he could find, caught him by the throat, **choked** him and bumped him and banged him till he grunted for **mercy**, and then threw him aside and attacked the next. You see, Kotick had never fasted for four months as the big seals did

THE JUNGLE STORY

"如果我赢了，你会跟我去吗？"科迪克问。他的眼里闪过一道绿光，因为他为不得不打架而感到十分气恼。

"很好，"年轻的海豹漫不经心地说，"如果你赢了，我就去。"

他没时间改变主意了，因为科迪克的脑袋已经探出来，他的牙齿深深地印在年轻的海豹脖子上的那块赘肉里了。然后他往后一仰蹲下来，把他的对手拖到沙滩上，摇晃着把他撞倒。然后科迪克对着其他海豹怒吼："我在这过去的五个季节以来一直在尽自己最大的努力找海岛。我已经找到了可以保证你们安全的海岛，但是除非你们愚蠢的脑袋从你们脖子上被拽了下来，否则你们是不会相信的。我要给你们点教训。你们自己小心点！"

林默辛告诉我在他的一生中从来没有见过——林默辛每年都见到上万头大海豹打架——在他短短的一生中从来没有见过像科迪克这样冲向海豹窝的。他朝他能找到的最大个子的海豹扑上去，掐住他的脖子让他透不过气，一阵拳打脚踢直到他咕咕求饶，然后把他扔到一边，再冲向另外一头。你知道，科迪克从来不像其他大海豹那样每年

---

charge v. 冲锋　　choke v. 使……透不过气　　mercy n. 怜悯，宽恕

every year, and his deep-sea swimming trips kept him in perfect condition, and, best of all, he had never fought before. His curly white mane stood up with rage, and his eyes flamed, and his big dog teeth glistened, and he was splendid to look at. Old Sea Catch, his father, saw him tearing past, hauling the grizzled old seals about as though they had been halibut, and upsetting the young bachelors in all directions; and Sea Catch gave a roar and shouted: "He may be a fool, but he is the best fighter on the beaches! Don't tackle your father, my son! He's with you!"

Kotick roared in answer, and old Sea Catch waddled in with his mustache on end, blowing like a locomotive, while Matkah and the seal that was going to marry Kotick cowered down and admired their men-folk. It was a gorgeous fight, for the two fought as long as there was a seal that dared lift up his head, and when there were none they paraded grandly up and down the beach side by side, bellowing.

At night, just as the Northern Lights were winking and flashing through the fog, Kotick climbed a bare rock and looked down on the scattered nurseries and the torn and bleeding seals. "Now," he said, "I've taught you your lesson."

THE JUNGLE STORY

禁食四个月。他在深海里的游行也让他的身体保持完美的状态。最重要的是,他以前从来没有打过架。他卷曲的白鬃毛气得竖立了起来,他的眼睛里冒着火,他的大犬牙闪着光,看上去神奇十足。他的爸爸老西卡其看着他飞奔过去,把灰色的老海豹们像大比目鱼一样拽来拽去,把周围一圈的年轻的单身汉都撞倒在地,怒吼了一声,喊道:"他也许是个傻瓜,但是他是所有的海滩上最棒的勇士!别打你爸爸,我的儿子!他和你是同一战线的!"

科迪克吼了一声作为回答,老西卡其摇摇摆摆地走过去,胡子都竖了起来,吼得像一个火车头。而马特卡和准备嫁给科迪克的那只海豹退到一旁,欣赏着他们的男人。这是一场精彩的战斗,因为他们两个一直打到没有一只海豹敢把头抬起来。然后他们肩并肩、大摇大摆地在海滩上走来走去,吼叫着。

晚上,当北极光在雾气中一闪一闪发亮的时候,科迪克爬上一块光秃秃的岩石,看着下面乱七八糟的小海豹窝和被咬得遍体鳞伤流着血的海豹们,"现在,"他说,"我已经给你们教训了。"

---

upset v. 打翻　　bachelor n. 单身汉　　tackle v. 对付　　parade v. 游行,招摇地走
wink v. 闪烁　　flash v. 闪亮

"My wig! " said old Sea Catch, boosting himself up stiffly, for he was fearfully mauled. "The Killer Whale himself could not have cut them up worse. Son, I'm proud of you, and what's more, I'll come with you to your island—if there is such a place."

"Hear you, fat pigs of the sea. Who comes with me to the Sea Cow's tunnel? Answer, or I shall teach you again," roared Kotick.

There was a murmur like the ripple of the tide all up and down the beaches. "We will come," said thousands of tired voices. "We will follow Kotick, the White Seal."

Then Kotick dropped his head between his shoulders and shut his eyes proudly. He was not a white seal any more, but red from head to tail. All the same he would have scorned to look at or touch one of his wounds.

A week later he and his army (nearly ten thousand holluschickie and old seals) went away north to the Sea Cow's tunnel, Kotick leading them, and the seals that stayed at Novastoshnah called them idiots. But next spring, when they all met off the fishing banks of the Pacific, Kotick's seals told such tales of the new beaches beyond Sea Cow's tunnel that more and more seals left Novastoshnah. Of course it was not all done at once, for the seals are not very clever,

THE JUNGLE STORY

"我的天哪!"老西卡其说,他费力地撑起身体,因为他伤得也很厉害。"虎鲸也不能把他们伤得再厉害了。儿子,我为你骄傲,而且,我要跟你到你的海岛上去——如果真的有这么一个地方。"

"你们听着,海里的肥猪们。谁要跟着我去海牛的坑道?回答,否则我会再教训你们的。"科迪克咆哮着说。

响起了一片细语声,就像海滩上潮水拍岸的涟漪。"我们跟你去,"成千上万个疲倦的声音说,"我们会跟随白海豹科迪克的。"

然后科迪克把脑袋埋在肩膀里,骄傲地闭上了眼睛。他不再是一头白海豹了,从头到尾都是红色的。即便这样,他也不屑于看一眼,或者舔一舔自己的伤口。

一个星期以后,他和他的部队(大约一万多头霍卢斯奇科和老海豹)往北出发去海牛的坑道,科迪克带领着他们,而那些留在诺瓦斯图夏纳的海豹称他们为白痴。第二年春天的时候,当所有的海豹在太平洋捕鱼区碰面的时候,科迪克的海豹们讲述着在海牛坑道那里的新海滩的故事,于是有更多的海豹离开了诺瓦斯图夏纳和洛卡农以及其他

---

murmur n. 轻声   ripple n. 涟漪   scorn v. 不屑   wound n. 伤口

and they need a long time to turn things over in their minds, but year after year more seals went away from Novastoshnah, and Lukannon, and the other nurseries, to the quiet, sheltered beaches where Kotick sits all the summer through, getting bigger and fatter and stronger each year, while the holluschickie play around him, in that sea where no man comes.

THE JUNGLE STORY

海豹窝,到那块宁静的、隐蔽的海滩去。科迪克每年夏天都坐在沙滩上,一年年变得更大、更胖、更壮。霍卢斯奇科们在他的身边玩耍,在人类没有到过的海里玩耍。

---

ashamed *a.* 羞愧的　　bleed *v.* 流血

Chapter 8 Lukannon

This is the great deep-sea song that all the St. Paul seals sing when they are heading back to their beaches in the summer. It is a sort of very sad seal National Anthem.

I met my mates in the morning (and, oh, but I am old!),
Where roaring on the ledges the summer ground-swell rolled;
I heard them lift the **chorus** that **drowned** the breakers' song—
The Beaches of Lukannon—two million voices strong.

The song of pleasant stations beside the salt lagoons,
The song of blowing squadrons that shuffled down the dunes,
The song of midnight dances that churned the sea to flame—
The Beaches of Lukannon—before the sealers came!

THE JUNGLE STORY

第八章　洛卡农

这是一首优美的深海歌曲，圣保罗所有的海豹们每年夏天返回他们的海滩时都会唱这首歌。那是一种非常忧伤的海豹的国歌。

早上我遇到了我的伙伴们（哦，但是我已经老了！），
他们在夏日沙滩的岩石上吼叫，打着滚；
我听到了他们的合唱，淹没了海浪声，
——洛卡农的沙滩啊——两百万个声音震天响。

盐水湖边的舒适的海豹窝之歌，
沙丘上嬉笑打闹的海豹之歌，
让海洋迸发热情的午夜舞曲，
——洛卡农的沙滩啊——在海豹猎人到来之前！

---

chorus n. 合唱　　drown v. 淹没，盖没

丛林的故事

I met my mates in the morning (I'll never meet them more!);
They came and went in legions that darkened all the shore.
And o'er the foam-flecked offing as far as voice could reach
We hailed the landing-parties and we sang them up the beach.

The Beaches of Lukannon—the winter wheat so tall—
The dripping, crinkled lichens, and the sea-fog drenching all!
The platforms of our playground, all shining smooth and worn!

The Beaches of Lukannon—the home where we were born!

I met my mates in the morning, a broken, scattered band.
Men shoot us in the water and club us on the land;
Men drive us to the Salt House like silly sheep and tame,
And still we sing Lukannon—before the sealers came.

Wheel down, wheel down to southward; oh, Gooverooska, go!

THE JUNGLE STORY

早上我遇到了我的伙伴们（我从没见过这么多头海豹！），
他们蜂拥而至，海滩上黑压压的一片！
歌声远远地飞到冒着点点泡沫的近海，
我们欢呼着举行派对庆贺，歌声飘扬在海滩上。

洛卡农的海滩啊——高高的冬季的小麦——
滴着露水的大片苔藓，海雾浸润了一切！
我们的游乐场，闪闪发光，磨得光又滑！
洛卡农的海滩啊——这是我们出生的家乡！

早上我遇到了我的伙伴们，一群伤痕累累东倒西歪的海豹们。
人类在水中射杀我们，在陆地上用棍子揍我们；
人类像赶愚蠢的母羊和羊羔一样把我们驱赶到撒尔特府邸，
我们仍然在歌唱洛卡农海滩——在海豹猎人到来之前！

我们往南去吧，往南去吧；哦，去古维卢斯卡，出发！

---

woe n. 不幸；灾难

丛林的故事

And tell the Deep-Sea Viceroys the story of our **woe**;

Ere, empty as the shark's egg the tempest flings ashore,

The Beaches of Lukannon shall know their sons no more!

THE JUNGLE STORY

把我们不幸的故事讲述给深海总督听；
暴风雨袭向海岸，沙滩空旷得像光溜溜的鲨鱼蛋，
洛卡农的海滩再也见不到他们的海豹孩子了！

中英对照

J.K.罗琳的读书单

丛林故事

THE JUNGLE STORY

[英] 吉卜林◎著

辛 静◎译

下

《哈里·波特》作者J.K.罗琳

最喜爱的英美经典文学名著

中国书籍出版社

图书在版编目（CIP）数据

丛林故事／（英）吉卜林著；辛静译．—北京：中国
书籍出版社，2007.1
（J. K. 罗琳的读书单）
书名原文：The Jungle Story
ISBN 978 - 7 - 5068 - 1721 - 9

Ⅰ. 丛... Ⅱ. ①吉...②辛... Ⅲ. ①英语—汉语—
对照读物②童话—作品集—英国—近代
Ⅳ. H319. 4：I

中国版本图书馆 CIP 数据核字（2006）第 159971 号

责任编辑／毕　磊　李立云
责任印制／熊　力　武雅彬
封面设计／汇智泉文化设计公司
出版发行／中国书籍出版社
　　　　　地　　址：北京市丰台区三路居路 97 号（邮编：100073）
　　　　　电　　话：(010)52257142(总编室)　　(010)52257154(发行部)
　　　　　电子邮箱：chinabp@ vip. sina. com
经　销／全国新华书店
印　刷／三河市杨庄镇明华印装厂
开　本／690 毫米×960 毫米　1/16
印　张／31
字　数／238 千字
版　次／2013 年第 1 月第 2 版，2013 第 2 次印刷
定　价／61. 80 元（上、中、下）

版权所有　翻印必究

目录

丛林的故事

Chapter 9 "Rikki-Tikki-Tavi"

At the hole where he went in,
Red-Eye called to Wrinkle-Skin.
Hear what little Red-Eye saith:
"Nag, come up and dance with death!"

Eye to eye and head to head,
(Keep the measure, Nag.)
This shall end when one is dead;
(At your pleasure, Nag.)
Turn for turn and twist for twist—
(Run and hide you, Nag.)
Hah! The hooded Death has missed!
(Woe betide you, Nag!)

This is the story of the great war that Rikki-tikki-tavi fought single-handed, through the bath-rooms of the big bungalow in

THE JUNGLE STORY

第九章 "里基—蒂基—塔维"

他钻进了那个洞,

"红眼睛"呼唤着"皱皮肤"。

小"红眼睛"这样说道:

"纳格,出来和死亡跳舞吧!"

眼对着眼,头对着头,

(跟上拍子,纳格。)

只有我们其中一个死去,舞蹈才会完结;

(悉听尊便,纳格。)

我转你也转,我扭你也扭——

(你快跑吧,躲起来,纳格。)

哈!死亡没有击中带头罩的!

(不幸得要降临了,纳格!)

这个故事讲述的是里基—蒂基—塔维在塞戈里营地一幢孟加拉式平房的浴室里单枪匹马进行的一次伟大的战役。长尾缝叶莺达齐帮

---

swrinkle n. 皱纹   saith v. 说   single-handed adv. 单枪匹马地

丛林的故事

Segowlee cantonment. Darzee, the Tailorbird, helped him, and Chuchundra, the musk-rat, who never comes out into the middle of the floor, but always creeps round by the wall, gave him advice, but Rikki-tikki did the real fighting.

He was a mongoose, rather like a little cat in his fur and his tail, but quite like a weasel in his head and his habits. His eyes and the end of his **restless** nose were pink. He could scratch himself anywhere he pleased with any leg, front or back, that he chose to use. He could fluff up his tail till it looked like a bottle brush, and his war cry as he scuttled through the long grass was: "Rikk-tikk-tikki-tikki-tchk!"

One day, a high summer flood washed him out of the burrow where he lived with his father and mother, and carried him, kicking and clucking, down a roadside ditch. He found a little wisp of grass floating there, and clung to it till he lost his senses. When he **revived**, he was lying in the hot sun on the middle of a garden path, very draggled indeed, and a small boy was saying, "Here's a dead mongoose. Let's have a **funeral**."

"No," said his mother, "let's take him in and dry him. Perhaps he isn't really dead."

They took him into the house, and a big man picked him up between his finger and **thumb** and said he was not dead but half

THE JUNGLE STORY

助了他,从来都只敢沿着墙边跑、不敢走到房间中央的麝鼠丘查德给他提了些建议,但是真正战斗的只有里基—蒂基一个人。

他是只獴,皮毛和尾巴都像只小猫,但是头部和习惯却像只黄鼠狼。他的眼睛和他永不宁静的鼻子顶端都是粉红色的。只要他高兴,他会用任何一条腿,不管前腿还是后腿,抓身上的任何一个地方。他会松开他的尾巴,把它变得像一把刷瓶子的刷子,他在长长的草丛里飞奔时发出的战斗口号是:"里基—蒂基—蒂基—蒂基—恰克!"

一天,夏季的一场大洪水把他从他和父母居住的地洞里冲了出来,他踢着腿,咯咯地叫着,洪水把他冲到了路边的沟里。他看到有一小簇草漂在那里,就紧紧地抱着它,直到失去知觉。等他恢复知觉的时候,烈日当空,他躺在一条花园小径的中央,全身又脏又湿,一个小男孩正在说,"这里有只死獴,让我们来举行葬礼吧。"

"不,"他妈妈说,"我们把他带到屋里去,把他擦干。也许他还没死呢。"

他们把他带进屋子里,一个高大的男人用拇指和食指把他拎了起来,说他还没有死,只是被水呛了。于是他们用棉絮把他裹起来,在一

---

restless a. 永不宁静的   revive v. 使苏醒,复苏
funeral n. 葬礼   thumb n. 大拇指

313

从林的故事

choked. So they wrapped him in cotton wool, and warmed him over a little fire, and he opened his eyes and sneezed.

"Now," said the big man (he was an Englishman who had just moved into the bungalow), "don't **frighten** him, and we'll see what he'll do."

It is the hardest thing in the world to frighten a mongoose, because he is eaten up from nose to tail with curiosity. The **motto** of all the mongoose family is "Run and find out," and Rikki-tikki was a true mongoose. He looked at the cotton wool, decided that it was not good to eat, ran all round the table, sat up and put his fur in order, scratched himself, and jumped on the small boy's shoulder.

"Don't be frightened, Teddy," said his father. "That's his way of making friends."

"Ouch! He's tickling under my chin," said Teddy.

Rikki-tikki looked down between the boy's collar and neck, snuffed at his ear, and climbed down to the floor, where he sat rubbing his nose.

"Good gracious," said Teddy's mother, "and that's a wild **creature**! I suppose he's so **tame** because we've been kind to him."

"All mongooses are like that," said her husband. "If Teddy doesn't pick him up by the tail, or try to put him in a cage, he'll run in and out of the house all day long. Let's give him something to

THE JUNGLE STORY

堆小火上面给他暖身子,他睁开了眼睛,打了个喷嚏。

"现在,"这个高大的男人说(他是刚刚搬进这个营地的英国人),"别吓到他,我们看看他要做什么。"

要吓倒一只獴恐怕是世界上最困难的事情了,因为他从鼻子到尾巴都充满了好奇。所有的獴家族的座右铭是:"跑去看看发生了什么事情。"而里基—蒂基是只地地道道的獴。他看着棉絮,认为这不好吃,于是绕着桌子跑了一圈,然后坐下来整理了一下自己的皮毛,又抓了抓痒,然后跳到了小男孩的肩膀上。

"别害怕,特迪,"他爸爸说,"那是他交朋友的方式。"

"唉呦! 他弄得我下巴很痒。"特迪说。

里基—蒂基往男孩的领口和脖子间瞧了瞧,在他的耳朵边嗅了嗅,然后爬下来坐在地板上,开始揉鼻子。

"天哪,"特迪的妈妈说,"这就是野生动物啊! 我猜他这么听话是因为我们对他很友好。"

"所有的獴都是这样的,"他丈夫说,"如果特迪不捏着他的尾巴把他拎起来,也不把他关到笼子里,他会整天在屋子里跑进跑出的。让我

---

choke v. (水、烟等)呛住   frighten v. 使惊恐,吓唬
creature n. 生物,动物   tame a. 驯服的,听话的

315

eat."

They gave him a little piece of raw meat. Rikki-tikki liked it immensely, and when it was finished he went out into the veranda and sat in the sunshine and fluffed up his fur to make it dry to the roots. Then he felt better.

"There are more things to find out about in this house," he said to himself, "than all my family could find out in all their lives. I shall certainly stay and find out."

He spent all that day roaming over the house. He nearly drowned himself in the bath-tubs, put his nose into the ink on a writing table, and burned it on the end of the big man's cigar, for he climbed up in the big man's lap to see how writing was done. At nightfall he ran into Teddy's nursery to watch how kerosene lamps were lighted, and when Teddy went to bed Rikki-tikki climbed up too. But he was a restless companion, because he had to get up and attend to every noise all through the night, and find out what made it. Teddy's mother and father came in, the last thing, to look at their boy, and Rikki-tikki was awake on the pillow. "I don't like that," said Teddy's mother. "He may bite the child." "He'll do no such thing," said the father. "Teddy's safer with that little beast than if he had a bloodhound to watch him. If a snake came into the nursery now—"

But Teddy's mother wouldn't think of anything so awful.

316

THE JUNGLE STORY

们给他点东西吃。"

他们给了他一小块生肉。里基—蒂基非常喜欢吃,吃完了他便跑到外面走廊里,坐在太阳下,蓬开了他的皮毛让它彻底晒干。然后他觉得舒服多了。

"这个屋子里有这么多事情可以探个究竟,"他心里想,"比我们一家人一辈子能看到的东西还要多。我肯定要留下来,看个究竟。"

他整天就在屋子里到处走。他差点让自己在浴缸里淹死,把鼻子放在写字台的墨水里,为了看字是怎么写的,他爬到那个高大的男人的大腿上,鼻子被大男人的雪茄烟头烫着了。夜晚降临了,他跑到特迪的儿童卧室里看煤油灯是怎样点燃的。特迪上床睡觉,里基—蒂基也爬了上去。但是他是个片刻不宁的伙伴,因为整个晚上只要有声响,他就得爬起来,看看声音究竟是从何而来。特迪的爸爸妈妈在睡觉前来看他们的孩子,这时里基—蒂基正醒着躺在枕头上。"我不喜欢那样,"特迪的妈妈说,"他可能会咬孩子的。""他不会做这样的事情,"爸爸说,"特迪和这个小野兽在一起很安全,比有一头大猎犬看着他还安全。现在如果有条蛇爬进儿童卧室——"

但是特迪妈妈不相信有这么可怕的事情。

---

drown v. 使淹死   awful a. 可怕的

Early in the morning Rikki-tikki came to early breakfast in the veranda riding on Teddy's shoulder, and they gave him banana and some boiled egg. He sat on all their laps one after the other, because every well-brought-up mongoose always hopes to be a house mongoose some day and have rooms to run about in; and Rikki-tikki's mother (she used to live in the **general**'s house at Segowlee) had carefully told Rikki what to do if ever he came across white men.

Then Rikki-tikki went out into the garden to see what was to be seen. It was a large garden, only half **cultivated**, with bushes, as big as summer-houses, of Marshal Niel roses, lime and orange trees, clumps of bamboos, and thickets of high grass. Rikki-tikki licked his lips. "This is a splendid hunting-ground," he said, and his tail grew bottle-brushy at the thought of it, and he scuttled up and down the garden, snuffing here and there till he heard very sorrowful voices in a thorn-bush.

It was Darzee, the Tailorbird, and his wife. They had made a beautiful nest by pulling two big leaves together and stitching them up the edges with fibers, and had filled the hollow with cotton and downy fluff. The nest swayed to and fro, as they sat on the rim and cried.

"What is the matter?" asked Rikki-tikki.

318

THE JUNGLE STORY

早晨,里基—蒂基骑在特迪的脖子上到走廊上吃早饭,他们给了他香蕉和一些煮蛋。他轮流坐到他们腿上,因为每一只有良好教养的獴都希望有一天能成为一只家养的獴,可以在房间里跑进跑出;里基—蒂基的妈妈(她过去曾住在塞戈里营地的将军家里)详细地告诉过他,如果他碰见白人该怎么做。

接着里基—蒂基跑到外面花园里,看看那里有什么好看的东西。这是个大花园,只有一半的面积种上了灌木,有像花园凉亭那么大的元帅尼尔玫瑰,酸橙树和橘树,竹丛和一丛丛茂盛的青草。里基—蒂基舔了舔嘴唇。"这是个打猎的好地方,"他一想到这个,尾巴就蓬开得像刷瓶子的刷子。他在花园里跑来跑去,这里嗅嗅,那里闻闻,直到他听到荆棘丛里传来悲痛的哭声。

那是长尾缝叶莺达齐和他的妻子。他们本来把两片大叶子合在一起,用细枝把叶子边上缝起来做成了一个漂亮的鸟巢,还在里面放上棉絮和松软的绒毛。但现在鸟巢在空中荡来荡去,他们坐在边上哭。

"发生什么事了?"里基—蒂基问。

---

general n. 将军   cultivate v. 耕种,耕作

319

丛林的故事

"We are very miserable," said Darzee. "One of our babies fell out of the nest yesterday and Nag ate him."

"H'm!" said Rikki-tikki, "that is very sad—but I am a stranger here. Who is Nag?"

Darzee and his wife only cowered down in the nest without answering, for from the thick grass at the foot of the bush there came a low hiss—a horrid cold sound that made Rikki-tikki jump back two clear feet. Then inch by inch out of the grass rose up the head and spread hood of Nag, the big black cobra, and he was five feet long from tongue to tail. When he had lifted one-third of himself clear of the ground, he stayed balancing to and fro exactly as a dandelion tuft balances in the wind, and he looked at Rikki-tikki with the wicked snake's eyes that never change their expression, whatever the snake may be thinking of.

"Who is Nag?" said he. "I am Nag. The great God Brahm put his mark upon all our people, when the first cobra spread his hood to keep the sun off Brahm as he slept. Look, and be afraid!"

He spread out his hood more than ever, and Rikki-tikki saw the spectacle-mark on the back of it that looks exactly like the eye part of a hook-and-eye fastening. He was afraid for the minute, but it is impossible for a mongoose to stay frightened for any length of time, and though Rikki-tikki had never met a live cobra before, his mother had fed him on dead ones, and he knew that all a grown

THE JUNGLE STORY

"我们真可怜，"达齐说，"昨天我们的一个孩子从鸟巢里掉了下去，被纳格吃掉了。"

"唔，"里基—蒂基说，"那真是很惨——但是我刚到这儿，谁是纳格啊？"

达齐和他的妻子没有回答，只是把身子蜷缩在鸟巢里，因为在灌木丛下茂密的草丛里传来一个低低的嘶声——这个可怕冰冷的声音让里基—蒂基往后整整跳了两英尺。然后大黑眼镜蛇纳格的脑袋和展开的颈部皮褶从草丛里一寸一寸地抬起来。他从舌头到尾巴一共有五英尺长。他把三分之一的身体抬离了地面，就像风中的蒲公英一样保持着平衡。他用邪恶的蛇眼看着里基—蒂基。蛇的表情总是一成不变的，不管他在想什么。

"谁是纳格？"他说，"我就是纳格。当第一条眼镜蛇为正在睡觉的神梵天展开脖子上的皮褶遮挡太阳的时候，伟大的梵天就在我们的家族身上留下了他的记号。看，别害怕！"

他把皮褶展开地更大了。里基—蒂基看到了他背上就像风纪扣的扣眼一样的眼镜记号。他害怕了一小会儿，但是要让一只獴害怕很长时间是不可能的。虽然里基—蒂基以前没有见过一条活的眼镜蛇，但是他妈妈用死的眼镜蛇喂过他，而且他知道一个成年獴一生中的主要

---

miserable a. 可怜的，悲惨的

mongoose's business in life was to fight and eat snakes. Nag knew that too and, at the bottom of his cold heart, he was afraid.

"Well," said Rikki-tikki, and his tail began to fluff up again, "marks or no marks, do you think it is right for you to eat fledglings out of a nest?"

Nag was thinking to himself, and watching the least little movement in the grass behind Rikki-tikki. He knew that mongooses in the garden meant death sooner or later for him and his family, but he wanted to get Rikki-tikki off his **guard**. So he dropped his head a little, and put it on one side.

"Let us talk," he said. "You eat eggs. Why should not I eat birds?"

"Behind you! Look behind you! " sang Darzee.

Rikki-tikki knew better than to waste time in staring. He jumped up in the air as high as he could go, and just under him whizzed by the head of Nagaina, Nag's wicked wife. She had crept up behind him as he was talking, to make an end of him. He heard her savage hiss as the **stroke** missed. He came down almost across her back, and if he had been an old mongoose he would have known that then was the time to break her back with one bite; but he was afraid of the terrible lashing return stroke of the cobra. He bit, indeed, but did not bite long enough, and he jumped clear of the whisking tail, leaving Nagaina torn and angry.

THE JUNGLE STORY

事情就是和蛇战斗,吃掉蛇。纳格也知道这点,所以在他冰冷的内心深处,还是害怕的。

"好吧,"里基—蒂基说,他的尾巴又一次蓬开了,"不管有记号还是没记号,你认为吃掉一只掉到鸟巢外面的小鸟是对的吗?"

纳格正在打着主意,注意着里基—蒂基身后草丛里的任何一个微小的动静。他知道花园里有獴意味着他和他的家族迟早得死,但是他想让里基—蒂基放松警惕。所以他低下头,把头弯向一边。

"让我们谈谈吧,"他说,"你吃鸡蛋。为什么我就不能吃鸟呢?"

"身后!小心你身后!"达齐叫道。

里基—蒂基当然知道不能浪费时间回头看,他立刻尽可能地高高跳起,纳加娜的脑袋,纳格邪恶的妻子,从他的身下飕地滑过。她在他说话的时候悄悄地爬到他身后,想结束他的性命。他听到了她一击没打中发出的恶毒的咝咝声。他跳下来几乎就在她的背上,如果他是只老獴的话,他就会知道那时是一口咬断她的背的最好时机;但是他害怕眼镜蛇可怕的一记回击。他的确咬了,但是咬的时间不够长。他跳着躲过了横扫过来的尾巴,被咬伤的纳加娜暴跳如雷。

---

guard n. 警戒　stroke n. 击,打

丛林的故事

"Wicked, wicked Darzee! " said Nag, lashing up as high as he could reach toward the nest in the thorn-bush. But Darzee had built it out of reach of snakes, and it only swayed to and fro.

Rikki-tikki felt his eyes growing red and hot (when a mongoose's eyes grow red, he is angry), and he sat back on his tail and hind legs like a little kangaroo, and looked all round him, and chattered with rage. But Nag and Nagaina had disappeared into the grass. When a snake misses its stroke, it never says anything or gives any sign of what it means to do next. Rikki-tikki did not care to follow them, for he did not feel sure that he could manage two snakes at once. So he trotted off to the gravel path near the house, and sat down to think. It was a serious matter for him.

If you read the old books of natural history, you will find they say that when the mongoose fights the snake and happens to get bitten, he runs off and eats some **herb** that cures him. That is not true. The victory is only a matter of quickness of eye and quickness of foot—snake's blow against mongoose's jump—and as no eye can follow the motion of a snake's head when it strikes, this makes things much more wonderful than any magic herb. Rikki-tikki knew he was a young mongoose, and it made him all the more pleased to think that he had managed to escape a blow from behind. It gave him **confidence** in himself, and when Teddy came running down the path, Rikki-tikki was ready to be petted.

THE JUNGLE STORY

　　"坏蛋,坏蛋达齐!"纳格叫道,把尾巴向着荆棘丛里的鸟巢用力高高地扫去。但是达齐把鸟巢筑在蛇够不到的地方,鸟巢只是在空中荡来荡去。

　　里基—蒂基觉得眼睛变红了,变热了(当一只獴的眼睛变红时,表明他生气了),他像一只袋鼠那样坐在自己的尾巴和后腿上,看着他的周围,发出生气的咕咕声。但是纳格和纳加娜已经消失在草丛里了。当一条蛇没击中目标时,他不会说什么,也不会表明他下一步打算做什么。里基—蒂基不想跟着他们,因为他不确定是否能一次应付两条蛇。于是他跑到屋子旁的砾石路上,坐下来思考。这对他来说是件重大的事情。

　　如果你读过关于自然历史的书,你会看到书上说,当獴和蛇打斗的时候碰巧被咬了,他就会跑开去吃一些药草来治疗。但那不是真的。要取得胜利的关键是眼疾脚快——蛇的攻击是针对獴的跳跃的——因为当蛇攻击的时候,没有什么眼睛能跟上蛇头的运动,这比神奇的草药更加令人惊叹。里基—蒂基知道他只是只小獴,一想到他躲过了蛇从身后的一击,就让他高兴极了。这给了自己信心。所以当特迪从小路上跑过来的时候,里基—蒂基准备好接受他的爱抚了。

---

herb n. 药草　　cure v. 治愈,治疗　　confidence n. 信心

But just as Teddy was **stooping**, something wriggled a little in the dust, and a tiny voice said: "Be careful. I am Death! " It was Karait, the dusty brown snakeling that lies for choice on the dusty earth; and his bite is as dangerous as the cobra's. But he is so small that nobody thinks of him, and so he does the more harm to people.

Rikki-tikki's eyes grew red again, and he danced up to Karait with the **peculiar** rocking, swaying motion that he had **inherited** from his family. It looks very funny, but it is so perfectly balanced a gait that you can fly off from it at any angle you please, and in dealing with snakes this is an **advantage**. If Rikki-tikki had only known, he was doing a much more dangerous thing than fighting Nag, for Karait is so small, and can turn so quickly, that unless Rikki bit him close to the back of the head, he would get the return stroke in his eye or his lip. But Rikki did not know. His eyes were all red, and he rocked back and forth, looking for a good place to hold. Karait struck out. Rikki jumped **sideways** and tried to run in, but the wicked little dusty gray head lashed within a **fraction** of his shoulder, and he had to jump over the body, and the head followed his heels close.

Teddy shouted to the house: "Oh, look here! Our mongoose is

326

THE JUNGLE STORY

但当特迪弯下腰的时候,尘土里有什么东西扭动了一下,一个细小的声音说:"小心啊,我是死神!"那是卡拉特,一种喜欢在尘土里生活,身上布满灰尘的棕色小蛇。他和眼镜蛇一样危险。但是由于他太小了,没有人注意到他,所以他对人类的危害更大。

里基—蒂基的眼睛又一次变红了,他以从他们家族继承来的独特的晃动摇摆姿势跳向卡拉特。这看上去很滑稽,但是这是一种非常平衡的步伐,可以让你从喜欢的任意方向跳出去,而对付一条蛇,这是一个有利条件。不过里基—蒂基不知道,他正在做一件比和纳格战斗要危险得多的事情。因为卡拉特太小了,而且转身非常迅速,所以除非里基在靠近头部的地方咬一口,否则他的眼睛或嘴唇上会挨一下反击。但是里基并不知道这一切。他的眼睛都是红的,他前后摇动着,寻找一个合适的地方下口。卡拉特猛得出击了。里基跳到一边,准备短兵相接进行搏斗,但是邪恶的、布满灰尘的灰脑袋突然一击,离他的肩膀只差了一点点。他不得不一跃跳过,蛇头紧紧追着他的脚后跟。

特迪对着屋子里喊:"哦,看这里!我们的獴正在杀一条蛇。"里

---

stoop v. 俯身,弯腰　　peculiar a. 特别的,独具的　　inherit v. 继承
advantage n. 有利条件　　sideways adv. 斜着　　fraction n. 一部分,一点儿

327

killing a snake." And Rikki-tikki heard a scream from Teddy's mother. His father ran out with a stick, but by the time he came up, Karait had lunged out once too far, and Rikki-tikki had sprung, jumped on the snake's back, dropped his head far between his forelegs, bitten as high up the back as he could get hold, and rolled away. That bite **paralyzed** Karait, and Rikki-tikki was just going to eat him up from the tail, after the custom of his family at dinner, when he remembered that a full meal makes a slow mongoose, and if he wanted all his strength and quickness ready, he must keep himself thin.

He went away for a dust bath under the castor-oil bushes, while Teddy's father beat the dead Karait. "What is the use of that?" thought Rikki-tikki. "I have settled it all;" and then Teddy's mother picked him up from the dust and hugged him, crying that he had saved Teddy from death, and Teddy's father said that he was a **providence**, and Teddy looked on with big scared eyes. Rikki-tikki was rather **amused** at all the **fuss**, which, of course, he did not understand. Teddy's mother might just as well have petted Teddy for playing in the dust. Rikki was thoroughly enjoying himself.

That night at dinner, walking to and fro among the wine-glasses

THE JUNGLE STORY

基—蒂基听到特迪妈妈发出一声尖叫。他爸爸拿着一根棍子跑出来，但等他跑到的时候，卡拉特由于一击击得太远，里基—蒂基已经跃起跳到蛇背上，把头在两条前腿中间低下，在他抓住的靠近头部的蛇背上大咬了一口，然后滚到一边。那口咬得卡拉特瘫痪了，里基—蒂基正要按照他们家族吃饭的习俗，从尾巴开始把猎物吃了，他突然想起，一顿饱餐会使獴行动缓慢，如果他想保持力量和敏捷，他就必须保持苗条。

他跑开去在蓖麻油树下享受了一下泥土浴，而特迪的爸爸还在鞭打死了的卡拉特。"那有什么用啊？"里基—蒂基想，"我都已经把他解决了。"然后特迪的妈妈把他从泥土中抱起来，搂着他哭着说，是他救了特迪的命。特迪的爸爸说他是上天派来的，而特迪则惊恐地瞪大了眼睛看着这一切。里基—蒂基对他们的大惊小怪感到很可笑，当然，他不理解这是怎么回事。特迪的妈妈也许也会因为特迪在泥土里玩而爱抚地拍拍他。里基在这里玩得高兴极了。

---

paralyze v. 使瘫痪　　providence n. 天意
amuse v. 逗……乐,逗……笑　　fuss n. 忙乱,大惊小怪

丛林的故事

on the table, he might have stuffed himself three times over with nice things. But he remembered Nag and Nagaina, and though it was very pleasant to be patted and petted by Teddy's mother, and to sit on Teddy's shoulder, his eyes would get red from time to time, and he would go off into his long war cry of "Rikk-tikk-tikki-tikki-tchk! "

Teddy carried him off to bed, and insisted on Rikki-tikki sleeping under his chin. Rikki-tikki was too well **bred** to bite or scratch, but as soon as Teddy was asleep he went off for his nightly walk round the house, and in the dark he ran up against Chuchundra, the musk-rat, creeping around by the wall. Chuchundra is a **broken-hearted** little beast. He whimpers and cheeps all the night, trying to make up his mind to run into the middle of the room. But he never gets there.

"Don't kill me," said Chuchundra, almost weeping. "Rikki-tikki, don't kill me! "

"Do you think a snake-killer kills muskrats?" said Rikki-tikki **scornfully.**

"Those who kill snakes get killed by snakes," said Chuchundra, more sorrowfully than ever. "And how am I to be sure that Nag won't mistake me for you some dark night?"

330

THE JUNGLE STORY

那晚吃饭的时候,他在桌子上的酒杯间走来走去,他本来完全可以用这些好吃的东西把自己塞得三倍满,但是他想起了纳格和纳加娜,虽然他觉得得到特迪母亲的轻拍和爱抚,坐在特迪的肩膀上让他很开心,他的眼睛还是不时地会变红,然后爆发出他长长的战斗嚎叫:"里基—蒂基—蒂基—蒂基—恰克!"

特迪把他抱到床上,坚持要里基—蒂基睡在他下巴底下。里基—蒂基有良好的教养,他从来不会咬人,不会抓人。但是特迪一睡着,他就起来在屋子周围进行每晚的散步。在黑暗中,他碰到了麝鼠丘查德,他正在墙边蹑手蹑脚地走来走去。丘查德是一只伤心的小野兽。他整夜呜咽着,吱吱地叫,虽下定决心跑到房间中央,但是他从来没到过那里。

"别杀我,"丘查德说,几乎是带着哭腔的。"里基—蒂基,别杀我!"

"你认为一个捕蛇者会杀麝鼠吗?"里基—蒂基轻蔑地说。

"杀蛇的人总会被蛇杀死。"丘查德更加悲伤地说,"而且我怎么能

---

breed v. 养育;教养   broken-hearted a. 极其伤心的;心碎的   scornfully adv. 轻蔑地

"There's not the least danger," said Rikki-tikki. "But Nag is in the garden, and I know you don't go there."

"My cousin Chua, the rat, told me—" said Chuchundra, and then he stopped.

"Told you what?"

"H'sh! Nag is everywhere, Rikki-tikki. You should have talked to Chua in the garden."

"I didn't—so you must tell me. Quick, Chuchundra, or I'll bite you! "

Chuchundra sat down and cried till the tears rolled off his whiskers. "I am a very poor man," he sobbed. "I never had spirit enough to run out into the middle of the room. H'sh! I mustn't tell you anything. Can't you hear, Rikki-tikki?"

Rikki-tikki listened. The house was as still as still, but he thought he could just catch the faintest scratch-scratch in the world—a noise as faint as that of a wasp walking on a window-pane—the dry scratch of a snake's scales on brick-work.

THE JUNGLE STORY

确定纳格不会在某个黑夜里错把我当成你呢？"

"这种危险一点也不存在，"里基—蒂基说，"纳格是在花园里的，而我知道你不去那里的。"

"我的堂兄老鼠丘阿告诉我——"丘查德说了一半就停下了。

"告诉你什么？"

"嘘！纳格无处不在，里基—蒂基。你应该和花园里的丘阿谈谈。"

"我没和他谈过——所以你得告诉我。快点，丘查德，否则我咬你了。"

丘查德坐下哭起来，直到眼泪从胡须上掉了下来。"我是个可怜的人。"他哭着说，"我从来没有足够的勇气跑到房子中间去。嘘！我不该告诉你任何事情的。你听得见吗？里基—蒂基？"

里基—蒂基竖起耳朵倾听。房间里一片寂静，但是他觉得他听到了世界上最微弱的沙沙声——声音小得像黄蜂在窗玻璃上爬——是蛇的鳞片蹭到砖墙上的沙沙声。

"That's Nag or Nagaina," he said to himself, "and he is crawling into the bath-room sluice. You're right, Chuchundra; I should have talked to Chua."

He stole off to Teddy's bath-room, but there was nothing there, and then to Teddy's mother's bathroom. At the bottom of the smooth plaster wall there was a brick pulled out to make a sluice for the bath water, and as Rikki-tikki stole in by the masonry curb where the bath is put, he heard Nag and Nagaina whispering together outside in the moonlight.

"When the house is emptied of people," said Nagaina to her husband, "he will have to go away, and then the garden will be our own again. Go in quietly, and remember that the big man who killed Karait is the first one to bite. Then come out and tell me, and we will hunt for Rikki-tikki together."

"But are you sure that there is anything to be gained by killing the people?" said Nag.

"Everything. When there were no people in the bungalow, did we have any mongoose in the garden? So long as the bungalow is empty, we are king and queen of the garden; and remember that as soon as our eggs in the melon bed hatch (as they may tomorrow), our children will need room and quiet."

"I had not thought of that," said Nag. "I will go, but there is no need that we should hunt for Rikki-tikki afterward. I will kill the big

THE JUNGLE STORY

"那是纳格，要么是纳加娜，"他自言自语道，"他正在爬到浴室的下水道里。你是对的，丘查德，我该去和丘阿谈谈。"

他悄悄地跑到特迪的浴室里，但是没发现什么，接着跑到特迪妈妈的浴室里。在光滑的灰泥墙墙角上，有一块砖头被挖出，做成浴室放水的下水道。当里基—蒂基悄悄地溜进浴室站在放澡盆的砖石槽旁边时，他听到了纳格和纳加娜在外面月光下的窃窃私语。

"当这个屋子没有人住的时候，"纳加娜对他丈夫说，"他就不得不离开这里了，然后花园就又是我们的天下了。悄悄地溜进去，记住，第一个就咬那个杀了卡拉特的高大男人。然后跑出来告诉我，我们一起去猎杀里基—蒂基。"

"但是你肯定杀死人对我们有好处吗？"纳格说。

"好处多了。以前平房里不住人的时候，我们会在花园里碰到獴吗？只要平房是空的，我们就是花园里的国王和王后。别忘了，等我们瓜地里的蛋孵化出来(可能明天他们就孵化出来了)，我们的孩子需要空间，也需要安静。"

，"我原本到没想到这个。"纳格说，"我去，但是之后我们不需要猎杀里基—蒂基。我会杀了那个高大的男人和他的妻子，如果可以的话，

---

stoop v. 俯身，弯腰   peculiar a. 特别的，独具的   inherit v. 继承
advantage n. 有利条件   afterward *adv.* 后来

man and his wife, and the child if I can, and come away quietly. Then the bungalow will be empty, and Rikki-tikki will go."

Rikki-tikki **tingled** all over with rage and **hatred** at this, and then Nag's head came through the sluice, and his five feet of cold body followed it. Angry as he was, Rikki-tikki was very frightened as he saw the size of the big cobra. Nag coiled himself up, raised his head, and looked into the bathroom in the dark, and Rikki could see his eyes **glitter**.

"Now, if I kill him here, Nagaina will know; and if I fight him on the open floor, the **odds** are in his favor. What am I to do?" said Rikki-tikki-tavi.

Nag waved to and fro, and then Rikki-tikki heard him drinking from the biggest water-jar that was used to fill the bath. "That is good," said the snake. "Now, when Karait was killed, the big man had a stick. He may have that stick still, but when he comes in to bathe in the morning he will not have a stick. I shall wait here till he comes. Nagaina—do you hear me?—I shall wait here in the cool till daytime."

There was no answer from outside, so Rikki-tikki knew Nagaina had gone away. Nag coiled himself down, coil by coil, round the bulge at the bottom of the water jar, and Rikki-tikki stayed still as death. After an hour he began to move, muscle by muscle, toward

THE JUNGLE STORY

还有他们的孩子,然后悄悄地溜走。然后平房就不会有人住了,里基—蒂基也一定会离开的。"

里基—蒂基听到这里又气又恨,浑身发抖,接着他看到纳格的脑袋从下水道里伸出来,紧跟着是他五英尺长的冰凉的身体。尽管他很生气,但当里基—蒂基看到大眼镜蛇巨大的身躯时,还是非常害怕。纳格把自己蜷起来,抬起头,在黑暗中看着浴室,里基能看到他闪闪发着光的眼睛。

"现在,如果我在这里杀了他,纳加娜马上就会知道的;如果我在开阔的空地上打,很有可能他就占了优势。我该怎么做呢?"里基—蒂基—塔维说。

纳格把身子摆来摆去,接着里基—蒂基听到他在喝用来给澡盆里添水的大水罐里的水。"那很好,"蛇说,"卡拉特被杀死的时候,高大的男人手里有一根棍子。现在他可能还留着那棍子,但是等他早上进来洗澡的时候,他不会带着棍子。我就在这里等着他进来。纳加娜,你听到我说的没有?——我找个凉快的地方等到天亮。"

外面没有回答他的声音,所以里基—蒂基知道纳加娜早就走了。纳格把自己在大水罐底部凸出的地方一圈一圈地盘起来,而里基—蒂基待在那里一动不动地,就像死了一样。过了一小时,他开始一点点向

---

tingle v. 震颤 hatred n. 憎恨 glitter v. 闪光 odds n. 可能性

the jar. Nag was asleep, and Rikki-tikki looked at his big back, wondering which would be the best place for a good hold. "If I don't break his back at the first jump," said Rikki, "he can still fight. And if he fights—O Rikki! " He looked at the thickness of the neck below the hood, but that was too much for him; and a bite near the tail would only make Nag savage.

"It must be the head" ' he said at last; "the head above the hood. And, when I am once there, I must not let go."

Then he jumped. The head was lying a little clear of the water jar, under the curve of it; and, as his teeth met, Rikki braced his back against the bulge of the red **earthenware** to hold down the head. This gave him just one second's purchase, and he made the most of it. Then he was battered to and fro as a rat is shaken by a dog—to and fro on the floor, up and down, and around in great circles, but his eyes were red and he held on as the body cart-whipped over the floor, upsetting the tin dipper and the soap dish and the flesh brush, and banged against the tin side of the bath. As he held he closed his jaws tighter and tighter, for he made sure he would be banged to death, and, for the honor of his family, he preferred to be found with his teeth locked. He was **dizzy**, aching, and felt shaken to pieces when something went off like a thunderclap just behind him. A hot wind knocked him senseless and

THE JUNGLE STORY

水罐移去。纳格睡着了,里基—蒂基盯着他大大的后背,思索着哪里是下口的最佳位置。

　　"如果我第一次跳起没有咬断他的背," 里基说,"他还是能战斗的。如果他还能战斗——哦,里基!"他看着眼镜蛇颈部皮褶下的粗脖子,这对他来说太困难了;如果一口咬在靠近尾巴的地方,只会让纳格发狂。

　　"一定是头部,"他终于想到了,"颈部皮褶上面的头部。而且一旦我咬住了,我就不会松口的。"

　　然后他跳了起来,头部就在离开水罐一点点的地方,在水罐颈部弯曲的地方下面;当他咬住的时候,里基把背靠在红色陶器凸起的地方,以便死死咬住蛇头。这只给了他一秒钟的时间,他也充分地利用了这个时间。然后他就像一只被狗在地板上甩来甩去的老鼠,被来来回回、上上下下得转着圈。但是他的眼睛红了,他咬住不松口。蛇身在地板上像赶马车的鞭子一样鞭打着地面,把锡勺、肥皂盒和洗澡刷都打翻了,还撞到了澡盆的锡边上。他咬住眼镜蛇的时候,越咬越紧,因为他认为自己一定会被撞死的,为了家族的荣誉,他希望人们发现他的时候,知道他死的时候也没有松口。他觉得头晕目眩,浑身疼痛,整个

---

earthenware *n.* 陶器

red fire **singed** his fur. The big man had been wakened by the noise, and had fired both barrels of a shotgun into Nag just behind the hood.

Rikki-tikki held on with his eyes shut, for now he was quite sure he was dead. But the head did not move, and the big man picked him up and said, "It's the mongoose again, Alice. The little chap has saved our lives now."

Then Teddy's mother came in with a very white face, and saw what was left of Nag, and Rikki-tikki dragged himself to Teddy's bedroom and spent half the rest of the night shaking himself **tenderly** to find out whether he really was broken into forty pieces, as he **fancied**.

When morning came he was very stiff, but well pleased with his doings. "Now I have Nagaina to settle with, and she will be worse than five Nags, and there's no knowing when the eggs she spoke of will hatch. Goodness! I must go and see Darzee," he said.

Without waiting for breakfast, Rikki-tikki ran to the thornbush where Darzee was singing a song of **triumph** at the top of his voice. The news of Nag's death was all over the garden, for the sweeper had thrown the body on the rubbish-heap.

"Oh, you stupid tuft of feathers! " said Rikki-tikki angrily. "Is this the time to sing?"

THE JUNGLE STORY

人好像被摇得散了架，而这时身后响起了如同晴天霹雳的一声巨响。一阵热风让他失去了知觉，红色的火焰烧焦了他的皮毛。原来那个高大的男人被吵醒了，用双管猎枪对着纳格颈部皮褶后面开了一枪。

里基—蒂基闭着眼睛，仍然死死得咬着不松口，因为他认为自己肯定死了。但是蛇头一动不动，高个人男人把他抱了起来说，"又是獴，艾丽思。现在这个小家伙救了我们的命。"

特迪的妈妈脸色苍白地走了进来，看了看纳格的尸体。里基—蒂基艰难地走回到特迪的卧室里，后半夜他都在轻轻地晃着身体，看看他自己是不是像自己想象的那样，被摇成了四十块。

早晨来临的时候，他还是全身疼痛，但是一想起自己所做的事情还是非常开心。"现在我只剩下纳加娜要对付了，她可比五个纳格还要难对付，而且不知道她所说的蛋什么时候会孵化出来。天哪，我必须得去见见达齐。"他说。

不等吃过早饭，他就跑到荆棘丛那里，达齐正在高声地唱着胜利之歌。纳格死了的消息已经传遍了整个花园，因为清洁工把尸体丢在了垃圾堆上。

"哦，你这个一堆羽毛的笨蛋！"里基—蒂基生气地说，"现在是唱歌的时候吗？"

---

dizzy .adv. 温柔地　　fancy v. 想象

"Nag is dead—is dead—is dead! " sang Darzee. "The **valiant** Rikki-tikki caught him by the head and held fast. The big man brought the bang-stick, and Nag fell in two pieces! He will never eat my babies again."

"All that's true enough. But where's Nagaina?" said Rikki-tikki, looking carefully round him.

"Nagaina came to the bathroom sluice and called for Nag," Darzee went on, "and Nag came out on the end of a stick—the sweeper picked him up on the end of a stick and threw him upon the rubbish heap. Let us sing about the great, the red-eyed Rikki-tikki! " And Darzee filled his throat and sang.

"If I could get up to your nest, I'd roll your babies out! " said Rikki-tikki. "You don't know when to do the right thing at the right time. You're safe enough in your nest there, but it's war for me down here. Stop singing a minute, Darzee."

"For the great, the beautiful Rikki-tikki's sake I will stop," said Darzee. "What is it, O Killer of the terrible Nag?"

"Where is Nagaina, for the third time?"

"On the rubbish heap by the stables, **mourning** for Nag. Great is Rikki-tikki with the white teeth."

"Bother my white teeth! Have you ever heard where she keeps her eggs?"

THE JUNGLE STORY

"纳格死了—死了—死了！"达齐唱道,"勇敢的里基—蒂基抓住了他的头,紧紧地咬着。高大的男人带来了砰砰作响的棍子,纳格就被打成了两半！他再也不能吃我们的孩子了。"

"那都是事实,但是纳加娜在哪里？"里基—蒂基边问边警惕地看着他的周围。

"纳加娜到浴室下水道去呼唤纳格,"达齐继续唱,"纳格被挑在棍子的一头上出来了——清洁工用棍子的一头挑起了他,把他扔在了垃圾堆上。让我们歌颂伟大的,红眼睛的里基—蒂基吧！"达齐吸了口气又唱起来。

"如果我可以爬上你的鸟巢,就把你的孩子都摇下来。"里基—蒂基说,"你不知道怎样在恰当的时间做恰当的事情。你在树上的鸟巢是很安全,但对下面的我来说是一场战争。停止一会你的唱歌吧,达齐。"

"为了伟大的、美丽的里基—蒂基,我会停止的,"达齐说,"有什么事情？杀死了可怕的纳格的猎手？"

"第三次问你了,纳加娜在哪里？"

"在牛棚旁边的垃圾堆上,在为纳格哀悼呢。有着洁白的牙齿的里基—蒂基真伟大！"

"别为我的白牙齿操心！你知道她把自己的蛇蛋藏在哪里了吗？"

---

triumph *n.* 胜利   valiant *a.* 勇敢的

"In the melon bed, on the end nearest the wall, where the sun strikes nearly all day. She hid them there weeks ago."

"And you never thought it worth while to tell me? The end nearest the wall, you said?"

"Rikki-tikki, you are not going to eat her eggs?"

"Not eat exactly; no. Darzee, if you have a **grain** of sense you will fly off to the stables and pretend that your wing is broken, and let Nagaina **chase** you away to this bush. I must get to the melon-bed, and if I went there now she'd see me."

Darzee was a feather-brained little fellow who could never hold more than one idea at a time in his head. And just because he knew that Nagaina's children were born in eggs like his own, he didn't think at first that it was fair to kill them. But his wife was a **sensible** bird, and she knew that cobra's eggs meant young cobras later on. So she flew off from the nest, and left Darzee to keep the babies warm, and continue his song about the death of Nag. Darzee was very like a man in some ways.

She **fluttered** in front of Nagaina by the rubbish heap and cried out, "Oh, my wing is broken! The boy in the house threw a stone at me and broke it." Then she fluttered more desperately than ever.

Nagaina lifted up her head and hissed, "You warned Rikki-tikki when I would have killed him. Indeed and truly, you've chosen a bad

THE JUNGLE STORY

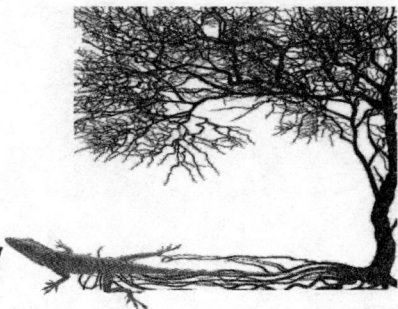

"在最靠近墙角的瓜地里。那里整天都晒得到太阳。她三个星期前藏在那里的。"

"你就从来没想过这值得告诉我吗？你是说，最靠近墙角的地方？"

"里基—蒂基,你不是打算去吃她的蛋吧?"

"确切地说,不是吃,不是,达齐,如果你有一点头脑的话,你就飞到牛棚那里,假装你的翅膀受伤了,让纳加娜追你到荆棘丛这里。我必须去瓜地,如果我现在去,她会看到我的。"

达齐是个头脑愚笨的小家伙,在他的脑袋里一次最多不能超过一个念头。正是因为他知道纳加娜的孩子和他的一样,是从蛋里孵出来的,所以最初的时候,他认为杀死他们是不公平的。但是他妻子是只聪明的鸟, 她知道眼镜蛇的蛋就意味着不久就会从那里长出来小眼镜蛇。所以她从鸟巢里飞出来,让达齐温暖着孩子们,继续歌唱着纳格的死亡。在有些方面达齐和男人非常相像。

她拍着翅膀飞到垃圾堆旁的纳加娜面前,喊道:"哦,我的翅膀折断了! 房子里的男孩朝我扔石头,折断了我的翅膀。"然后她更加绝望地拍打着翅膀。

纳加娜抬起头, 发出唑唑的声音,"本来我可以杀死他的时候,是你警告了里基—蒂基。说真的,你选择了一个糟糕的地方来折断你的

---

mourn *v.* 哀悼　　grain *n.* 一点儿　　chase *v.* 追逐

345

place to be lame in." And she moved toward Darzee's wife, slipping along over the dust.

"The boy broke it with a stone! " shrieked Darzee's wife.

"Well! It may be some **consolation** to you when you're dead to know that I shall settle accounts with the boy. My husband lies on the rubbish heap this morning, but before night the boy in the house will lie very still. What is the use of running away? I am sure to catch you. Little fool, look at me! "

Darzee's wife knew better than to do that, for a bird who looks at a snake's eyes gets so frightened that she cannot move. Darzee's wife fluttered on, piping sorrowfully, and never leaving the ground, and Nagaina quickened her **pace**.

Rikki-tikki heard them going up the path from the stables, and he raced for the end of the melon patch near the wall. There, in the warm litter above the melons, very cunningly hidden, he found twenty-five eggs, about the size of a bantam's eggs, but with whitish skin instead of shell.

"I was not a day too soon," he said, for he could see the baby cobras curled up inside the skin, and he knew that the minute they were hatched they could each kill a man or a mongoose. He bit off the tops of the eggs as fast as he could, taking care to **crush** the young cobras, and turned over the litter from time to time to see

翅膀。"然后她在尘土上朝着达齐的妻子滑过去。

"男孩用石头把它折断的！"达齐的妻子尖叫着。

"很好！告诉你我会去和那男孩算帐的,这足以在你死的时候得到些安慰了。今天早上我的丈夫躺在垃圾堆上了,但是在天黑以前,屋子里的男孩也会安静地躺着。跑有什么用？我肯定能抓到你。小笨蛋,看着我！"

达齐的妻子当然知道不能这么做,因为一只鸟看着蛇的眼睛会吓得迈不了步子。达齐的妻子继续拍着翅膀,尖着嗓子哀伤地嚎叫着。她没有飞离地面,于是纳加娜加快了她的步伐。

里基—蒂基听到她们离开了牛棚,往小路上去了,于是飞快地跑到墙边的瓜地尽头。他在那里找到了二十五只蛋,巧妙地藏在瓜地上的暖褥草堆里。这些蛋都像矮脚鸡的鸡蛋那么大,但是代替蛋壳的,是一层白色的皮。

"我来的正是时候。"他说,因为他可以看到蜷缩在皮下的小眼镜蛇,他知道一旦他们孵出来,他们就可以杀死一个人或者一只獴。他飞快地咬掉蛋壳的顶部,仔细地把小蛇都碾碎,他还不时地翻转褥草,看看他有没有漏下一只。最后只剩下三只蛇蛋了,里基—蒂基开

---

sensible *a.* 明智的　　flutter *v.* 振翼,拍翅　　consolation *n.* 安慰

whether he had missed any. At last there were only three eggs left, and Rikki-tikki began to chuckle to himself, when he heard Darzee's wife screaming:

"Rikki-tikki, I led Nagaina toward the house, and she has gone into the veranda, and—oh, come quickly—she means killing! "

Rikki-tikki smashed two eggs, and tumbled **backward** down the melon-bed with the third egg in his mouth, and scuttled to the veranda as hard as he could put foot to the ground. Teddy and his mother and father were there at early breakfast, but Rikki-tikki saw that they were not eating anything. They sat stone-still, and their faces were white. Nagaina was coiled up on the matting by Teddy's chair, within easy striking distance of Teddy's **bare** leg, and she was swaying to and fro, singing a song of triumph.

"Son of the big man that killed Nag," she hissed, "stay still. I am not ready yet. Wait a little. Keep very still, all you three! If you move I strike, and if you do not move I strike. Oh, foolish people, who killed my Nag! "

Teddy's eyes were fixed on his father, and all his father could do was to whisper, "Sit still, Teddy. You mustn't move. Teddy, keep still."

Then Rikki-tikki came up and cried, "Turn round, Nagaina.

THE JUNGLE STORY

始对着自己咯咯地笑了。这时,他听到达齐的妻子在喊:

"里基—蒂基,我把纳加娜引到房子那去了,她跑到走廊里去了,哦,快点来,她要咬人了!"

里基—蒂基碾碎了剩下的两只蛋,把第三只蛋衔在嘴里,往后一个倒翻滚翻下瓜地,快步跑到走廊里。特迪和他妈妈、爸爸正在那儿吃早饭,但是里基—蒂基看到他们现在什么都没吃。他们一动不动地坐在那里,脸色发白。纳加娜在特迪椅子旁的草席上蜷着身子,从那里她可以轻易地咬到特迪赤裸裸的大腿。她的身子晃来晃去,唱着胜利的歌。

"杀死纳格的高大男人的儿子,"她咝咝地叫着,"呆着别动。我还没准备好,再等一下。你们三个,都别动!如果你动了,我就咬了,如果你不动,我还是会咬。哦,愚蠢的人,杀了我的纳格!"

特迪的眼睛盯着他的爸爸,而他爸爸能做的只是小声地说,"坐着别动,特迪。你不能动。特迪,呆着别动。"

这时里基—蒂基跑上前来叫道,"转过身来,纳加娜。转过身来打

---

pace *n.* 步伐   crush *v.* 碾碎

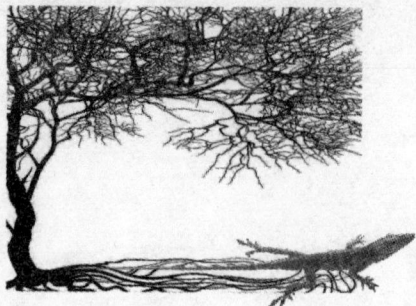

Turn and fight! "

"All in good time," said she, without moving her eyes. "I will settle my account with you presently. Look at your friends, Rikki-tikki. They are still and white. They are afraid. They dare not move, and if you come a step nearer I strike."

"Look at your eggs," said Rikki-tikki, "in the melon bed near the wall. Go and look, Nagaina! "

The big snake turned half around, and saw the egg on the veranda. "Ah-h! Give it to me," she said.

Rikki-tikki put his paws one on each side of the egg, and his eyes were blood-red. "What price for a snake's egg? For a young cobra? For a young king cobra? For the last—the very last of the brood? The ants are eating all the others down by the melon bed."

Nagaina spun clear round, forgetting everything for the sake of the one egg. Rikki-tikki saw Teddy's father shoot out a big hand, catch Teddy by the shoulder, and drag him across the little table with the tea-cups, safe and out of reach of Nagaina.

"Tricked! Tricked! Tricked! Rikk-tck-tck! " chuckled Rikki-tikki. "The boy is safe, and it was I—I—I that caught Nag by the hood last night in the bathroom." Then he began to jump up and down, all four feet together, his head close to the floor. "He threw

THE JUNGLE STORY

一架！"

"我会的，"她没有移开她的目光，"我一会再和你算帐。看看你的朋友们，里基—蒂基。他们一动也不敢动，面色苍白。他们都害怕了。他们动也不敢动，如果你再走进一步，我就咬了。"

"去看看你的蛋，"里基—蒂基说，"墙边的瓜地里。快点去看看，纳加娜！"

大蛇转过半个身子，看到了走廊里的蛇蛋。"啊！把它给我！"她说。

里基—蒂基用两只爪子抓住蛇蛋，他的眼睛变红了。"为了一只蛇蛋你会付出什么代价？为了一条小蛇？为了一条小眼睛蛇？为了最后一只——你这一窝里的最后一只蛇蛋？瓜地里蚂蚁正在吞噬其他的蛇蛋。"

纳加娜完全转过了身子，因为那只蛋她把其他的事情都抛之脑后了。里基—蒂基看到特迪的爸爸伸出一只大手，抓住特迪的肩膀，把他从放茶杯的桌子上抱了过去，到了纳加娜安全地够不着的地方。

"上当了！上当了！上当了！里基—恰克—恰克！"里基—蒂基咯咯地笑了。"男孩已经安全了。昨天晚上在浴室里，是我——我咬住了

---

backward *adv.* 向后　　bare *a.* 光秃秃的，赤裸的

me to and fro, but he could not shake me off. He was dead before the big man blew him in two. I did it! Rikki-tikki-tck-tck! Come then, Nagaina. Come and fight with me. You shall not be a widow long."

Nagaina saw that she had lost her chance of killing Teddy, and the egg lay between Rikki-tikki's paws. "Give me the egg, Rikki-tikki. Give me the last of my eggs, and I will go away and never come back," she said, lowering her hood.

"Yes, you will go away, and you will never come back. For you will go to the rubbish heap with Nag. Fight, widow! The big man has gone for his gun! Fight! "

Rikki-tikki was bounding all round Nagaina, keeping just out of reach of her stroke, his little eyes like hot coals. Nagaina gathered herself together and flung out at him. Rikki-tikki jumped up and backward. Again and again and again she struck, and each time her head came with a whack on the matting of the veranda and she gathered herself together like a watch **spring**. Then Rikki-tikki danced in a circle to get behind her, and Nagaina spun round to keep her head to his head, so that the rustle of her tail on the matting sounded like dry leaves blown along by the wind.

He had forgotten the egg. It still lay on the veranda, and Nagaina came nearer and nearer to it, till at last, while Rikki-tikki

纳格的颈部皮褶。"然后他开始上串下跳地蹦,四条腿并拢,头靠着地面。"他把我甩来甩去,但是没能把我甩掉。在高个子男人开枪把他打成两半之前他就已经死了。是我干的!里基—蒂基—恰克—恰克!来吧,纳加娜。来跟我作战吧。你做寡妇也做不了多久了。"

纳加娜知道她已经错过了杀死特迪的机会,而蛋还躺在里基—蒂基的爪子中间。"把蛋给我,里基—蒂基。把最后一个蛇蛋还给我,我马上离开,永远不再回来,"她低下头说。

"是的,你会马上离开的,而且永远不再回来。因为你将和纳格一起待在垃圾堆上。战斗吧,寡妇!高个子男人已经去拿枪了!战斗吧!"

里基—蒂基在纳加娜身边跳来跳去,刚好在她咬不到的地方,他的小眼睛就像烧红的煤炭一样。纳加娜打起精神,朝他扑了过去。里基—蒂基跳起来往后退。她一次又一次地攻击,每次她的头都重重地撞在走廊的草席上,就像个钟表弹簧一样被弹回来。然后里基—蒂基就绕着圈跳到她身后,而纳加娜则转过身让她的头正对着他的头,所以她的尾巴啪啪地打在草席上,发出的声音就像风中吹起的干树叶。

里基已经忘了那只蛇蛋。它静静地躺在走廊上,纳加娜越走越近,最后,趁着里基—蒂基喘气的功夫,她猛地把蛋衔在嘴里,转身向走廊

---

brood *n.* 一窝   spin *v.* 使快速旋转;扭转

was drawing breath, she caught it in her mouth, turned to the veranda steps, and flew like an arrow down the path, with Rikki-tikki behind her. When the cobra runs for her life, she goes like a whip-lash **flicked** across a horse's neck.

Rikki-tikki knew that he must catch her, or all the trouble would begin again. She headed straight for the long grass by the thorn-bush, and as he was running Rikki-tikki heard Darzee still singing his foolish little song of triumph. But Darzee's wife was wiser. She flew off her nest as Nagaina came along, and flapped her wings about Nagaina's head. If Darzee had helped they might have turned her, but Nagaina only lowered her hood and went on. Still, the **instant**'s delay brought Rikki-tikki up to her, and as she **plunged** into the rat-hole where she and Nag used to live, his little white teeth were **clenched** on her tail, and he went down with her—and very few mongooses, however wise and old they may be, care to follow a cobra into its hole. It was dark in the hole; and Rikki-tikki never knew when it might open out and give Nagaina room to turn and strike at him. He held on savagely, and stuck out his feet to act as **brakes** on the dark slope of the hot, **moist** earth.

Then the grass by the mouth of the hole stopped waving, and Darzee said, "It is all over with Rikki-tikki! We must sing his death song. Valiant Rikki-tikki is dead! For Nagaina will surely kill him

THE JUNGLE STORY

的台阶游去,像一枝箭一样沿着小路逃了下去,里基—蒂基在身后紧追不舍。当一条眼镜蛇逃命的时候,她跑得就像一匹背上挨了马鞭狂奔的马。

里基—蒂基知道他必须抓住她,否则所有的麻烦又会重头再来。她径直向荆棘丛旁边的高高的草地游去,里基—蒂基一路追去。在追的时候,他听到达齐还在唱着他那首愚蠢的胜利之歌。但是达齐的妻子就比他聪明多了。看到纳加娜跑过来,她飞到纳加娜头部上方,拍打着翅膀。如果达齐也帮下忙的话,他们也许可以拦住她,但是纳加娜只是把头一低,继续逃命。然而,就是这一会儿的迟疑让里基—蒂基赶上了她。在她正要跃入她和纳格曾经居住的老鼠洞里时,他小小的白牙齿就一口咬住了她的尾巴,于是他随着纳加娜一起进了洞里——不管有多聪明的獴还是年长的獴,很少有人愿意追眼镜蛇追到洞里。洞里很黑;里基—蒂基也不知道什么地方洞里会豁然开阔,让纳加娜有地方可以转身攻击他。他死死地咬着不放,伸出自己的脚抵在闷热、潮湿、黑暗的斜坡上,当作刹车。

后来洞口的草停止了摇摆,达齐说,"里基—蒂基肯定完蛋了!我们得为他唱哀歌了。勇敢的里基—蒂基死了!因为纳加娜一定会在地

---

spring n. 弹簧

underground."

So he sang a very mournful song that he made up on the spur of the minute, and just as he got to the most touching part, the grass quivered again, and Rikki-tikki, covered with dirt, dragged himself out of the hole leg by leg, licking his whiskers. Darzee stopped with a little shout. Rikki-tikki shook some of the dust out of his fur and sneezed. "It is all over," he said. "The widow will never come out again." And the red ants that live between the grass stems heard him, and began to troop down one after another to see if he had spoken the truth.

Rikki-tikki curled himself up in the grass and slept where he was—slept and slept till it was late in the afternoon, for he had done a hard day's work.

"Now," he said, when he awoke, "I will go back to the house. Tell the Coppersmith, Darzee, and he will tell the garden that Nagaina is dead."

The Coppersmith is a bird who makes a noise exactly like the beating of a little hammer on a copper pot; and the reason he is always making it is because he is the town crier to every Indian garden, and tells all the news to everybody who cares to listen. As Rikki-tikki went up the path, he heard his "attention" notes like a tiny dinner gong, and then the steady "Ding-dong-tock! Nag is

THE JUNGLE STORY

底下把他杀了。"

于是他唱起了一首他临时编造的、非常凄凉的悲歌。正当他唱到最感人的部分，草儿又一次微微颤动了，里基—蒂基舐着他的胡子，浑身是泥的从洞里一步一步艰难地走出来。达齐轻轻地叫了一声，停止了唱歌。里基—蒂基把皮毛上的泥抖落下来，打了个喷嚏。"一切都结束了，"他说，"那寡妇再也不会出来了。"住在草根中央的那些红蚂蚁听到了他说的话，开始一个接一个地排着队到洞里看看他说的是不是实话。

里基—蒂基在草地里把自己蜷起来，就地躺下睡着了——睡啊睡啊一直睡到傍晚，因为他已经完成了一天辛苦的工作。

"现在，"他醒了以后说道，"我要回到屋子里去了。把这消息告诉铜匠鸟，达齐，他会让整个花园都知道纳加娜死了。"

铜匠鸟是一种鸟，他发出的声音就像小锤子击打铜罐的声音一样；而他总是发出这样的声音是因为他是印度每个花园的公告传报员，把所有的消息告诉每一个愿意听的人。当里基—蒂基跑到小路上的时候，听到他就像一只小小的就餐铜锣发出"注意"的声音。然后是平稳的"叮—咚—珰！纳格已经死了！纳加娜也死了！叮—咚—珰！"那个消息让花园里所有的鸟儿歌唱了起来，青蛙呱呱地叫了起来，因

---

flick v. 轻打　　instant n. 瞬息　　plunge v. 投入，跳入　　clench v. 咬紧(牙齿)

dead—dong! Nagaina is dead! Ding-dong-tock! " That set all the birds in the garden singing, and the frogs croaking, for Nag and Nagaina used to eat frogs as well as little birds.

When Rikki got to the house, Teddy and Teddy's mother (she looked very white still, for she had been fainting) and Teddy's father came out and almost cried over him; and that night he ate all that was given him till he could eat no more, and went to bed on Teddy's shoulder, where Teddy's mother saw him when she came to look late at night.

"He saved our lives and Teddy's life," she said to her husband. "Just think, he saved all our lives."

Rikki-tikki woke up with a jump, for the mongooses are light sleepers.

"Oh, it's you," said he. "What are you bothering for? All the cobras are dead. And if they weren't, I'm here."

Rikki-tikki had a right to be proud of himself. But he did not grow too proud, and he kept that garden as a mongoose should keep it, with tooth and jump and spring and bite, till never a cobra dared show its head inside the walls.

THE JUNGLE STORY

为纳格和纳加娜过去都吃过青蛙和小鸟。

当里基跑到屋子里的时候,特迪和特迪的妈妈(她还是脸色发白,因为她刚才晕过去了)、特迪的爸爸都跑了出来,几乎抱着他哭起来。那天晚上他把所有给他吃的东西都吃掉了,直到再也吃不下为止,然后在特迪的肩膀上睡着了。等特迪妈妈晚上很晚进来看他的时候,他仍然躺在特迪的肩膀上呼呼睡大觉。

"他救了我们的命和特迪的命。"她对她丈夫说,"想想,他救了我们大家。"

里基—蒂基猛得跳了起来,醒了,因为獴都是容易惊醒的动物。

"哦,是你们啊,"他说,"你们还在担心什么？所有的眼镜蛇都死了。如果没死,有我在这里。"

里基—蒂基有权利为自己感到骄傲。但是他没有太得意忘形,他就像一只獴该做的那样,用牙齿、跳跃、嘶咬保护着花园,之后再也没有眼镜蛇敢在围墙内露面了。

---

brake *n.* 刹车　　moist *a.* 潮湿的　　underground *adv.* 在地下
touching *adj.* 动人的,感人的　　quiver *v.* 颤抖

Chapter 10 Darzee's Chant

(Sung in honor of Rikki-tikki-tavi)

Singer and tailor am I—
Doubled the joys that I know—
Proud of my lilt to the sky,
Proud of the house that I sew—
Over and under, so weave I my music—so weave I the house
that I sew.

Sing to your fledglings again,
Mother, oh lift up your head!
Evil that **plagued** us is slain,
Death in the garden lies dead.
Terror that hid in the roses is impotent—flung on the dung-hill
and dead!

THE JUNGLE STORY

第十章　达齐的歌

(为了歌颂里基–蒂基–恰克)

我是歌唱家，也是裁缝——
这给了我双倍的快乐——
我以向天轻声歌唱感到骄傲，
也为我筑的鸟巢感到自豪——
树上树下，我编织着我的音乐——我编织着我的鸟巢。

再给你的小鸟们唱一首吧，
妈妈，哦，抬起你的头！
困扰我们的坏蛋已经被杀死了，
尸体静静地躺在花园里。
躲在玫瑰花里的恶魔再也不能使坏了——他被抛到垃圾堆里，
已经死了！

---

plague *v.* 折磨；烦扰

丛林的故事

Who has delivered us, who?

Tell me his nest and his name.

Rikki, the valiant, the true,

Tikki, with eyeballs of flame,

Rikk-tikki-tikki, the **ivory**-fanged, the hunter with eyeballs of flame!

Give him the Thanks of the Birds,

Bowing with tail feathers spread!

Praise him with nightingale words—

Nay, I will praise him instead.

Hear! I will sing you the praise of the bottle-tailed Rikki, with eyeballs of red!

(Here Rikki-tikki interrupted, and the rest of the song is lost.)

THE JUNGLE STORY

是谁解救了我们，是谁？

告诉我他的住所和名字。

里基，勇士，忠诚的朋友，

蒂基，他有双火焰般通红的眼睛，

里基－蒂基－恰克，有着象牙般的尖牙，有双火焰般通红的眼睛
的猎人！

向他表达鸟儿们的谢意，

展开尾部的羽毛向他鞠躬！

用夜莺的歌唱赞美他——

不，让我的歌声来赞美他。

听！我将歌唱带着一束尾巴的里基，有着一双火红眼睛的里
基！

(唱到这里，里基－蒂基打断了他，后面的歌我们就无从知晓
了）

---

ivory n. 象牙

Chapter 11　Toomai of the Elephants

I will remember what I was,
I am sick of rope and chain—
I will remember my old strength and all my forest affairs.
I will not sell my back to man for a bundle of sugar-cane:
I will go out to my own kind, and the wood-folk in their lairs.
I will go out until the day, until the morning break—
Out to the wind's untainted kiss, the water's clean caress;
I will forget my ankle-ring and snap my picket stake.
I will revisit my lost loves, and playmates masterless!

Kala Nag, which means Black Snake, had served the Indian Government in every way that an elephant could serve it for forty-seven years, and as he was fully twenty years old when he was caught, that makes him nearly seventy—a ripe age for an elephant. He remembered pushing, with a big leather pad on his forehead, at a gun stuck in deep mud, and that was before the Afghan War of 1842, and he had not then come to his full strength.

His mother Radha Pyari,—Radha the darling,—who had been caught in the same drive with Kala Nag, told him, before his little

THE JUNGLE STORY

第十一章　大象们的图梅

我会记得我是什么，

我厌倦了绳索和锁链——

我会记得我以前的力量和所有丛林里的事情。

我将不会为了一捆甘蔗为人类卖力干活；

我要出去回到我的同类那里，回到兽穴里的丛林兽民那里。

白天来临的时候，破晓时分，我将走出去——

出去接受激风清白无瑕的吻，接受海水纯洁的爱抚；

我会忘记我脚踝上的铁环，会折断栓着我的尖木桩。

我会再去找寻我失去的爱情和没有主人的玩伴！

　　卡拉·纳格，意思是"黑蛇"，以一头大象能够尽职的各种方式为印度政府服务了四十七年。而他被抓获的那一年，他刚二十岁——对一头大象来说是个成熟的年龄了，现在他快七十岁了。他记得曾经靠前额上垫着的一块皮垫推着陷在烂泥里的钢炮，那是在1842年阿富汗战争之前，那时他的力气还没长足。

　　他的妈妈拉德哈·皮艾——亲爱的拉德哈——和卡拉·纳格是在同一次围捕中被捉的。在他的小白长牙长出来之前，他妈妈就告诉他

---

ripe *adj.* 成熟的

milk tusks had dropped out, that elephants who were afraid always got hurt. Kala Nag knew that that advice was good, for the first time that he saw a shell burst he backed, screaming, into a stand of piled rifles, and the bayonets pricked him in all his softest places. So, before he was twenty-five, he gave up being afraid, and so he was the best-loved and the best-looked-after elephant in the service of the Government of India. He had carried tents, twelve hundred pounds' weight of tents, on the **march** in Upper India. He had been hoisted into a ship at the end of a steam crane and taken for days across the water, and made to carry a mortar on his back in a strange and rocky country very far from India, and had seen the Emperor Theodore lying dead in Magdala, and had come back again in the steamer **entitled**, so the soldiers said, to the Abyssinian War medal. He had seen his fellow elephants die of cold and epilepsy and **starvation** and sunstroke up at a place called Ali Musjid, ten years later; and afterward he had been sent down thousands of miles south to haul and pile big balks of teak in the timberyards at Moulmein. There he had half killed an **insubordinate** young elephant who was shirking his fair share of work.

After that he was taken off timber-hauling, and employed, with a few score other elephants who were trained to the business, in helping to catch wild elephants among the Garo hills. Elephants are

THE JUNGLE STORY

害怕的大象总是会受到伤害。卡拉·纳格知道这是个善意的忠告,因为他第一次看到他背的一枚炮弹爆炸时,他尖叫着退到一个堆放着步枪的台子上,刺刀把他身上最软软的地方都戳破了。所以在他二十五岁之前,他就不再害怕了,因此他在为印度政府服务期间是最受宠爱的,得到了最好的照顾。他在去印度的行军途中驮过帐篷,一千两百多磅重的帐篷。他被蒸气机吊车吊到船上,在海上航行数日,然后在一座远离印度、陌生的、到处是岩石的国家里,用背驮着迫击炮。在马戈达拉,他看到了葬在那里的皇帝西多尔。然后他又被赶回到船上,听船员们说,那艘船被授予了阿比西尼亚战争奖章。十年以后,他亲眼见到他的大象同伴们因为寒冷、癫痫、饥饿而死去;在一个叫做阿里·莫斯基德的地方他中过暑;后来他被往南送到几千里外的莫尔梅贮木场运送和堆积大块大块的柚木。在那里他差点杀死了一头不听话的年轻小象,那头象干活偷懒,逃避自己分内的工作。

在那之后,他不再运送木材了,和其他几十头大象一起,接受专门的训练帮助人们在加鲁山上捕捉野象。大象受到印度政府的严格保护。有一个部门,别的什么也不干,专门捕猎大象,抓住他们后,让他

---

march *n.* 行军   entitle *v.* 授予   starvation *n.* 饥饿   insubordinate *adj.* 不顺从的

very strictly **preserved** by the Indian Government. There is one whole department which does nothing else but hunt them, and catch them, and break them in, and send them up and down the country as they are needed for work.

Kala Nag stood ten fair feet at the shoulders, and his tusks had been cut off short at five feet, and bound round the ends, to prevent them splitting, with bands of copper; but he could do more with those stumps than any untrained elephant could do with the real sharpened ones. When, after weeks and weeks of **cautious** driving of scattered elephants across the hills, the forty or fifty wild monsters were driven into the last stockade, and the big drop gate, made of tree trunks lashed together, jarred down behind them, Kala Nag, at the word of **command**, would go into that flaring, trumpeting pandemonium (generally at night, when the flicker of the torches made it difficult to judge distances), and, picking out the biggest and wildest tusker of the mob, would hammer him and hustle him into quiet while the men on the backs of the other elephants roped and tied the smaller ones.

There was nothing in the way of fighting that Kala Nag, the old wise Black Snake, did not know, for he had stood up more than once in his time to the charge of the wounded tiger, and, curling up his soft trunk to be out of harm's way, had knocked the springing

们接受训练,在需要他们干活的时候把他们送到全国各地。

卡拉·纳格站起来,到肩膀足有十英尺高。他的尖牙被截短到五英尺长,为了防止他们裂开,尖牙末端用铜箍缚住,但是他用残余的尖牙干的活要比那些没有受过训练但有着真正锋利尖牙的大象还要多。经过几个星期,他们把山上分散的大象小心地驱赶到一起,四五十只野象被赶进最后的围场里。用树干扎起来的大吊门唰地一声落下关上了。卡拉·纳格,随着一声命令,会走进灯火闪烁的、怒吼着的乱哄哄的象群(通常是在晚上,摇曳的火把让他很难判断距离),在象群中挑出有着最大最粗的尖牙的大象,又捶又打逼他们安静下来,而骑在其他大象背上的人们用绳索绑住弱小些的大象。

在打架方面,卡拉·纳格,聪明的老"黑蛇",几乎无所不知,因为在他的一生中,他曾经不止一次站起身来攻击受伤的老虎。他把自己软软的长鼻子卷起来以免受到伤害,然后从侧面撞向跃起的老虎,用他

---

preserve *v.* 保护   cautious adj. 小心谨慎的   command *n.* 命令

369

丛林的故事

brute sideways in mid-air with a quick sickle cut of his head, that he had invented all by himself; had knocked him over, and kneeled upon him with his huge knees till the life went out with a gasp and a howl, and there was only a fluffy striped thing on the ground for Kala Nag to pull by the tail.

"Yes," said Big Toomai, his driver, the son of Black Toomai who had taken him to Abyssinia, and grandson of Toomai of the Elephants who had seen him caught, "there is nothing that the Black Snake fears except me. He has seen three generations of us feed him and groom him, and he will live to see four."

"He is afraid of me also," said Little Toomai, standing up to his full height of four feet, with only one rag upon him. He was ten years old, the eldest son of Big Toomai, and, according to custom, he would take his father's place on Kala Nag's neck when he grew up, and would handle the heavy iron ankus, the elephant goad, that had been worn smooth by his father, and his grandfather, and his great-grandfather.

He knew what he was talking of; for he had been born under Kala Nag's shadow, had played with the end of his trunk before he could walk, had taken him down to water as soon as he could walk, and Kala Nag would no more have dreamed of disobeying his shrill little orders than he would have dreamed of killing him on that day

THE JUNGLE STORY

自己发明的、用脑袋作出一个快速镰刀砍的动作,把老虎撞到半空中。把他撞倒以后,他把自己庞大的膝盖压在老虎身上,直到老虎喘息着、嚎叫着死去,地上只剩下一个软绵绵、长着条纹的东西,等着卡拉·纳格去拖他的尾巴。

"是的,"他的赶象人大图梅说。他是带卡拉·纳格到阿比西尼亚的黑图梅的儿子,也是亲眼目睹卡拉被捉的图梅的孙子。"'黑蛇'除了我,什么都不害怕。他看着我们三代人喂养、照料他,而且他会活着看到我们的第四代。"

"他也怕我,"小图梅说,他站直身子已经有四英尺高了,身上只披了块碎布。他已经十岁了,是大图梅的长子。按照习俗,等他长大了,他要代替他的爸爸坐在卡拉·纳格的脖子上,手拿沉重的驯象用的铁刺棒。那根刺棒已经被他的爸爸、他的祖父和他的曾祖父磨得光溜溜的了。

他听得懂卡拉的话,因为他是在卡拉·纳格的影子底下出生的;在他学会走路以前,他就在象鼻尖上玩耍;他一学会走路,就把卡拉带到水里;卡拉·纳格从来没有想过不听从他尖着嗓子发出的小小命令;那天当大图梅把这个小小的棕色肌肤的娃娃放在卡拉·纳格象牙下,让

---

sideways *adv.* 斜着,在一边　　generation *n.* 一代　　disobey *v.* 不服从,不顺从

when Big Toomai carried the little brown baby under Kala Nag's tusks, and told him to **salute** his master that was to be.

"Yes," said Little Toomai, "he is afraid of me," and he took long strides up to Kala Nag, called him a fat old pig, and made him lift up his feet one after the other.

"Wah! " said Little Toomai, "you are a big elephant," and he wagged his fluffy head, **quoting** his father. "The Government may pay for elephants, but they belong to us mahouts. When you are old, Kala Nag, there will come some rich rajah, and he will buy you from the Government, on account of your size and your manners, and then you will have nothing to do but to carry gold earrings in your ears, and a gold howdah on your back, and a red cloth covered with gold on your sides, and walk at the head of the **processions** of the King. Then I shall sit on your neck, O Kala Nag, with a silver ankus, and men will run before us with golden sticks, crying, 'Room for the King's elephant! ' That will be good, Kala Nag, but not so good as this hunting in the jungles."

"Umph! " said Big Toomai. "Thou art a boy, and as wild as a buffalo-calf. This running up and down among the hills is not the best Government service. I am getting old, and I do not love wild elephants. Give me brick elephant lines, one stall to each elephant, and big stumps to tie them to safely, and flat, broad roads to

THE JUNGLE STORY

他向未来主人行礼时,他也没想过要踩死他。

"是的,"小图梅说,"他怕我。"他大踏步地走向卡拉·纳格,喊他老肥猪,命令他一只一只地抬起他的脚。

"哇呜!"小图梅说,"你是一头高大的象,"他摇摇自己头发蓬松的脑袋,学着他爸爸的语气说话。"政府可能会为大象付钱,但是他们是属于我们赶象人的。等你老了,卡拉·纳格,会有一个有钱的酋长因为你的个头和规矩,把你从政府那里买下来。然后你就没什么事情可做了,只要耳朵上带着金耳环,背上背个金象轿,身上披个镶金的红布头,走在首领队伍的最前头。那时,我坐在你的脖子上,哦,卡拉·纳格,手拿着银象棒,还有一些手持金棍的人走在我们前面喊着:'给首领的大象让路!'那该多好啊,卡拉·纳格,但是还是比不上在丛林里打猎好。"

"哼!"大图梅说,"你是个男孩子,像水牛犊这么野的孩子。在这些山上跑上跑下可不是政府最好的差事。我越来越老了,我可不喜欢野象。给我砖砌的象场,一头象一个象棚,有大大的木桩可以安全地拴着大象,有平坦宽阔的大路可以训练大象,而不是这种临时的帐篷。啊

---

salute *v.* 行礼   quote *v.* 引用   procession *n.* 行列,队伍

exercise upon, instead of this come-and-go camping. Aha, the Cawnpore barracks were good. There was a bazaar close by, and only three hours' work a day."

Little Toomai remembered the Cawnpore elephant-lines and said nothing. He very much preferred the camp life, and hated those broad, flat roads, with the daily grubbing for grass in the forage reserve, and the long hours when there was nothing to do except to watch Kala Nag fidgeting in his pickets.

What Little Toomai liked was to scramble up bridle paths that only an elephant could take; the dip into the valley below; the glimpses of the wild elephants browsing miles away; the rush of the frightened pig and peacock under Kala Nag's feet; the blinding warm rains, when all the hills and valleys smoked; the beautiful misty mornings when nobody knew where they would camp that night; the steady, cautious drive of the wild elephants, and the mad rush and blaze and hullabaloo of the last night's drive, when the elephants poured into the stockade like boulders in a landslide, found that they could not get out, and flung themselves at the heavy posts only to be driven back by yells and flaring torches and volleys of blank cartridge.

Even a little boy could be of use there, and Toomai was as useful as three boys. He would get his torch and wave it, and yell

哈,科恩波尔的营房就不错,旁边还有街市,一天只要工作三个小时。"

小图梅记得科恩波尔象场,但他没再说什么。他更喜欢营地的生活,讨厌那些宽阔的光滑的大路,讨厌每天得在储备的饲料里搜寻草料,讨厌那些漫长的时光无事可做,只能看着卡拉·纳格被栓在桩上烦躁不安。

小图梅喜欢的是爬上只有一头象能通过的马道;爬到下面的山谷;看着几里外野象吃草;看着卡拉·纳格脚下受惊的猪和孔雀跑来跑去;那使人头晕眼花的暖雨,所有的山和山谷都变得烟雾缭绕;那笼罩着薄雾的美丽早晨,没有人知道昨晚他们在哪里露营;喜欢坚定而小心地驱赶野象,喜欢昨天夜里赶象时疯狂的奔跑、熊熊燃烧的火焰和喧嚣声,当时大象就像山崩时落下的巨石涌进围场,当他们发现自己出不去了,就往粗重的木桩上撞,喊叫声、燃烧的火把和发射的空子弹壳才把他们赶了回去。

即使是一个小娃娃在那里也是有用的,而且图梅抵得上三个男孩子。他会拿上火把,挥舞着,拼命地喊叫。但是真正激动的时候是把大

reserve n. 储备   glimpse n. 一瞥,一看

375

with the best. But the really good time came when the driving out began, and the Keddah—that is, the stockade— looked like a picture of the end of the world, and men had to make signs to one another, because they could not hear themselves speak. Then Little Toomai would climb up to the top of one of the **quivering** stockade posts, his sun-bleached brown hair flying **loose** all over his shoulders, and he looking like a goblin in the torch-light. And as soon as there was a lull you could hear his high-pitched yells of encouragement to Kala Nag, above the trumpeting and crashing, and snapping of ropes, and groans of the tethered elephants. "Mael, mael, Kala Nag! (Go on, go on, Black Snake!) Dant do! (Give him the tusk!) Somalo! Somalo! (Careful, careful!) Maro! Mar! (Hit him, hit him!) Mind the post! Arre! Arre! Hai! Yai! Kya-a-ah!" he would shout, and the big fight between Kala Nag and the wild elephant would sway to and fro across the Keddah, and the old elephant catchers would wipe the sweat out of their eyes, and find time to nod to Little Toomai wriggling with joy on the top of the posts.

He did more than wriggle. One night he **slid** down from the post and **slipped** in between the elephants and threw up the loose end of a rope, which had dropped, to a driver who was trying to get a purchase on the leg of a kicking young calf (calves always give

THE JUNGLE STORY

象赶出去的时候。那时,科达——就是围场——就像一副世界末日的画,人们只能互相打着手势,因为他们听不到彼此说话。那时,小图梅就会爬上一根摇晃的围场柱子顶端,他那被太阳晒得褪色的棕色头发松散地飘在肩头,在火把的照耀下,就像一个小妖精。等稍稍安静些的时候,你就能听到他尖声的鼓励卡拉·纳格的声音,那声音盖过了大象的吼叫声、撞击声、猛咬绳索的声音和被拴着的大象的咕哝声。"加油,加油,黑蛇!咬他!小心,小心!打他,打他!小心柱子!啊!啊!嗨!呀!驾啊!"他大声得喊,卡拉·纳格和野象之间的大战在科达围场内来回地进行着,老捕象人不时地擦去他们眼角的汗水,找机会向在柱子顶端快乐地扭动着的小图梅点点头。

他能做的不只是扭动身体。一天晚上,他从柱子上滑下来,溜到大象里面,把掉落的绳索松开的一头往上扔给一个赶象人,他正设法紧紧地抓住一头乱踢乱蹭的小象的腿 (小象总是比成年的动物更加麻烦)。卡拉看到他,用长鼻子抓住他,把他交给了大图梅。大图梅当时就

---

quiver *v.* 颤抖　　loose *a.* 松散的　　slide *v.* 滑落　　slip *v.* 滑行,滑动

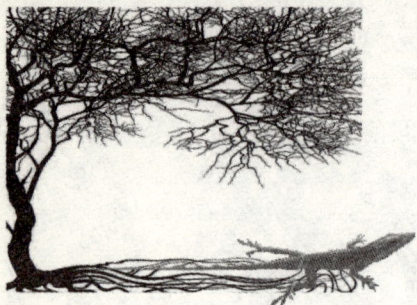

more trouble than full-grown animals). Kala Nag saw him, caught him in his trunk, and handed him up to Big Toomai, who slapped him then and there, and put him back on the post.

Next morning he gave him a **scolding** and said, "Are not good brick elephant lines and a little tent carrying enough, that you must needs go elephant catching on your own account, little worthless? Now those foolish hunters, whose pay is less than my pay, have spoken to Petersen Sahib of the matter." Little Toomai was frightened. He did not know much of white men, but Petersen Sahib was the greatest white man in the world to him. He was the head of all the Keddah operations—the man who caught all the elephants for the Government of India, and who knew more about the ways of elephants than any living man.

"What—what will happen?" said Little Toomai.

"Happen! The worst that can happen. Petersen Sahib is a madman. Else why should he go hunting these wild devils? He may even require you to be an elephant catcher, to sleep anywhere in these fever-filled jungles, and at last to be trampled to death in the Keddah. It is well that this nonsense ends safely. Next week the catching is over, and we of the **plains** are sent back to our stations. Then we will march on smooth roads, and forget all this hunting. But, son, I am angry that you shouldst **meddle** in the business that

THE JUNGLE STORY

拍了拍他,把他拴回木桩上了。

第二天早上,大图梅骂了他一顿,他说,"砖砌的象场和稍微搬点帐篷还不够好吗?你非得自己去捕象吗?没用的小东西?现在这些收入比我少的、愚蠢的猎人把这事告诉彼得森·萨希博了。"小图梅吓坏了。他对白人了解不多,但是对他来说,彼得森·萨希博是世界上最了不起的白人。他是科达围场的首领——印度政府的所有大象都是他捕捉的,他比任何人都了解大象的生活习性。

"什么——会发生什么事情?"小图梅问。

"发生什么事!最糟糕的事情都会发生的。彼得森·萨希博是个疯子。要不然他为什么要捕猎这些野家伙呢?他甚至可能会要求你去当捕象人,在这个充满热病的丛林随地而睡,最后在科达象场里被践踏至死。还好这种胡说八道已经平息下去了,一切平安无事。下个星期围捕就结束了,我们这些从平原上来的人就要被送回自己的车站了。然后我们会在平坦的大路上行进,忘记所有关于打猎的事情。但是,儿

---

scolding *n.* 责骂　　plain *n.* 平原　　meddle *v.* 干涉

belongs to these dirty Assamese jungle folk. Kala Nag will obey none but me, so I must go with him into the Keddah, but he is only a fighting elephant, and he does not help to rope them. So I sit at my ease, as befits a mahout,—not a mere hunter,—a mahout, I say, and a man who gets a **pension** at the end of his service. Is the family of Toomai of the Elephants to be trodden underfoot in the dirt of a Keddah? Bad one! Wicked one! Worthless son! Go and wash Kala Nag and attend to his ears, and see that there are no thorns in his feet. Or else Petersen Sahib will surely catch you and make you a wild hunter—a follower of elephant's foot tracks, a jungle bear. Bah! Shame! Go! "

Little Toomai went off without saying a word, but he told Kala Nag all his **grievances** while he was examining his feet. "No matter," said Little Toomai, turning up the fringe of Kala Nag's huge right ear. "They have said my name to Petersen Sahib, and perhaps—and perhaps—and perhaps—who knows? Hai! That is a big thorn that I have pulled out! "

The next few days were spent in getting the elephants together, in walking the newly caught wild elephants up and down between a couple of tame ones to prevent them giving too much trouble on the downward march to the plains, and in taking stock of the blankets and ropes and things that had been worn out or lost in the

THE JUNGLE STORY

子,你干涉那些本属于肮脏的阿萨姆丛林居民的事情,让我很生气。卡拉·纳格只会听我的话,所以我必须和他一起去科达象场,但是他只是一个斗象,他不会帮忙用绳索拴野象。所以我挺安心的,作为一个称职的赶象人,——不仅仅是个捕猎人,——我是说,一个赶象人,一个服役期满后就能得到养老金的人。大象图梅家族会在科达象场的尘土里被踩在脚下吗?坏孩子!淘气包!没用的儿子!去给卡拉·纳格洗洗身子,照料下他的耳朵,看看脚上有没有扎到刺。不然的话,彼得森·萨希博一定会抓住你,让你做一个野象猎人——一个追寻大象足迹的人,一只丛林熊。呸!丢人!去吧!"

小图梅一句话没说就走了,但是当他在给卡拉·纳格检查脚的时候,他把所有的不满都告诉卡拉·纳格了。"没关系,"小图梅一边翻转着卡拉·纳格硕大的右耳,一边说。"他们已经把我的名字告诉彼得森·萨希博了,也许——也许——也许——谁知道?嗨!我拔出了一个好大的刺!"

接下来的几天,他把大象赶到一块,把新抓来的大象夹在两只温顺的大象中间来回走,以防他们在走到平原的路上惹麻烦,他还清点

---

pension *n.* 养老金   grievance *n.* 不满

forest.

Petersen Sahib came in on his clever she-elephant Pudmini; he had been paying off other camps among the hills, for the season was coming to an end, and there was a native clerk sitting at a table under a tree, to pay the drivers their **wages**. As each man was paid he went back to his elephant, and joined the line that stood ready to start. The catchers, and hunters, and beaters, the men of the regular Keddah, who stayed in the jungle year in and year out, sat on the backs of the elephants that belonged to Petersen Sahib's **permanent** force, or **leaned** against the trees with their guns across their arms, and made fun of the drivers who were going away, and laughed when the newly caught elephants broke the line and ran about.

Big Toomai went up to the clerk with Little Toomai behind him, and Machua Appa, the head tracker, said in an **undertone** to a friend of his, "There goes one piece of good elephant stuff at least. 'Tis a pity to send that young jungle-cock to molt in the plains."

Now Petersen Sahib had ears all over him, as a man must have who listens to the most silent of all living things—the wild elephant. He turned where he was lying all along on Pudmini's back and said, "What is that? I did not know of a man among the plains-drivers who had **wit** enough to rope even a dead elephant."

THE JUNGLE STORY

了剩下的毯子、绳索和破旧的东西和森林里丢失的东西。

彼得森·萨希博坐着他聪明的母象珀得米尼进来了。他在把山上其他营地的工资付清，因为捕猎的季节马上就要结束了。树下桌子旁坐着一个当地的职员，在给赶象人支付工资。每个人拿到钱后，就走回到自己的大象旁，加入到站在那里等着出发的队伍中。那些捕象人、狩猎人和捕兽人都是科达的长工，年复一年地待在丛林里。他们坐在属于彼得森·萨希博的永久财产的象背上，或是手里挎着枪靠在树上，和那些走开的赶象人开开玩笑，看到有新捕获的大象冲出队伍到处乱跑时，他们就哈哈大笑。

大图梅走到职员跟前，小图梅跟在他身后。追捕者的首领马丘阿·阿帕低声对他的一个朋友说："至少有了一块好象材。真可惜，要让这个丛林小公鸡在平原上脱毛了。"

作为一个必须能听到所有生物中最安静的动物——野象的人，彼得森·萨希博全身都是耳朵。一直躺在珀得米尼背上的他转过身来说："怎么回事？我不知道平原赶象人中有一个男人，聪明到去拴一头死象。"

---

wage n. 工资　permanent adj. 永久的　lean v. 斜靠
undertone n. 低声，小声　wit v. 知道

丛林的故事

"This is not a man, but a boy. He went into the Keddah at the last drive, and threw Barmao there the rope, when we were trying to get that young calf with the blotch on his shoulder away from his mother."

Machua Appa pointed at Little Toomai, and Petersen Sahib looked, and Little Toomai bowed to the earth.

"He throw a rope? He is smaller than a picket-pin. Little one, what is your name?" said Petersen Sahib.

Little Toomai was too frightened to speak, but Kala Nag was behind him, and Toomai made a sign with his hand, and the elephant caught him up in his trunk and held him level with Pudmini's forehead, in front of the great Petersen Sahib. Then Little Toomai covered his face with his hands, for he was only a child, and except where elephants were concerned, he was just as bashful as a child could be.

"Oho! " said Petersen Sahib, smiling underneath his mustache, "and why didst you teach your elephant that trick? Was it to help you steal green corn from the roofs of the houses when the ears are put out to dry?"

"Not green corn, Protector of the Poor,—melons," said Little Toomai, and all the men sitting about broke into a roar of laughter. Most of them had taught their elephants that trick when they were

THE JUNGLE STORY

    "这不是一个男人，是个男孩。他是最后一次围捕中进入科达的。我们正设法让肩膀上有斑点的小象离开他妈妈，他把绳子扔给了巴冒。"

    码丘阿·阿帕指了指小图梅，彼得森·萨希博朝他看了一眼，小图梅深深地鞠了一躬。

    "他扔了根绳子？他还没有一个木桩尖高。小家伙，你叫什么名字？"彼得森·萨希博问道。

    小图梅吓得说不出话来，但是卡拉·纳格就在他身后，图梅用手做了个手势，大象用鼻子把他卷起来，抬到和珀得米尼前额一样的高度，正对着了不起的彼得森·萨希博。小图梅双手捂着脸，毕竟他还是个孩子，除了和大象有关的事情，他和所有的孩子一样会害羞。

    "啊哈！"彼得森·萨希博微笑着在胡子底下说，"你为什么教大象那种本领？是等晒玉米穗的时候，帮你偷屋顶上的青玉米吗？"

    "不是青玉米，穷人的保护者，——是瓜，"小图梅说，坐在四周的人都大笑起来。他们中的大多数人在他们还是孩子的时候都教过大象

---

concern *v.* 涉及   trick *n.* 诡计，把戏   roar *n.* 大笑声

boys. Little Toomai was hanging eight feet up in the air, and he wished very much that he were eight feet underground.

"He is Toomai, my son, Sahib," said Big Toomai, scowling. "He is a very bad boy, and he will end in a jail, Sahib."

"Of that I have my doubts," said Petersen Sahib. "A boy who can face a full Keddah at his age does not end in jails. See, little one, here are four annas to spend in sweetmeats because you have a little head under that great thatch of hair. In time you mayest become a hunter too." Big Toomai scowled more than ever. "Remember, though, that Keddahs are not good for children to play in," Petersen Sahib went on.

"Must I never go there, Sahib?" asked Little Toomai with a big gasp.

"Yes." Petersen Sahib smiled again. "When you have seen the elephants dance. That is the proper time. Come to me when you have seen the elephants dance, and then I will let you go into all the Keddahs."

There was another roar of laughter, for that is an old joke among elephant-catchers, and it means just never. There are great cleared flat places hidden away in the forests that are called elephants' ball-rooms, but even these are only found by accident, and no man has ever seen the elephants dance. When a driver

386

THE JUNGLE STORY

这种本领。小图梅被举起空中八英尺高,但是他真希望他是在地下八英尺的地方。

"他是图梅,我的儿子,萨希博。"大图梅皱着眉说,"他是个坏孩子,以后会入大牢的,萨希博。"

"对此我表示怀疑。"彼得森·萨希博说,"一个在他这种年纪就能面对整个科达象场的男孩以后是不会入大牢的。看,小家伙,这里有四安那给你买糖吃,因为你那头浓密的头发下有个小脑袋。以后你也会成为一个狩猎人。"大图梅的眉头皱得更紧了。"不过,记住,科达不是孩子玩的好地方。"彼得森·萨希博继续说。

"我永远都不能去那儿吗,萨希博?"小图梅大声得喘着气说。

"是的,"彼得森·萨希博又笑了。"等你看到大象跳舞,那就是恰当的时候了。等你看到大象跳舞就来找我,那时我会让你进入所有的象场的。"

又是一阵大笑,因为那是一个在捕象人中流传已久的笑话,它的意思就是永远不可能。在森林里隐藏着空旷的平地,被称为大象的舞厅,但是它们只是偶尔被人们所发现,没有人亲眼看到过大象跳舞。当有赶象人吹嘘自己的技艺和勇敢时,其他赶象人总会说,"你什么时候

---

scowle *v.* 皱眉　　jail *n.* 监狱

boasts of his skill and **bravery** the other drivers say, "And when didst you see the elephants dance?"

Kala Nag put Little Toomai down, and he bowed to the earth again and went away with his father, and gave the silver four-anna piece to his mother, who was nursing his baby brother, and they all were put up on Kala Nag's back, and the line of grunting, squealing elephants rolled down the hill path to the plains. It was a very lively march on account of the new elephants, who gave trouble at every ford, and needed **coaxing** or beating every other minute.

Big Toomai prodded Kala Nag spitefully, for he was very angry, but Little Toomai was too happy to speak. Petersen Sahib had noticed him, and given him money, so he felt as a private soldier would feel if he had been called out of the ranks and praised by his commander-in-chief.

"What did Petersen Sahib mean by the elephant dance?" he said, at last, softly to his mother.

Big Toomai heard him and grunted. "That you shouldst never be one of these hill buffaloes of trackers. That was what he meant. Oh, you in front, what is **blocking** the way?"

An Assamese driver, two or three elephants ahead, turned round angrily, crying: "Bring up Kala Nag, and knock this youngster of mine into good behavior. Why should Petersen Sahib have

THE JUNGLE STORY

见过大象跳舞？"

卡拉·纳格把小图梅放回到地上,他又深深地鞠了一躬,就和他父亲一起离开了。他把四个安那给了他正在喂养弟弟的母亲。然后他们都坐上了卡拉·纳格的背,一列咕哝着、尖叫着的大象队伍摇摇摆摆地走下山,往平原出发。由于有新捕的大象,这段行程颇为惊险。每次有浅滩的时候,他们总是惹出点麻烦,不时需要哄骗或者鞭打。

大图梅怀恨地戳着卡拉·纳格,因为他非常生气,但是小图梅却高兴得说不出话来。彼得森·萨希博注意到了他,还给了他钱,所以他感觉就像一名被叫出队伍的列兵,受到了司令的赞扬。

"彼得森·萨希博说大象跳舞是什么意思?"终于,他轻轻地问他的母亲。

大图梅听到了,咕哝着说:"是说你永远成不了追捕者。那就是他的意思。哦,你们前面的,什么东西挡住了路?"

在两三头大象前头一个阿萨姆赶象人转过身来生气地喊道:"把卡拉·纳格带上来,让我的这头年轻小象规矩点。彼得森·萨希博为什

---

boast v. 自夸;自豪   bravery n. 大胆,勇敢   coax v. 哄,劝诱   block v. 堵塞,阻碍

丛林的故事

chosen me to go down with you donkeys of the rice fields? Lay your beast alongside, Toomai, and let him prod with his tusks. By all the Gods of the Hills, these new elephants are **possessed**, or else they can smell their **companions** in the jungle." Kala Nag hit the new elephant in the ribs and knocked the wind out of him, as Big Toomai said, "We have swept the hills of wild elephants at the last catch. It is only your carelessness in driving. Must I keep order along the whole line?"

"Hear him! " said the other driver. "We have swept the hills! Ho! Ho! You are very wise, you plains people. Anyone but a mud-head who never saw the jungle would know that they know that the drives are ended for the season. Therefore all the wild elephants tonight will—but why should I waste wisdom on a river-turtle?"

"What will they do?" Little Toomai called out.

"Ohe, little one. Art you there? Well, I will tell you, for you have a cool head. They will dance, and it **behooves** your father, who has swept all the hills of all the elephants, to double-chain his pickets tonight."

"What talk is this?" said Big Toomai. "For forty years, father and son, we have tended elephants, and we have never heard such moonshine about dances."

390

么选了我和你们这些稻田里的蠢驴一起下山？把你的大象赶到一边，图梅，让他用象牙戳。我以山神发誓，这些新捕的大象都着魔了，要不就是他们能闻到丛林里同伴的味道。"卡拉·纳格撞向新捕大象的肋骨，把他的傲气给撞没了。这时，大图梅说，"我们最后一次围捕的时候已经把山上的野象都清除了。这只是你赶象的时候不当心罢了。非得让我维持整支队伍的秩序吗？"

"听听他说的，"另一个赶象人说，"我们清除了整座山！嗬！嗬！你可真聪明，平原人。除了从没见过丛林的烂泥脑袋，每个人都知道捕猎季节结束了。所以今天晚上，所有的野象将——但是我干嘛在一只河龟身上浪费我的智慧呢？"

"他们将做什么？"小图梅喊道。

"呃，小家伙，你在那里吗？好吧，我告诉你，因为你有冷静的头脑。他们将跳舞，而你父亲，清除了整座山上所有野象的人，今晚有必要用双链锁着木桩。"

"这是什么话？"大图梅说，"四十年来，我们几代父子照看着大象，我们从来没有听说过这种关于跳舞的胡话。"

---

possessed *adj.* 着魔的   companion *n.* 同伴   behoove *v.* 对……有必要

丛林的故事

"Yes; but a plainsman who lives in a hut knows only the four walls of his hut. Well, leave your elephants **unshackled** tonight and see what comes. As for their dancing, I have seen the place where—Bapree-bap! How many windings has the Dihang River? Here is another ford, and we must swim the calves. Stop still, you behind there."

And in this way, talking and **wrangling** and splashing through the rivers, they made their first march to a sort of receiving camp for the new elephants. But they lost their tempers long before they got there.

Then the elephants were chained by their hind legs to their big stumps of pickets, and extra ropes were fitted to the new elephants, and the fodder was piled before them, and the hill drivers went back to Petersen Sahib through the afternoon light, telling the plains drivers to be extra careful that night, and laughing when the plains drivers asked the reason.

Little Toomai attended to Kala Nag's supper, and as evening fell, wandered through the camp, unspeakably happy, in search of a tom-tom. When an Indian child's heart is full, he does not run about and make a noise in an **irregular** fashion. He sits down to a sort of revel all by himself. And Little Toomai had been spoken to by Petersen Sahib! If he had not found what he wanted, I believe he

THE JUNGLE STORY

　　"是的，但是一个住在小棚屋里的平原人只知道他小棚屋的四面墙。好吧,今晚松开大象的锁链,看看会发生什么事情。至于他们跳舞,我见过那个地方——巴普里-巴卜!迪罕河有几个弯啊?这里又有一个浅滩,我们必须让小象游过去。你们后面的,停在那儿。"

　　就这样,他们说着话,争吵着,溅着水花过了河,他们踏上了第一段行程,去一个接收新捕大象的营地。但是在他们还远没有到达那里以前,大象就发起了脾气。

　　于是用链条锁着大象的后腿拴在尖木桩上,那些特大的绳索用来拴新捕的大象,把饲料堆放在他们面前。山里的赶象人下午时分就回到彼得森·萨希博那里去了,叮嘱平原赶象人那晚得特别小心,当平原赶象人问起原因的时候,他们就大笑起来。

　　小图梅照料卡拉·纳格的晚饭。随着夜晚的降临,他心里有难以言状的快乐,于是他就在营地里到处寻找一只手鼓。当一个印度孩子心情激动的时候,他不会以不寻常的方式到处吵吵闹闹乱跑,他会独自一个人坐下狂欢。彼得森·萨希博和他说话了!如果他没有找到他想要

---

unshackle v. 松开……的桎梏　　wrangle v. 争吵　　irregular adj. 不规则的,不合常规的

would have been ill. But the sweetmeat seller in the camp lent him a little tom-tom—a drum beaten with the flat of the hand—and he sat down, cross-legged, before Kala Nag as the stars began to come out, the tom-tom in his lap, and he thumped and he thumped and he thumped, and the more he thought of the great honor that had been done to him, the more he thumped, all alone among the elephant fodder. There was no tune and no words, but the thumping made him happy.

The new elephants strained at their ropes, and squealed and trumpeted from time to time, and he could hear his mother in the camp hut putting his small brother to sleep with an old, old song about the great God Shiv, who once told all the animals what they should eat. It is a very soothing lullaby, and the first verse says:

Shiv, who poured the harvest and made the winds to blow,
Sitting at the doorways of a day of long ago,
Gave to each his portion, food and toil and fate,
From the King upon the guddee to the Beggar at the gate.
All things made he—Shiva the Preserver.
Mahadeo! Mahadeo! He made all—
Thorn for the camel, fodder for the kine,
And mother's heart for sleepy head,
O little son of mine!

THE JUNGLE STORY

的东西,我想他一定会不高兴的。幸好营地里卖糖的小贩借给他一个小手鼓————一种用手掌拍打的鼓————他在卡拉·纳格面前盘着腿坐下来。当天上的星星出来的时候,他把手鼓放在大腿上,敲啊,敲啊,敲啊,越是想到他得到的巨大荣耀,就敲得越欢,只有他一个人坐在大象草料堆里。虽然没有调子,没有歌词,敲鼓让他觉得很高兴。

新捕的大象拉紧了拴他们的绳索,不时地尖叫着,吼叫着。他能听到营地木棚屋里他妈妈在用一首非常非常古老的关于伟大的湿婆的歌谣哄他的小弟弟入睡。湿婆曾经告诉所有的动物它们应该吃什么。这是一首催人入睡的摇篮曲,第一段是这样的:

湿婆,带来了收获,让风吹拂,
很久以前的某一天,他坐在门口,
让每一个人分享他的食物、劳苦和命运,
从宝座上的国王到门口的乞丐。
他所做的一切让他成为————湿婆,保护神。
神啊!神啊!他创造了一切————
骆驼的荆棘丛,母牛的草料,
还有拥抱瞌睡的小脑袋的母亲的怀抱,
哦,我的小儿子!

---

lap *n.* 大腿   verse *n.* 诗句,诗行   doorway *n.* 门口   portion *n.* 一部分,一份

丛林的故事

Little Toomai came in with a joyous tunk-a-tunk at the end of each verse, till he felt sleepy and stretched himself on the fodder at Kala Nag's side. At last the elephants began to lie down one after another as is their custom, till only Kala Nag at the right of the line was left standing up; and he rocked slowly from side to side, his ears put forward to listen to the night wind as it blew very slowly across the hills. The air was full of all the night noises that, taken together, make one big silence— the click of one bamboo stem against the other, the rustle of something alive in the undergrowth, the scratch and squawk of a half-waked bird (birds are awake in the night much more often than we imagine), and the fall of water ever so far away. Little Toomai slept for some time, and when he waked it was brilliant moonlight, and Kala Nag was still standing up with his ears cocked. Little Toomai turned, rustling in the fodder, and watched the curve of his big back against half the stars in heaven, and while he watched he heard, so far away that it sounded no more than a pinhole of noise pricked through the stillness, the "hoot-toot" of a wild elephant.

All the elephants in the lines jumped up as if they had been shot, and their grunts at last waked the sleeping mahouts, and they came out and drove in the picket pegs with big mallets, and tightened this rope and knotted that till all was quiet. One new

THE JUNGLE STORY

　　每一段歌末尾欢乐的咚咚声让小图梅越来越入迷,直到他觉得困了,在卡拉·纳格旁边的草料堆上舒展开身子。再后来,大象按照他们的习惯,一个接一个躺了下来,最后只剩下卡拉·纳格在队伍的右边站着。他慢慢地左右摇晃着,风柔柔地吹过山群,他的耳朵伸向前,听着夜风的声音。空中充满了夜晚各种各样的声音,这些声音一起让夜晚显得更加宁静——一根竹竿碰到另外一根竹竿发出的咔哒声,灌木丛里活的东西发出的沙沙声,半梦半醒的鸟儿搔抓、受惊大叫的声音(鸟儿在晚上醒着的时间比我们想象得要多多了),还有远处的流水声。小图梅睡着了一会儿。等他醒来的时候,已经是月光皎洁了。卡拉·纳格还是竖着耳朵站在那里。小图梅翻了个身,弄得草料沙沙地响,他看着卡拉宽大的背部曲线,挡住了天空中半边的星星。看着看着,他听到一只野象发出"呜—嘟"的声音,遥远得就像一个小孔的噪音刺穿了黑夜的寂静。

　　象场里所有的大象就像被枪击中一样,跳了起来。他们的咕哝声最终吵醒了睡着了的赶象人,他们走到外面,用大头锤敲紧了桩钉,拉

---

　　curve *n.* 曲线　　　heaven *n.* 天,天空

elephant had nearly grubbed up his picket, and Big Toomai took off Kala Nag's leg chain and shackled that elephant fore-foot to hind-foot, but slipped a loop of grass string round Kala Nag's leg, and told him to remember that he was tied fast. He knew that he and his father and his grandfather had done the very same thing hundreds of times before. Kala Nag did not answer to the order by gurgling, as he usually did. He stood still, looking out across the moonlight, his head a little raised and his ears spread like fans, up to the great folds of the Garo hills.

"Tend to him if he grows restless in the night," said Big Toomai to Little Toomai, and he went into the hut and slept. Little Toomai was just going to sleep, too, when he heard the coir string snap with a little "tang," and Kala Nag rolled out of his pickets as slowly and as silently as a cloud rolls out of the mouth of a valley. Little Toomai pattered after him, barefooted, down the road in the moonlight, calling under his breath, "Kala Nag! Kala Nag! Take me with you, O Kala Nag! " The elephant turned, without a sound, took three strides back to the boy in the moonlight, put down his trunk, swung him up to his neck, and almost before Little Toomai had settled his knees, slipped into the forest.

There was one blast of furious trumpeting from the lines, and then the silence shut down on everything, and Kala Nag began to

THE JUNGLE STORY

紧了绳索,打紧了结头,直到一切都安静下来。一头新捕的大象差点把木桩给拱了出来,大图梅松开了卡拉·纳格腿上的链条,把那头大象从前腿到后腿都缚起来,而只在卡拉·纳格腿上栓了根草绳,并且告诉他要记住,他被拴得很紧。他知道他和他的父亲还有他的祖父以前做过这样的事情已经几百次了。卡拉·纳格没有象往常一样,用咯咯声来回答命令。他静静地站着,穿过月光往外看,他的头微微抬起,耳朵像扇子一样摊开着,眺望着重重叠叠的加鲁山。

"看着他晚上是不是会变得不安,"大图梅对小图梅说,然后他就走进小棚屋里睡觉了。小图梅正要睡着的时候,他听到椰子壳的粗纤维绳口当的一声折断了,卡拉·纳格就像一朵飘出山谷口的云慢慢地却坚定地挣脱开木桩走了出去。小图梅光着脚啪嗒啪嗒地跟在后面,在月光下沿着大路跑着,压低着声音喊道:"卡拉·纳格!卡拉·纳格!带上我,哦,卡拉·纳格!"大象转过身子,一声不吭,在月光下往回走了三步,走到男孩面前,伸出他的长鼻子把他放到背上。小图梅的双脚还没放稳,大象就悄悄地走进了森林里。

象场里发出一阵愤怒的吼声,接着一切又归于平静,卡拉·纳格开始往前走了。有时一束高高的青草擦过他的身子,就像海浪拍打着船

---

fold *n.* 折叠　　restless *adj.* 不安的,焦虑的
barefooted *adv.* 光着脚的　furious *adj.* 狂暴的

move. Sometimes a tuft of high grass washed along his sides as a wave washes along the sides of a ship, and sometimes a cluster of wild-pepper vines would scrape along his back, or a bamboo would creak where his shoulder touched it. But between those times he moved absolutely without any sound, drifting through the thick Garo forest as though it had been smoke. He was going uphill, but though Little Toomai watched the stars in the rifts of the trees, he could not tell in what direction.

Then Kala Nag reached the crest of the ascent and stopped for a minute, and Little Toomai could see the tops of the trees lying all speckled and furry under the moonlight for miles and miles, and the blue-white mist over the river in the hollow. Toomai leaned forward and looked, and he felt that the forest was awake below him— awake and alive and crowded. A big brown fruit-eating bat brushed past his ear; a porcupine's quills rattled in the thicket; and in the darkness between the tree stems he heard a hog-bear digging hard in the moist warm earth, and snuffing as it digged.

Then the branches closed over his head again, and Kala Nag began to go down into the valley—not quietly this time, but as a runaway gun goes down a steep bank—in one rush. The huge limbs moved as steadily as pistons, eight feet to each stride, and the wrinkled skin of the elbow points rustled. The undergrowth on

THE JUNGLE STORY

舷。有时一束野生胡椒的藤蔓会擦过他的背,或者他的肩膀碰到一枝毛竹,发出吱吱嘎嘎的声音。但是除了这些时候,他走的时候几乎没有一点声音,他轻轻地穿过茂密的加鲁森林,仿佛森林都变得不存在了。他往山上走去,虽然小图梅透过树木的缝隙看着天上的星星,但还是不知道他们朝着哪个方向。

然后,卡拉·纳格到达了山顶,稍稍停留了一下。小图梅可以看到树林的顶端在月光下斑斑点点、连绵数里,青色的雾气笼罩着山谷里的小河。图梅把身子往前倾看着,他觉得下面的森林都醒了——醒了,充满生气,热热闹闹。一只大大的棕色的吃水果的蝙蝠掠过他的耳边;豪猪的刺在灌木丛里发出咯咯的声音;在黑乎乎的树干之间,小熊在潮湿温暖的土壤里拼命挖土的声音,边挖边用鼻子嗅着。

接着树枝又淹没了他的脑袋,卡拉·纳格开始往下走向山谷——这次不是静悄悄的,而是像一个逃跑的猎手匆忙地跑下陡峭的山坡。他硕大的腿像活塞一样坚定的摆动着,每一大步八英尺远,肘部皱起的皮肤发出沙沙的声音。两边的灌木丛发出扯破帆布的声响,他用肩

---

cluster *n.* 一束,一串

401

either side of him ripped with a noise like torn canvas, and the saplings that he heaved away right and left with his shoulders sprang back again and banged him on the flank, and great trails of creepers, all matted together, hung from his tusks as he threw his head from side to side and plowed out his pathway. Then Little Toomai laid himself down close to the great neck lest a swinging bough should sweep him to the ground, and he wished that he were back in the lines again.

The grass began to get squashy, and Kala Nag's feet sucked and squelched as he put them down, and the night mist at the bottom of the valley chilled Little Toomai. There was a splash and a trample, and the rush of running water, and Kala Nag strode through the bed of a river, feeling his way at each step. Above the noise of the water, as it swirled round the elephant's legs, Little Toomai could hear more splashing and some trumpeting both upstream and down—great grunts and angry snortings, and all the mist about him seemed to be full of rolling, wavy shadows.

"Ai! " he said, half aloud, his teeth chattering. "The elephant-folk are out tonight. It is the dance, then! "

Kala Nag swashed out of the water, blew his trunk clear, and began another climb. But this time he was not alone, and he had not to make his path. That was made already, six feet wide, in front

THE JUNGLE STORY

膀左右撞开倒向一边的小树又都弹了回来,撞到他的身上。他左右甩头奋力开路的时候, 一串串杂生在一起的匍匐植物缠在了他的象牙上。于是小图梅贴着大象的大脖子躺了下来,以免被摇晃的树枝扫到地上,他真希望再次回到象场。

草地开始变得又湿又软,卡拉·纳格一踩上去,脚就陷了下去,还发出嘎吱嘎吱的响声。山谷底部的夜雾让小图梅感到寒冷。有溅水声,践踏声和湍急的流水声。卡拉·纳格小心地一步步摸索着趟过河床。河水绕着大象腿打着旋,在这水声之上,小图梅听到了上游下游更多的溅水声和大象吼叫声——大声的咕哝声和生气的哼哼声,环绕着他的雾气中似乎充满了起伏的影子。

"啊!"他几乎要大喊起来,牙齿带着哆嗦。"象群今晚都出来了。然后他们就要跳舞了。"

卡拉·纳格咆哮着从水里走出来,擤干鼻子,开始了另一次攀登。但是这次他不是一个人了,而且不用自己开路了。在他面前,已经有一

---

lest *conj.* 免得   bough *n.* 树枝   chill *v.* 使感到冷   upstream *adv.* 在上游

403

of him, where the bent jungle-grass was trying to recover itself and stand up. Many elephants must have gone that way only a few minutes before. Little Toomai looked back, and behind him a great wild tusker with his little pig's eyes glowing like hot coals was just lifting himself out of the misty river. Then the trees closed up again, and they went on and up, with trumpetings and crashings, and the sound of breaking branches on every side of them.

At last Kala Nag stood still between two tree-trunks at the very top of the hill. They were part of a circle of trees that grew round an irregular space of some three or four acres, and in all that space, as Little Toomai could see, the ground had been trampled down as hard as a brick floor. Some trees grew in the center of the clearing, but their bark was rubbed away, and the white wood beneath showed all shiny and **polished** in the patches of moonlight. There were creepers hanging from the upper branches, and the bells of the flowers of the creepers, great **waxy** white things like convolvuluses, hung down fast asleep. But within the limits of the clearing there was not a single blade of green— nothing but the trampled earth.

The moonlight showed it all iron gray, except where some elephants stood upon it, and their shadows were **inky** black. Little Toomai looked, holding his breath, with his eyes **starting** out of his

THE JUNGLE STORY

条六英尺宽的路了,两边被压弯的小草在逐渐地恢复原状,直立起来。几分钟前一定有许多大象经过这里。小图梅回头望去,身后有一头巨大的野象正从烟雾弥漫的小河里走上来,他小猪般的眼睛像烧红的煤炭一样发光。接着树木再次合拢了,他们继续往上走着,一边走一边不断地发出吼叫声、撞击声和踩碎两边树枝的声音。

最后卡拉·纳格在山顶的两根树干中间停住不动了。这两棵树是长在大约三到四英亩一片不规则的空地上的一圈树当中的两棵。小图梅看到,在那块空地上,土地被踩得像砖地一样结实。有几颗树长在空地的中央,但是它们的树皮被磨光了,露出下面的白木头,在月光下闪着光。树枝上挂下来一些爬山虎,爬山虎钟型的花朵,像旋花那样大大的蜡白色的东西,垂挂下来一动不动。但是在空地的范围以内,见不到一片绿叶——什么也没有,只有被踏平的土地。

月光把那里照得一片铁灰色,除了几头大象站着的地方,他们的影子一片漆黑。小图梅屏住呼吸看着这一切,眼睛都要从脑袋里瞪出

---

polished *adj.* 擦亮的,磨光的   waxy *adj.* 蜡制的   inky *adj.* 漆黑的   start *v.* 突出,鼓出

head, and as he looked, more and more and more elephants swung out into the open from between the tree trunks. Little Toomai could only count up to ten, and he counted again and again on his fingers till he lost count of the tens, and his head began to swim. Outside the clearing he could hear them crashing in the undergrowth as they worked their way up the hillside, but as soon as they were within the circle of the tree trunks they moved like ghosts.

There were white-tusked wild males, with fallen leaves and nuts and twigs lying in the wrinkles of their necks and the folds of their ears; fat, slow-footed she-elephants, with restless, little pinky black calves only three or four feet high running under their stomachs; young elephants with their tusks just beginning to show, and very proud of them; lanky, scraggy old-maid elephants, with their hollow anxious faces, and trunks like **rough** bark; savage old bull elephants, scarred from shoulder to flank with great weals and cuts of **bygone** fights, and the caked dirt of their **solitary** mud baths dropping from their shoulders; and there was one with a broken tusk and the marks of the full-stroke, the terrible drawing scrape, of a tiger's claws on his side.

They were standing head to head, or walking to and fro across the ground in **couples,** or rocking and swaying all by themselves—scores and scores of elephants.

THE JUNGLE STORY

来了。他看着看着,越来越多的大象从树干中摇摇晃晃地走出来走到空地里。小图梅数数还只会数到十,他一遍一遍地板着手指头数,直到他也忘了数到第几个十了,他的脑袋开始发昏。他能听到在空地外面大象上山开路,践踏着灌木丛的声音,但是一旦他们走到那圈树里来,他们移动起来就像幽灵一样。

他们当中有长着白牙的野公象,在他们脖子的皱褶处和耳朵的褶层处都是落叶、坚果和小树枝;有步履缓慢的肥胖的母象,带着他们不安分的、稍带粉红色的黑小象,小象们只有三到四英尺高,在母象肚子下奔跑着;还有些刚开始长象牙的年轻小象,他们为自己的象牙颇为自豪;那些皮包骨头又瘦又长的老母象,凹陷的脸上带着焦虑的表情,象鼻就像粗糙的树皮;有野蛮的老公象,从肩膀到腹肋都是过去打架留下的伤痕伤疤,他们独自去洗泥澡时沾上的一块块泥巴,从肩膀上掉落下来;还有一头象,象牙断了,身上有老虎留下的清晰可见的、可怕的抓痕。

他们头碰头的站着,或者成双地在空地上走来走去,或者独自摇来晃去——数不清的大象。

---

rough *adj.* 粗糙的   bygone *adj.* 过去的   solitary *adj.* 独自的
couple *n.* 一对;几个,两三个

丛林的故事

Toomai knew that so long as he lay still on Kala Nag's neck nothing would happen to him, for even in the rush and scramble of a Keddah drive a wild elephant does not reach up with his trunk and drag a man off the neck of a tame elephant. And these elephants were not thinking of men that night. Once they started and put their ears forward when they heard the chinking of a leg iron in the forest, but it was Pudmini, Petersen Sahib's pet elephant, her chain snapped short off, grunting, snuffling up the hillside. She must have broken her pickets and come straight from Petersen Sahib's camp; and Little Toomai saw another elephant, one that he did not know, with deep rope galls on his back and breast. He, too, must have run away from some camp in the hills about.

At last there was no sound of any more elephants moving in the forest, and Kala Nag rolled out from his station between the trees and went into the middle of the crowd, clucking and gurgling, and all the elephants began to talk in their own **tongue**, and to move about.

Still lying down, Little Toomai looked down upon scores and scores of broad backs, and wagging ears, and tossing trunks, and little rolling eyes. He heard the click of tusks as they crossed other tusks by accident, and the dry rustle of trunks twined together, and the chafing of **enormous** sides and shoulders in the crowd, and the

THE JUNGLE STORY

　　图梅知道,只要他安静地趴在卡拉·纳格脖子上,他就不会出什么事,因为即使在科达围捕的混乱匆忙中,野象也不会把鼻子伸到一头驯服的大象脖子上把人给拽下来。而且那晚,大象压根也没考虑到会有人。一次,他们听到森林里发出脚镣的叮当声,吓了一跳,都把耳朵往前伸。不过那只是彼得森·萨希博的宠象珀得米尼,她的链锁喀嚓一下折断了,咕哝着呼哧呼哧地跑上山。她一定是从彼得森·萨希博的营地里挣脱了木桩,径直跑到这里来的;小图梅还看到另外一头他不认识的大象,背上、胸前都有深深的绳索勒痕。他肯定也是从山边某个营地逃出来的。

　　终于再没有任何大象在森林里走动的声音了。卡拉·纳格摇摇晃晃地从他在树木间待的地方走出来,到象圈的中央,咯咯地叫着。所有的大象开始用他们自己的语言交谈,开始走来走去。

　　小图梅仍然躺着,往下看着数不清的宽大的象背,摇摆的耳朵,挥动的象鼻和滚动的小眼睛。他听到象牙偶然碰撞发出的咔哒声,象鼻缠绕在一起发出的粗糙的沙沙声;象群里大象巨大的身躯、肩膀互相摩擦的声音;大尾巴不停地轻拍和唑唑的声音。然后一朵云遮住了月

---

　　tongue *n.* 语言　　enormous *adj.* 巨大的;庞大的

incessant flick and hissh of the great tails. Then a cloud came over the moon, and he sat in black darkness. But the quiet, steady hustling and pushing and gurgling went on just the same. He knew that there were elephants all round Kala Nag, and that there was no chance of backing him out of the assembly; so he set his teeth and shivered. In a Keddah at least there was torchlight and shouting, but here he was all alone in the dark, and once a trunk came up and touched him on the knee.

Then an elephant trumpeted, and they all took it up for five or ten terrible seconds. The dew from the trees above spattered down like rain on the unseen backs, and a dull booming noise began, not very loud at first, and Little Toomai could not tell what it was. But it grew and grew, and Kala Nag lifted up one forefoot and then the other, and brought them down on the ground —one-two, one-two, as steadily as trip-hammers. The elephants were stamping all together now, and it sounded like a war drum beaten at the mouth of a cave. The dew fell from the trees till there was no more left to fall, and the booming went on, and the ground rocked and shivered, and Little Toomai put his hands up to his ears to shut out the sound. But it was all one gigantic jar that ran through him—this stamp of hundreds of heavy feet on the raw earth. Once or twice he could feel Kala Nag and all the others surge forward a few strides,

THE JUNGLE STORY

亮,他就坐在黑暗中。但是那静静的,不断的推攘声和咯咯的叫声依然持续着。他知道所有的大象都围着卡拉·纳格,他没机会退出这个集会,所以他咬紧牙关,打着寒战。在科达,至少还有火把和喊叫声,但是这里只有他独自一个人在黑暗中,甚至有一次一头大象还把鼻子伸上来,碰到了他的膝盖。

不久,一头大象吼叫起来,其他大象也都吼了起来,可怕的吼声一直持续了五到十秒钟。树上的露水象雨水般落到看不见的象背上,然后响起了一阵隆隆的声音,起初不太响,小图梅听不清那是什么声音。但是后来越来越响,卡拉·纳格举起了一只前脚,然后另外一只,再把两脚同时放下——一、二,一、二,就像杵锤一样有规律。现在所有的大象都一起踏着脚,听上去就像山洞洞口敲起战鼓。露水从树上掉下来,掉得一点不剩,但是这隆隆声还在继续,地面摇晃、颤抖着。小图梅用手捂着耳朵,挡住那声音。但是一阵巨大的刺耳声穿透了他——几百只笨重的大脚踏在湿冷的土地上。有一两次,他能感觉到卡拉·纳格和

---

incessant *adj.* 不停的,连续的   assembly *n.* 集合   gigantic *adj.* 巨大的,庞大的

and the thumping would change to the crushing sound of juicy green things being bruised, but in a minute or two the boom of feet on hard earth began again. A tree was creaking and groaning somewhere near him. He put out his arm and felt the bark, but Kala Nag moved forward, still tramping, and he could not tell where he was in the clearing. There was no sound from the elephants, except once, when two or three little calves squeaked together. Then he heard a thump and a shuffle, and the booming went on. It must have lasted fully two hours, and Little Toomai ached in every nerve, but he knew by the smell of the night air that the dawn was coming.

The morning broke in one sheet of pale yellow behind the green hills, and the booming stopped with the first ray, as though the light had been an order. Before Little Toomai had got the ringing out of his head, before even he had shifted his position, there was not an elephant in sight except Kala Nag, Pudmini, and the elephant with the rope-galls, and there was neither sign nor rustle nor whisper down the hillsides to show where the others had gone.

Little Toomai stared again and again. The clearing, as he remembered it, had grown in the night. More trees stood in the middle of it, but the undergrowth and the jungle grass at the sides had been rolled back. Little Toomai stared once more. Now he

THE JUNGLE STORY

其他大象一起往前走了几步,而且撞击声变成了绿色多汁的东西被捣碎的声音。但是一两分钟以后又变成了脚踩在坚实的土地上的声音。在他旁边某个地方有棵树发出吱吱嘎嘎的声音,他伸出手去摸到了树皮,但是卡拉·纳格往前挪动了,还在踩着脚,小图梅也不知道自己在空地的哪个位置。大象们都没有发出声音,除了一次,有两三只小象一起尖叫起来。然后他听到一声重锤和脚拖地的声音,接着隆隆声又继续响了起来。这一定持续了足足两个小时,小图梅的每个神经都疼痛了起来,但是他从夜晚的空气中感觉到黎明就要来了。

清晨给绿色的的后山带来了一抹淡淡的黄色,当第一道阳光出现的时候,隆隆声就停止了,好像阳光就是一道命令。还没等小图梅摆脱脑袋里的嗡嗡声,甚至他还来不及变换一下姿势,他已经一头象也看不见了,只剩下卡拉·纳格、珀得米尼和有绳索勒痕的那头象。下山的路上没有任何迹象,也没有窸窣声和耳语声,不知道其他的大象都去了哪里。

小图梅瞪着眼睛看了又看。空地一夜之间比他记忆中的要大多了。空地中间的树更多了,但是周围的灌木丛和丛林野草都往后退了。小图梅瞪着眼睛又看了看。现在他明白那踩地声是怎么回事了。大象

---

juicy *adj.* 多汁的   pale *adj.* 淡的   ray *n.* 光线,光亮   shift *v.* 改变,移动

understood the trampling. The elephants had stamped out more room—had stamped the thick grass and juicy cane to trash, the trash into slivers, the slivers into tiny fibers, and the fibers into hard earth.

"Wah! " said Little Toomai, and his eyes were very heavy. "Kala Nag, my lord, let us keep by Pudmini and go to Petersen Sahib's camp, or I shall drop from your neck."

The third elephant watched the two go away, snorted, wheeled round, and took his own path. He may have belonged to some little native king's establishment, fifty or sixty or a hundred miles away.

Two hours later, as Petersen Sahib was eating early breakfast, his elephants, who had been double chained that night, began to trumpet, and Pudmini, mired to the shoulders, with Kala Nag, very footsore, shambled into the camp. Little Toomai's face was gray and pinched, and his hair was full of leaves and drenched with dew, but he tried to salute Petersen Sahib, and cried faintly: "The dance—the elephant dance! I have seen it, and—I die! " As Kala Nag sat down, he slid off his neck in a dead faint.

But, since native children have no nerves worth speaking of, in two hours he was lying very contentedly in Petersen Sahib's hammock with Petersen Sahib's shooting-coat under his head, and a glass of warm milk, a little brandy, with a dash of quinine, inside

们踩出了更大的空地——把茂密的野草和多汁的甘蔗踩成残渣,残渣又被踩成碎片,碎片又被踩成小纤维,小纤维又被踩成了坚实的土地。

"哇呜!"小图梅说,他的眼皮很沉。"卡拉·纳格,我的大王啊,让我们走到珀得米尼旁边去,跟着她到彼得森·萨希博的营地里,否则我要从你的脖子上掉下去了。"

第三头大象看着另外两头走了,噗哧噗哧地转了个圈,也走到了自己的路上。他可能来自五六十英里远的当地某个土著首领的领地。

两小时以后, 彼得森·萨希博正在给昨晚被双重锁链锁住的大象们喂早饭,他们开始吼叫起来,肩膀以下都溅满了污泥的珀得米尼和走得脚发痛的卡拉·纳格蹒跚着走进营地。小图梅的脸色苍白,头发上满是落叶,已经被露水都浸湿了,但是他还是设法向彼得森·萨希博行礼,虚弱地哭喊着:"跳舞——大象跳舞了!我见过了,我要——死了!"卡拉·纳格蹲了下来,他就从他的脖子上滑了下来,晕死过去。

但是,因为当地孩子都毫无精神紧张可言,所以两小时以后他就心满意足地趟在彼得森·萨希博的吊床里了,头下枕着彼得森·萨希博的猎服,一杯热牛奶、一点白兰地和少量的奎宁已经下肚了。在他面

---

footsore *adj.* 脚痛的,脚酸的　　shamble *v.* 蹒跚　　drench *v.* 使湿透
faintly *adv.* 虚弱的,衰弱的　　contentedly *adv.* 满足地　　dash *n.* 少量

of him, and while the old hairy, scarred hunters of the jungles sat three deep before him, looking at him as though he were a spirit, he told his tale in short words, as a child will, and wound up with:

"Now, if I lie in one word, send men to see, and they will find that the elephant folk have trampled down more room in their dance-room, and they will find ten and ten, and many times ten, tracks leading to that dance-room. They made more room with their feet. I have seen it. Kala Nag took me, and I saw. Also Kala Nag is very leg-weary! "

Little Toomai lay back and slept all through the long afternoon and into the twilight, and while he slept Petersen Sahib and Machua Appa followed the track of the two elephants for fifteen miles across the hills. Petersen Sahib had spent eighteen years in catching elephants, and he had only once before found such a dance-place. Machua Appa had no need to look twice at the clearing to see what had been done there, or to scratch with his toe in the packed, rammed earth.

"The child speaks truth," said he. "All this was done last night, and I have counted seventy tracks crossing the river. See, Sahib, where Pudmini's leg-iron cut the bark of that tree! Yes; she was there too."

They looked at one another and up and down, and they

THE JUNGLE STORY

前坐着三排粗鲁的、满身伤疤的丛林老猎人，像看着幽灵一样看着他。他简短地讲述了他的故事，一个孩子总是这样，最后他说：

"好了，如果我有一句谎话，那就派人去看，他们会发现象群在他们的舞场里踩出了更大的空间，他们会发现有十条，十条，许多个十条路通向舞场。他们用脚踩出了更大的空间。我亲眼见到了。卡拉·纳格带我去的，我看到了。卡拉·纳格也走得腿很酸了。"

小图梅又躺了回去，整个长长的下午都在睡觉，一直睡到黄昏时分。他在睡觉的时候，彼得森·萨希博和玛丘阿·阿帕跟着两头大象的足迹穿过小山走了十五英里。彼得森·萨希博花了十八年捕象，以前他也只有一次发现了这样一个跳舞的地方。玛丘阿·阿帕无需再次去看那块空地上发生了什么事情，或者用脚趾头挖那压紧踩实的土地。

"那孩子说的是真的，"他说，"这些都是昨晚干的，我已经数过了，有七十条小路穿过河流。看，萨希博，珀得米尼腿上的铁链把那棵树上的树皮刮掉了！是的，她来过这里。"

他们互相看了一眼，上下打量了一番，他们很惊讶。因为大象的做

wondered. For the ways of elephants are beyond the wit of any man, black or white, to fathom.

"Forty years and five," said Machua Appa, "have I followed my lord, the elephant, but never have I heard that any child of man had seen what this child has seen. By all the Gods of the Hills, it is— what can we say?" and he shook his head.

When they got back to camp it was time for the evening meal. Petersen Sahib ate alone in his tent, but he gave orders that the camp should have two sheep and some fowls, as well as a double ration of flour and rice and salt, for he knew that there would be a feast.

Big Toomai had come up **hotfoot** from the camp in the plains to search for his son and his elephant, and now that he had found them he looked at them as though he were afraid of them both. And there was a feast by the blazing campfires in front of the lines of picketed elephants, and Little Toomai was the hero of it all. And the big brown elephant catchers, the trackers and drivers and ropers, and the men who know all the secrets of breaking the wildest elephants, passed him from one to the other, and they marked his forehead with blood from the breast of a newly killed jungle-cock, to show that he was a forester, **initiated** and free of all the jungles.

THE JUNGLE STORY

法比任何人,不管是黑人还是白人,都要聪明得多。

"四十五年了,"玛丘阿·阿帕说,"我都跟着我的象王,但是从来没有听说过有哪个孩子见过这个孩子见过的东西。我以所有的山神发誓,这是——我们能怎么说呢?"他摇着头。

等他们回到营地的时候,已经是晚饭的时间了。彼得森·萨希博一个人在自己的帐篷里吃饭,但是他下了命令,营地里要有两头羊和一些家禽,还要有双倍量的面粉、米和盐,因为他知道将会有一次盛宴。

大图梅匆匆忙忙地从平原里的营地跑来,寻找他的儿子和大象。现在他找到了他们,他看着他们却好像很怕他们似的。在燃烧的营火旁,在拴在尖木桩上的大象前,他们正在举行着盛宴,小图梅是整个盛宴上的英雄。高大的棕色捕象人、追象人、赶象人和拴象人,以及那些通晓驯服野象所有秘密的人,把小图梅从大家的手中一个接一个地传递,他们用新宰杀的一只丛林公鸡胸口的鲜血涂在他的前额上,以表明他是一个来自丛林而又是丛林以外的丛林人。

---

feast *n.* 盛宴   hotfoot *adv.* 匆忙地   initiate *v.* 开始;创始;发起

丛林的故事

And at last, when the flames died down, and the red light of the logs made the elephants look as though they had been dipped in blood too, Machua Appa, the head of all the drivers of all the Keddahs—Machua Appa, Petersen Sahib's other self, who had never seen a made road in forty years: Machua Appa, who was so great that he had no other name than Machua Appa,—leaped to his feet, with Little Toomai held high in the air above his head, and shouted: "Listen, my brothers. Listen, too, you my lords in the lines there, for I, Machua Appa, am speaking! This little one shall no more be called Little Toomai, but Toomai of the Elephants, as his great-grandfather was called before him. What never man has seen he has seen through the long night, and the favor of the elephant-folk and of the Gods of the Jungles is with him. He shall become a great tracker. He shall become greater than I, even I, Machua Appa! He shall follow the new trail, and the stale trail, and the mixed trail, with a clear eye! He shall take no harm in the Keddah when he runs under their bellies to rope the wild tuskers; and if he slips before the feet of the charging bull elephant, the bull elephant shall know who he is and shall not crush him. Aihai! my lords in the chains,"—he whirled up the line of pickets—"here is the little one that has seen your dances in your hidden places,—the sight that never man saw! Give him honor, my lords! Salaam karo, my

THE JUNGLE STORY

　　最后火焰熄灭了，木头的红光让大象看上去好像浸在血中一样。玛丘阿·阿帕，所有的科达赶象人的首领，另一个彼得森·萨希博，四十年来都没见过一条踏出来的路：玛丘阿·阿帕，他太了不起了，除了玛丘阿·阿帕，他没有其他名字——他一下子跳了起来，把小图梅高高地举过头顶，喊道："听着，我的兄弟们。你们也听着，营地里的象王们，因为我，玛丘阿·阿帕要说话了！这个小家伙不再叫小图梅了，而叫大象们的图梅，就像他曾祖父曾被称呼的那样。他在长夜里见到了从来没有人见到过的东西。他得到了象群和丛林诸神的宠爱。他将来会成为一个伟大的追象人。他会比我还了不起，比我，玛丘阿·阿帕更了不起！他将以锐利的眼光追踪新的足迹、陈旧的足迹和混合的足迹！在科达象场，他在大象肚子下奔跑去捡野象，不会受到伤害；如果他在冲锋的公象脚下滑倒了，公象会知道他是谁，不会撞到他。啊哈！我带着锁链的象王们，"——他急速地走到拴大象的木桩前——"这就是见到你们在自己秘密的地方跳舞的小家伙，——这是没有人曾经见过的景象！

---

flame *n.* 火焰　　belly *n.* 肚，腹

children. Make your salute to Toomai of the Elephants! Gunga Pershad, ahaa! Hira Guj, Birchi Guj, Kuttar Guj, ahaa! Pudmini,— you have seen him at the dance, and you too, Kala Nag, my pearl among elephants! —ahaa! Together! To Toomai of the Elephants. Barrao! ”

And at that last wild yell the whole line flung up their trunks till the tips touched their foreheads, and broke out into the full salute— the crashing trumpet-peal that only the Viceroy of India hears, the Salaamut of the Keddah.

But it was all for the sake of Little Toomai, who had seen what never man had seen before—the dance of the elephants at night and alone in the heart of the Garo hills!

THE JUNGLE STORY

给他荣耀，我的象王们！敬礼，我的孩子们！向大象的图梅敬礼！冈盖·珀夏德，啊哈！希拉·盖伊，伯奇·盖伊，库塔·盖伊，啊哈！珀得米尼，——你在跳舞的时候见过他了，还有你，卡拉·纳格，大象中的我的宝贝！——啊哈！一起！向大象的图梅致意！"

随着最后那一声狂叫，整排大象都把鼻子甩起，一直到鼻尖碰到前额，然后爆发出了完美的敬礼——那只有印度总督听到过的洪亮持久的吼叫声，整个科达象场的敬礼。

然而这一切都是为了小图梅，他见到了人类以前从没见过的景象——夜晚独自一人在加鲁山的中心看到了大象在跳舞。

---

pearl *n.* 珍珠

Chapter 12　Shiv and the Grasshopper

(The song that Toomai's mother sang to the baby)

Shiv, who poured the harvest and made the winds to blow,
Sitting at the doorways of a day of long ago,
Gave to each his portion, food and toil and fate,
From the King upon the guddee to the Beggar at the gate.

All things made he—Shiva the Preserver.
Mahadeo! Mahadeo! He made all,—
Thorn for the camel, fodder for the kine,
And mother's heart for sleepy head,
O little son of mine!

Wheat he gave to rich folk, millet to the poor,
Broken scraps for holy men that beg from door to door;

THE JUNGLE STORY

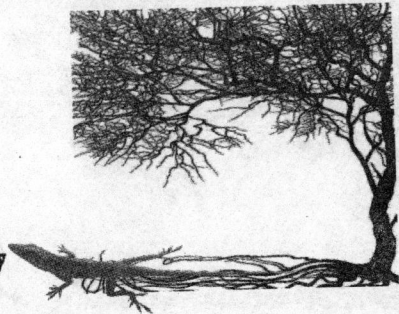

第十二章　湿婆和蚱蜢

(图梅的妈妈唱给小娃娃听的歌)

湿婆，带来了收获，让风吹拂，
很久以前的一天，他坐在门口，
让每一个人分享他的食物、劳苦和命运，
从宝座上的国王到门口的乞丐。

他所做的一切让他成为——湿婆，保护神。
神啊！神啊！他创造了一切——
骆驼的荆棘丛，母牛的草料，
还有拥抱瞌睡的小脑袋的母亲的怀抱，
哦，我的小儿子！

他把小麦给了富人，把谷子给了穷人，
把残羹剩饭赐给了挨家挨户乞讨的人；

---

grasshopper *n.* 蚱蜢

425

丛林的故事

Battle to the tiger, carrion to the kite,
And rags and bones to wicked wolves without the wall at night.

Naught he found too lofty, none he saw too low—
Parbati beside him watched them come and go;
Thought to cheat her husband, turning Shiv to jest—
Stole the little grasshopper and hid it in her breast.

So she tricked him, Shiva the Preserver.
Mahadeo! Mahadeo! Turn and see.
Tall are the camels, heavy are the kine,
But this was Least of Little Things,
O little son of mine!

When the dole was ended, laughingly she said,
Master, of a million mouths, is not one unfed?"
Laughing, Shiv made answer,
"All have had their part,
Even he, the little one, hidden 'neath your heart."
From her breast she plucked it,

THE JUNGLE STORY

他给老虎带来争斗，给鸢鹰带来腐肉，
夜晚让无拘无束的恶狼吞食了收废品的行贩。

在他眼里，没有贵贱——
他身边的帕巴蒂看着他们来来往往，
心想着要欺骗一下她的丈夫，和湿婆开个玩笑——
她偷了一只小蚱蜢，悄悄地藏在怀里。

就这样她戏弄了他，湿婆，保护神。
神啊！神啊！转过身来看看。
高高的是骆驼，笨重的是母牛，
但是这是小生物里最小的，
哦，我的小儿子！

当施舍结束的时候，她笑着说，
主啊，在一百万张嘴中，有没有还没有喂食的？
湿婆笑着回答，
"每一个都得到了自己的一份了，
即使是他，这个躲在你胸口的小家伙。"
她从怀里把小蚱蜢拽了出来，

---

naught *n.* 没有什么　　lofty *adj.* 崇高的,高尚的　　jest *n.* 玩笑,笑料
trick *v.* 哄骗,诈骗,恶作剧

丛林的故事

Parbati the thief,
Saw the Least of Little Things gnawed a new-grown leaf!
Saw and feared and wondered, making prayer to Shiv,

Who hath surely given meat to all that live.
All things made he—Shiva the Preserver.
Mahadeo! Mahadeo! He made all,—
Thorn for the camel, fodder for the kine,
And mother's heart for sleepy head,
O little son of mine!

THE JUNGLE STORY

帕巴蒂，这个小偷，
看到这个小家伙嘴里居然咬着一片新长的叶子！
她看着心生敬畏，惊叹不已，向湿婆祈祷。

毫无疑问，湿婆赐予了所有生命食物。
这一切让他成为——湿婆，保护神。
神啊！神啊！他创造了一切——
骆驼的荆棘丛，母牛的草料，
还有拥抱瞌睡的小脑袋的母亲的怀抱，
哦，我的小儿子！

---

prayer *n.* 祈祷，祈求

Chapter 13   Her Majesty's Servants

You can work it out by Fractions or by simple Rule of Three,
But the way of Tweedle-dum is not the way of Tweedle-dee.
You can twist it, you can turn it, you can plait it till you drop,
But the way of Pilly Winky's not the way of Winkie Pop!

It had been raining heavily for one whole month—raining on a camp of thirty thousand men and thousands of camels, elephants, horses, bullocks, and mules all gathered together at a place called Rawal Pindi, to be reviewed by the Viceroy of India. He was receiving a visit from the Amir of Afghanistan—a wild king of a very wild country. The Amir had brought with him for a bodyguard eight hundred men and horses who had never seen a camp or a locomotive before in their lives—savage men and savage horses from somewhere at the back of Central Asia. Every night a mob of these horses would be sure to break their heel ropes and stampede up and down the camp through the mud in the dark, or the camels would break loose and run about and fall over the ropes of the tents, and you can imagine how pleasant that was for men trying to

THE JUNGLE STORY

第十三章　女王陛下的仆人

你可以用分数或是简单的比例法算出，
但是特威德尔达姆与特威德尔迪用的不是同一个方法。
你可以捻它，可以转它，可以把它折起来，直到你停止。
但是皮利·威基和威齐·波普用的不是同一个方法。

大雨下了整整一个月——一个聚集了三万个人、几千头骆驼、大象、马匹、公牛和骡子的营地一直下着雨。所有的人聚集在一个叫作罗沃·平迪的地方，准备接受印度总督的检阅。他正在接待来自阿富汗的埃米尔的来访——一个来自非常野蛮的国家的野蛮的君主。埃米尔带来了一支八百人马的警卫队，在他们这一生中从未见过营地或是一辆火车——来自中亚后面的某个地方的野蛮人和野蛮马。每天晚上总是会有马群挣断它们腿上的绳索，在黑暗的营地里，穿过泥地到处乱窜，要不就是骆驼挣脱绳索，到处乱跑，被帐篷的绳子绊倒。你可以想象这

---

fraction *n.* 分数　　review *v.* 检阅　　bodyguard *n.* 警卫　　loose *adj.* 松的，松散的

丛林的故事

go to sleep. My tent lay far away from the camel lines, and I thought it was safe. But one night a man **popped** his head in and shouted, "Get out, quick! They're coming! My tent's gone! "

I knew who "they" were, so I put on my boots and **waterproof** and scuttled out into the slush. Little Vixen, my fox terrier, went out through the other side; and then there was a roaring and a grunting and bubbling, and I saw the tent cave in, as the pole snapped, and begin to dance about like a mad ghost. A camel had **blundered** into it, and wet and angry as I was, I could not help laughing. Then I ran on, because I did not know how many camels might have got loose, and before long I was out of sight of the camp, plowing my way through the mud.

At last I fell over the tail-end of a gun, and by that knew I was somewhere near the artillery lines where the cannon were stacked at night. As I did not want to plowter about any more in the **drizzle** and the dark, I put my waterproof over the muzzle of one gun, and made a sort of wigwam with two or three rammers that I found, and lay along the tail of another gun, wondering where Vixen had got to, and where I might be.

Just as I was getting ready to go to sleep I heard a **jingle** of harness and a grunt, and a mule passed me shaking his wet ears. He belonged to a screw-gun battery, for I could hear the rattle of

THE JUNGLE STORY

对那些打算入睡的人来说,是多么"愉快"的事情。我的帐篷在远离骆驼队的地方,因此我认为自己很安全。但是一天晚上,一个脑袋突然伸进帐篷,大喊:"出来,快点!他们来了!我的帐篷已经倒了!"

我知道"他们"指的是谁,所以我穿上靴子、雨衣匆匆地跑到烂泥里。我的猎狐小维克森从另外一边冲了出去。然后听到一阵喧闹声、咕哝声和汩汩的流水声,眼看着帐篷竿子喀嚓一声断了,然后帐篷塌了下来,像个疯狂的幽灵一样乱舞。原来是一头骆驼跌跌撞撞地走进了帐篷。虽然我全身湿透又气恼,还是禁不住大笑起来。接着,我拔腿就跑,因为我不知道还有多少头骆驼可能挣脱了绳索。我在泥地里奋力开路,很快就看不到骆驼了。

跑着跑着,我被一门大炮的末端绊倒了,于是我知道我到了晚上堆放大炮的炮兵营附近了。因为我不想再在阴雨绵绵的黑夜中跑来跑去,于是我把雨衣放在大炮炮口上,用找来的两三根撞杆搭了一个简陋小屋,沿着旁边一门炮的炮尾躺了下来,心里琢磨着维克森去了哪里,我又可能在哪里。

正当我要入睡的时候,我听到了马具的叮当声和咕哝声,一头骡子甩着他的湿耳朵从我身边经过。他从属于一个螺旋式炮兵连,因为

---

pop v. 突然放入,突然推撞;突然或出乎意料地放入或插入   waterproof n. 雨衣
blunder v. 跌跌撞撞地走,踉踉跄跄地走   drizzle n. 毛毛雨   jingle n. 叮当响

the straps and rings and chains and things on his saddle pad. The screw-guns are tiny little cannon made in two pieces, that are screwed together when the time comes to use them. They are taken up mountains, anywhere that a mule can find a road, and they are very useful for fighting in rocky country.

Behind the mule there was a camel, with his big soft feet squelching and slipping in the mud, and his neck bobbing to and fro like a **strayed** hen's. Luckily, I knew enough of beast language—not wild-beast language, but camp-beast language, of course—from the natives to know what he was saying.

He must have been the one that flopped into my tent, for he called to the mule, "What shall I do? Where shall I go? I have fought with a white thing that waved, and it took a stick and hit me on the neck." (That was my broken tent pole, and I was very glad to know it.) "Shall we run on?"

"Oh, it was you," said the mule, "you and your friends, that have been disturbing the camp? All right. You'll be beaten for this in the morning. But I may as well give you something on account now."

I heard the harness jingle as the mule backed and caught the camel two kicks in the ribs that rang like a drum. "Another time," he said, "you'll know better than to run through a mule battery at

THE JUNGLE STORY

我能听到他鞍垫上的皮带、圈子、链子和其他东西发出的吵闹声。螺旋式炮是非常小的炮,由两部分组成,用的时候,把两部分拧紧。它们被运到山上,运到骡子能找到路的地方。在一个到处是岩石的国家打仗,它们是十分有用的。

骡子旁边是一头骆驼,他那大大的软软的脚吱吱嘎嘎的滑进泥里,他的脖子像一只迷路的母鸡来回晃动。幸好,我从当地人那里学会了野生动物的语言——当然,不是野兽的语言,而是营地里动物的语言——我知道他们在说什么。

他一定就是那头重重地掉落在我帐篷里的骆驼,因为他对骡子说,"我该怎么做呢?我该去哪里呢?我和一个晃动的白东西打了一仗,它拿了根棍子打在我脖子上。"(其实那是我断了的帐篷杆子,知道这个让我非常高兴。)"我们该继续跑吗?"

"哦,是你啊,"骡子说,"大闹营地的是你和你的朋友们吗?好吧,为这事你们早上要挨打了。但是,现在我要赊给你们一些东西。"

我听到马具的叮当声。骡子后退了几步,然后在骆驼的肋骨处踢了两脚,咚咚的像敲鼓。"下次,"他说,"你就会明白最好别晚上在骡子炮兵连乱闯,还喊着'小偷啊,着火啦!',坐下,别动你的傻脖子了。"

---

stray *v.* 迷路

435

night, shouting 'Thieves and fire! ' Sit down, and keep your silly neck quiet."

The camel doubled up camel-fashion, like a two-foot rule, and sat down whimpering. There was a regular beat of hoofs in the darkness, and a big troop-horse cantered up as steadily as though he were on parade, jumped a gun tail, and landed close to the mule.

"It's disgraceful," he said, blowing out his nostrils. "Those camels have racketed through our lines again—the third time this week. How's a horse to keep his condition if he isn't allowed to sleep. Who's here?"

"I'm the breech-piece mule of number two gun of the First Screw Battery," said the mule, "and the other's one of your friends. He's waked me up too. Who are you?"

"Number Fifteen, E troop, Ninth Lancers—Dick Cunliffe's horse. Stand over a little, there."

"Oh, beg your pardon," said the mule. "It's too dark to see much. Aren't these camels too sickening for anything? I walked out of my lines to get a little peace and quiet here."

"My lords," said the camel humbly, "we dreamed bad dreams in the night, and we were very much afraid. I am only a baggage camel of the 39th Native Infantry, and I am not as brave as you are, my lords."

THE JUNGLE STORY

骆驼以骆驼的方式弯下身子,就像一把两脚尺,坐下来啜泣起来。黑暗中响起一阵有规律的蹄子踢打的声音。接着,一头高大的军马稳健地慢跑过来,好像他在接受检阅似的。他跳过一门炮的炮尾,落在骡子的旁边。

"这可真丢脸,"他说,鼻孔里喘着粗气,"这些骆驼又吵吵闹闹地穿过我们的营地——这个星期已经第三次了。如果不让马睡觉的话,怎么能保持他的状态呢?谁在这里?"

"我是第一螺旋式炮兵连第二门炮炮尾的骡子,"骡子说,"另外一个是你的朋友。他把我也吵醒了。你是谁?"

"第九长矛轻骑团,E骑兵连,十五号——迪克·坎利弗的坐骑。往那边站过去点。"

"哦,对不起,"骡子说,"太黑了看不太清楚。这些骆驼是不是太让人讨厌了?我从军营里出来到这里来图个清净。"

"我的老爷们,"骆驼谦卑地说,"我们晚上做恶梦,害怕极了。我只是第三十九步兵团驮行李的骆驼,我可没有你们这么勇敢,我的老爷们。"

---

whimper v. 啜泣   canter v. 慢跑   parade n. 游行,检阅
disgraceful adj. 可耻的   nostril n. 鼻孔   racket v. 喧嚷

从林的故事

"Then why didn't you stay and carry baggage for the 39th Native Infantry, instead of running all round the camp?" said the mule.

"They were such very bad dreams," said the camel. "I am sorry. Listen! What is that? Shall we run on again?"

"Sit down," said the mule, "or you'll snap your long stick-legs between the guns." He cocked one ear and listened. "Bullocks!" he said. "Gun bullocks. On my word, you and your friends have waked the camp very thoroughly. It takes a good deal of prodding to put up a gun-bullock."

I heard a chain dragging along the ground, and a yoke of the great sulky white bullocks that drag the heavy siege guns when the elephants won't go any nearer to the firing, came shouldering along together. And almost stepping on the chain was another battery mule, calling wildly for "Billy."

"That's one of our recruits," said the old mule to the troop horse. "He's calling for me. Here, youngster, stop squealing. The dark never hurt anybody yet."

The gun-bullocks lay down together and began chewing the cud, but the young mule huddled close to Billy.

"Things!" he said. "Fearful and horrible, Billy! They came into our lines while we were asleep. D'you think they'll kill us?"

438

THE JUNGLE STORY

"那么你为什么不待在三十九步兵团里驮行李，而要在军营里跑来跑去呢？"骡子问。

"那些恶梦太可怕了，"骆驼说，"真对不起。听！那是什么？我们要不要再跑啊？"

"坐下！"骡子说，"否则你会在大炮间把你棍子般的长腿折断的。"他竖起一只耳朵仔细听着。"公牛！"他说，"大炮公牛。以我的名誉担保，你和你的朋友把整个军营都彻底吵醒了。要惊扰到一头大炮公牛得有多大的举动啊。"

我听到一条链子拖地的声音，一对愠怒的大公牛拖着重重的攻城加农炮，肩并肩地走过来，因为当时大象不愿意往着火的地方去。另外一头炮兵连骡子差点踩在链子上，他拼命地喊着"比利！"

"那是我们一个新入伍的，"老骡子对军马说，"他在叫我。我在这儿，年轻人，别喊了。黑夜从来不会伤到任何人。"

两头大炮公牛躺了下来，开始咀嚼反刍的食物，那头年轻的骡子向比利那边挤过去。

"那些东西！"他说，"真是可怕，真吓人，比利！我们睡觉的时候他们闯进我们的营地里，你认为他们会不会杀了我们？"

---

recruit *n.* 新兵　　huddle *v.* 挤作一团

丛林的故事

"I've a very great mind to give you a number-one kicking," said Billy. "The idea of a fourteen-hand mule with your training disgracing the battery before this gentleman! "

"Gently, gently! " said the troop-horse. "Remember they are always like this to begin with. The first time I ever saw a man (it was in Australia when I was a three-year-old) I ran for half a day, and if I'd seen a camel, I should have been running still."

Nearly all our horses for the English cavalry are brought to India from Australia, and are broken in by the troopers themselves.

"True enough," said Billy. "Stop shaking, youngster. The first time they put the full harness with all its chains on my back I stood on my forelegs and kicked every bit of it off. I hadn't learned the real science of kicking then, but the battery said they had never seen anything like it."

"But this wasn't harness or anything that jingled," said the young mule. "You know I don't mind that now, Billy. It was Things like trees, and they fell up and down the lines and **bubbled**; and my head-rope broke, and I couldn't find my driver, and I couldn't find you, Billy, so I ran off with—with these gentlemen."

"H'm! " said Billy. "As soon as I heard the camels were loose I came away on my own account. When a battery—a screw-gun mule calls gun-bullocks gentlemen, he must be very badly **shaken** up. Who

440

THE JUNGLE STORY

"我真想狠狠地踢你一脚，"比利说，"一想到你这么训练有素的、十四手宽的骡子居然在这个绅士前给炮兵连丢脸。"

"别发火，别发火！"军马说，"别忘了一开始他们总是这样的。我第一次见到人的时候(那是我三岁在澳大利亚的时候)，我奔跑了半天，如果当时我见到的是一头骆驼的话，也会那么跑的。"

英国骑兵团的几乎所有的马匹都是从澳大利亚带到印度的，然后由骑兵们自己训练。

"的确是这样，"比利说，"别发抖了，年轻人。第一次他们把带锁链的整套马具放在我背上的时候，我用前脚站了起来，把它全踢掉了。那时我还没真正学会踢人，但是炮兵连的人说他们从没见过这样的。"

"但这叮当响的可不是马具什么的，"年轻的骡子说，"你知道我现在已经不介意那些东西了，比利。那是像树一样的东西，他们在营地里一起一伏地发出噗噗的声音，我头上的绳子断了，我找不到赶我的人，也找不到你了，比利，所以我就跑了——和这些绅士们一起跑了。"

"哼！"比利说，"我一听到骆驼松开了，就自己跑了。当一个炮兵连——一个螺旋式炮的骡子称大炮公牛为绅士，他肯定是吓坏了。那

---

bubble *v.* 发噗噗声　　shake *v.* 使震惊；打扰

are you fellows on the ground there?"

The gun bullocks rolled their cuds, and answered both together: "The seventh yoke of the first gun of the Big Gun Battery. We were asleep when the camels came, but when we were **trampled** on we got up and walked away. It is better to lie quiet in the mud than to be disturbed on good **bedding**. We told your friend here that there was nothing to be afraid of, but he knew so much that he thought otherwise. Wah! "

They went on chewing.

"That comes of being afraid," said Billy. "You get laughed at by gun-bullocks. I hope you like it, young un."

The young mule's teeth snapped, and I heard him say something about not being afraid of any **beefy** old bullock in the world. But the bullocks only clicked their horns together and went on chewing.

"Now, don't be angry after you've been afraid. That's the worst kind of **cowardice**," said the troop-horse. "Anybody can be forgiven for being scared in the night, I think, if they see things they don't understand. We've broken out of our pickets, again and again, four hundred and fifty of us, just because a new recruit got to telling tales of whip snakes at home in Australia till we were scared to death of the loose ends of our head-ropes."

442

THE JUNGLE STORY

边的两个家伙,你们究竟是谁?"

　　那对大炮公牛咀嚼着反刍的食物,一起回答道,"大炮连第一门炮的第七对公牛。骆驼来的时候,我们正在睡觉,但是当我们被踩到的时候,就起来走开了。安静地躺在泥地里总比在舒服的褥草上睡觉被打扰要好。我们对你们这里的朋友说,没什么好害怕的,但是他知道的太多了,所以并不这么想。哇!"

　　他们继续咀嚼着。

　　"那是因为害怕,"比利说,"大炮公牛都嘲笑你了。我希望你喜欢这样,年轻人。"

　　年轻骡子的牙齿突然"啪"的一声合上了,我听到他说了些不害怕世界上任何一头结实的老公牛之类的话。但是那对公牛只是碰了碰牛角,继续咀嚼着。

　　"好了,害怕过了就别生气了。那是最糟糕的一种胆怯,"军马说,"我想,任何人如果晚上看到了他们不理解的东西而感到害怕,都是可以谅解的。我们四百五十匹马一遍遍地挣脱拴我们的木桩,就是因为一个新入伍的马讲了好多关于澳大利亚家里的鞭蛇的故事,听得我们连看到头上松开的绳索头,都吓得要死。"

---

　　trample *v.* 踩,践踏　　bedding *n.* 褥草　　beefy *adj.* 结实的　　cowardice *n.* 胆小,怯懦

丛林的故事

"That's all very well in camp," said Billy. "I'm not above stampeding myself, for the fun of the thing, when I haven't been out for a day or two. But what do you do on active service?"

"Oh, that's quite another set of new shoes," said the troop horse. "Dick Cunliffe's on my back then, and drives his knees into me, and all I have to do is to watch where I am putting my feet, and to keep my hind legs well under me, and be bridle-wise."

"What's bridle-wise?" said the young mule.

"By the Blue Gums of the Back Blocks," snorted the troop-horse, "do you mean to say that you aren't taught to be bridle-wise in your business? How can you do anything, unless you can spin round at once when the rein is pressed on your neck? It means life or death to your man, and of course that's life and death to you. Get round with your hind legs under you the instant you feel the rein on your neck. If you haven't room to swing round, rear up a little and come round on your hind legs. That's being bridle-wise."

"We aren't taught that way," said Billy the mule stiffly. "We're taught to obey the man at our head: step off when he says so, and step in when he says so. I suppose it comes to the same thing. Now, with all this fine fancy business and rearing, which must be very bad for your hocks, what do you do?"

"That depends," said the troop-horse. "Generally I have to go

444

THE JUNGLE STORY

"营地里都还挺好的，"比利说，"我还不至于把自己吓地乱跑，只是为了好玩，每当我一两天没有出去的时候。但是在服役当中，你能怎么办？"

"哦，那是完全另外一回事了，"军马说，"那时迪克·坎利弗正在我背上，用膝盖夹得我紧紧的。我所能做的，就是注意把脚放在什么地方，把后腿在身下放好，听从缰绳的指挥。"

"什么是听从缰绳的指挥？"年轻的骡子问。

"以腹地的蓝桉起誓，"军马哼着鼻子说，"你的意思是说，在你的职责训练里你没学过听从缰绳指挥？除非缰绳在你脖子上拉紧的时候你能立刻转过身，否则你能做什么事情呢？这关系到你的骑手的生死，当然也关系到你的生死。你感觉到脖子上的缰绳一动，用身下的后腿一转，转过身来。如果没有足够的空间转过来，用后腿稍稍直立转过身。这才是听从缰绳的指挥。"

"不是那样教我们的，"骡子比利表情僵硬地说，"教我们要服从前面的人命令：他说齐步走，就齐步走，他说进去，就进去。我想这是一回事。那么，这种难度高超的本事和直立，对你的跗关节一定很不好，你怎么做呢？"

"那要看情况，"军马说，"通常，我得走到一群大喊大叫、粗鲁的拿

---

rein *n.* 缰绳　instant *n.* （某一）时刻　fancy *adj.* 难度高的，需要复杂技巧的

in among a lot of yelling, hairy men with knives—long shiny knives, worse than the farrier's knives—and I have to take care that Dick's boot is just touching the next man's boot without crushing it. I can see Dick's lance to the right of my right eye, and I know I'm safe. I shouldn't care to be the man or horse that stood up to Dick and me when we're in a hurry."

"Don't the knives hurt?" said the young mule.

"Well, I got one cut across the chest once, but that wasn't Dick's fault—"

"A lot I should have cared whose fault it was, if it hurt! " said the young mule.

"You must," said the troop horse. "If you don't trust your man, you may as well run away at once. That's what some of our horses do, and I don't blame them. As I was saying, it wasn't Dick's fault. The man was lying on the ground, and I stretched myself not to tread on him, and he slashed up at me. Next time I have to go over a man lying down I shall step on him—hard."

"H'm! " said Billy. "It sounds very foolish. Knives are dirty things at any time. The proper thing to do is to climb up a mountain with a well-balanced saddle, hang on by all four feet and your ears too, and creep and crawl and wriggle along, till you come out hundreds of feet above anyone else on a ledge where there's

THE JUNGLE STORY

着刀子的人群中间——比管马军士的刀还要糟糕的、长长的闪着光的刀——而且我得留心使迪克·坎利弗的靴子正好挨着旁边一个人的靴子,而没有踩到它。我能看到迪克的长矛在我右眼的右边,就知道我是安全的。在匆忙之中时,我可不愿意当那个勇敢的面对迪克和我的人或是马。"

"那些刀不会伤人吗?"年轻的骡子问。

"嗯,我有一次胸口划了一道,但是那不是迪克的错——"

"如果它伤了人,那么我特别关心的是到底是谁的错!"年轻的骡子问。

"你一定得关心,"军马说,"如果你不信任你的骑士,那么你还是立刻跑掉的好。我们有些马匹就是这么做的,我不怪他们。正如我说的,那不是迪克的错。那个人躺在地上,我拉直身体尽力不踩到他,他却一刀向我砍来。第二次我要越过一个躺在地上的人时,我就踩上去了——狠狠地踩了上去。"

"哼!"比利说,"听起来真是愚蠢。刀在任何时候都是卑劣的东西。恰当的做法是你带着匀称的马鞍爬上山,靠你的四只脚还有耳朵,缓慢地、徐徐地蜿蜒前进,直到你到了高出别人几百英尺的岩层,那里刚

---

fault *n.* 责任,过失　　**blame** *v.* 责备,谴责　　**slash** *v.* 砍
creep *v.* 缓慢行进　　**wriggle** *v.* 蜿蜒行进

just room enough for your hoofs. Then you stand still and keep quiet—never ask a man to hold your head, young un—keep quiet while the guns are being put together, and then you watch the little poppy shells drop down into the tree-tops ever so far below."

"Don't you ever trip?" said the troop-horse.

"They say that when a mule trips you can split a hen's ear," said Billy. "Now and again perhaps a badly packed saddle will upset a mule, but it's very seldom. I wish I could show you our business. It's beautiful. Why, it took me three years to find out what the men were driving at. The science of the thing is never to show up against the sky line, because, if you do, you may get fired at. Remember that, young un. Always keep hidden as much as possible, even if you have to go a mile out of your way. I lead the battery when it comes to that sort of climbing."

"Fired at without the chance of running into the people who are firing! " said the troop-horse, thinking hard. "I couldn't stand that. I should want to charge—with Dick."

"Oh, no, you wouldn't. You know that as soon as the guns are in **position** they'll do all the charging. That's scientific and neat. But knives—pah! "

The baggage-camel had been bobbing his head to and fro for some time past, anxious to get a word in **edgewise**. Then I heard

448

THE JUNGLE STORY

好有足够的空间可以放下你的蹄子。然后你在那里静静地站着——永远别让人来拉着你的头，年轻人——当大炮被组装起来的时候，保持安静，然后看着小小的罂粟壳掉到下面远远的树顶中间。"

"你摔倒过吗？"军马问。

"他们说，当一头骡子摔倒了，你就可以把一只母鸡的耳朵撕开了，"比利说，"也许偶尔会有骡子因为驮载的马鞍没放好而心烦意乱，但是那是很少的情况。我希望我可以向你展示一下我们的动作，可优美了。嗯，我花了三年的时间才了解了人们的意图。这个动作的技巧在于，永远不要在地平线上显露出来，因为，如果你这样做了，可能会挨枪子的。记住这点，年轻人。永远要尽可能地躲起来，即使你得偏离自己的道路一英里远。碰到需要那样爬山的时候，我都在前面给炮兵连带队。

"还没机会跑到开火的人群中，就被子弹打中了！"军马说，一边深思着。"我可受不了这个。我想和迪克一起冲锋。"

"哦，不，你不会的。你知道那些大炮只要一就位，他们就会装好弹药，动作娴熟，干净利落。但是刀——呸！"

驮包裹的骆驼一直上下地摆动他的头好一会了，急切地希望插上

---

position *n.* 位置　　edgewise *adv.* 从旁边

丛林的故事

him say, as he cleared his throat, nervously:

"I—I—I have fought a little, but not in that climbing way or that running way."

"No. Now you mention it," said Billy, "you don't look as though you were made for climbing or running—much. Well, how was it, old Hay-bales?"

"The proper way," said the camel. "We all sat down—"

"Oh, my crupper and breastplate! " said the troop-horse under his breath. "Sat down! "

"We sat down—a hundred of us," the camel went on, "in a big square, and the men piled our packs and saddles, outside the square, and they fired over our backs, the men did, on all sides of the square."

"What sort of men? Any men that came along?" said the troop-horse. "They teach us in riding school to lie down and let our masters fire across us, but Dick Cunliffe is the only man I'd trust to do that. It tickles my girths, and, besides, I can't see with my head on the ground."

"What does it matter who fires across you?" said the camel. "There are plenty of men and plenty of other camels close by, and a great many clouds of smoke. I am not frightened then. I sit still and wait."

THE JUNGLE STORY

一句话。接着,我听到他清了清嗓子,紧张地说:

"我——我——我打过一些仗,但不是那种爬山或者奔跑的方式。"

"是啊,既然你提到了,"比利说,"你看上去不像生来就能爬山或者跑步的。那么,是怎么样的呢,老草包?"

"以我们特有的方式,"骆驼说,"我们都趴下来——"

"哦,我的尾革茵和胸铠!"军马轻声说道,"趴下!"

"我们就都趴下——一百头,"骆驼继续说,"在一个大的操练场上,人们把我们驮的包裹和马鞍堆放起来。在操练场外面,他们隔着我们的背朝外开枪,人们就是这样做的,朝操练场的各个方向开枪。"

"什么样的人?任何一个来这儿的人吗?"军马说,"在骑术学校他们教我们趴下来,让我们的主人从我们的背上开枪,但是迪克·坎利弗是我惟一信任的能让他这样做的人。枪碰到我的肚带,痒痒的,而且,我的头朝着地面,什么也看不见。"

"谁在你背上开枪有什么关系呢?"骆驼说,"旁边有好多人和好多其他骆驼,而且烟雾缭绕。当时我并不害怕,我趴着一动不动,等待着。"

---

proper *adj.* 特有的   pile *v.* 堆积   tickle *v.* 使觉得痒

丛林的故事

"And yet," said Billy, "you dream bad dreams and upset the camp at night. Well, well! Before I'd lie down, not to speak of sitting down, and let a man fire across me, my heels and his head would have something to say to each other. Did you ever hear anything so awful as that?"

There was a long silence, and then one of the gun bullocks lifted up his big head and said, "This is very foolish indeed. There is only one way of fighting."

"Oh, go on," said Billy. "Please don't mind me. I suppose you fellows fight standing on your tails?"

"Only one way," said the two together. (They must have been twins.) "This is that way. To put all twenty yoke of us to the big gun as soon as Two Tails trumpets." ("Two Tails" is camp slang for the elephant.)

"What does Two Tails trumpet for?" said the young mule.

"To show that he is not going any nearer to the smoke on the other side. Two Tails is a great coward. Then we tug the big gun all together—Heya—Hullah! Heeyah! Hullah! We do not climb like cats nor run like calves. We go across the level plain, twenty yoke of us, till we are unyoked again, and we graze while the big guns talk across the plain to some town with mud walls, and pieces of the wall fall out, and the dust goes up as though many cattle were

452

THE JUNGLE STORY

"但是，"比利说，"你晚上做恶梦，还扰得整个军营不得安宁。好啦，好啦！在我躺下来之前，别再说趴下了，让人隔着我开枪，我的后脚和他的脑袋彼此有话要说呢。你有没有听到过这么可怕的事情？"

接着是长长的一段时间的沉默，然后一头大炮公牛抬起他的大脑袋，说道，"这真的是非常愚蠢。只有一种打仗的方式。"

"哦，继续说，"比利说，"请别在意我。我想你们两个是站在一起打仗的吧？"

"只有一种方式，"他们两个异口同声说道(他们两个一定是双胞胎)"就是这样的。等'双尾巴'一吼叫，我们二十对都赶到大炮旁。"("双尾巴"是营地对大象的称呼。)

"'双尾巴'为什么要吼叫呢？"年轻的骡子问。

"那是表明他不再往另一边的烟雾靠近了。'双尾巴'是个大大的胆小鬼。然后，我们一起用力拖大炮，——嘿呀——嘿呦！嘿嗬！嘿呦！我们不像猫那样爬，也不像小鹿那样奔跑。我们二十对公牛穿过平原，直到再次卸下挽具。我们在草地上吃着草，此时大炮呼啸着穿越平原飞到围着泥墙的某个城镇，泥墙一块块掉落下来，仰起阵阵尘土，好像

---

slang *n.* 俚语，行话

丛林的故事

coming home."

"Oh! And you choose that time for grazing?" said the young mule.

"That time or any other. Eating is always good. We eat till we are yoked up again and tug the gun back to where Two Tails is waiting for it. Sometimes there are big guns in the city that speak back, and some of us are killed, and then there is all the more grazing for those that are left. This is Fate. None the less, Two Tails is a great coward. That is the proper way to fight. We are brothers from Hapur. Our father was a **sacred** bull of Shiva. We have spoken."

"Well, I've certainly learned something tonight," said the troop-horse. "Do you gentlemen of the screw-gun battery feel **inclined** to eat when you are being fired at with big guns, and Two Tails is behind you?"

"About as much as we feel inclined to sit down and let men **sprawl** all over us, or run into people with knives. I never heard such **stuff**. A mountain ledge, a well-balanced load, a driver you can trust to let you pick your own way, and I'm your mule. But— the other things—no! " said Billy, with a **stamp** of his foot.

"Of course," said the troop horse, "everyone is not made in the same way, and I can quite see that your family, on your father's

THE JUNGLE STORY

许多牛正在往家跑。"

"哦！你们挑了那个时间吃草？"年轻的骡子问。

"选那个时候，或者其他任何时候。吃总是美好的。我们一直吃啊吃，直到再次被套上挽具，然后把大炮拖回'双尾巴'等着的地方。有时候，城里的大炮有回应，我们中的有些人就被打死了。那么剩下的就有更多的草吃了。那就是命运。但不管怎么说，'双尾巴'还是个大大的胆小鬼。那就是我们特有的打仗方式。我们是来自哈珀的两兄弟。我们的父亲是一头湿婆神牛。我们已经说过了。"

"好吧，我今晚学到了一些东西，"军马说，"当大炮在朝你们开火的时候，'双尾巴'在你们身后，你们螺旋式炮炮兵连的绅士们都还觉得想吃草吗？"

"想吃，就像我们想躺下来，让人们横七竖八地躺在我们身上，或者冲进拿着刀子的人群。我从来没听到过这种话。一块岩层、一个放稳的担子、一个可以让你自由选择道路的可以信赖的马夫，我就是你的骡子。但是——其他事情——没门！"比利说着跺了一下脚。

"当然，"军马说，"并不是每一个人都按照同一种方式造出来的，

455

side, would fail to understand a great many things."

"Never you mind my family on my father's side," said Billy angrily, for every mule hates to be reminded that his father was a donkey. "My father was a Southern gentleman, and he could pull down and bite and kick into rags every horse he came across. Remember that, you big brown Brumby! "

Brumby means wild horse without any breeding. Imagine the feelings of Sunol if a car-horse called her a "skate," and you can imagine how the Australian horse felt. I saw the white of his eye glitter in the dark.

"See here, you son of an **imported** Malaga jackass," he said between his teeth, "I'd have you know that I'm **related** on my mother's side to Carbine, winner of the Melbourne Cup, and where I come from we aren't **accustomed** to being ridden over roughshod by any parrot-mouthed, pig-headed mule in a pop-gun pea-shooter battery. Are you ready?"

"On your hind legs! " squealed Billy. They both reared up facing each other, and I was expecting a furious fight, when a gurgly, rumbly voice, called out of the darkness to the right— "Children, what are you fighting about there? Be quiet."

Both beasts dropped down with a snort of disgust, for neither horse nor mule can bear to listen to an elephant's voice.

THE JUNGLE STORY

我能清楚地了解,你父亲这边的家庭不能理解许多东西。"

"你别老是提起我父亲这边的家庭,"比利生气地说,因为每一头骡子都讨厌人家提醒他他父亲是头驴。"我父亲是南方的一个绅士,他能把碰到的每匹马都拉倒,又咬又踢地把他扯成碎片。记住了,你这个棕色大布鲁比!"

布鲁比指的是没有经过驯养的野马。想象一下如果一匹拉车的马管苏诺尔叫"不中用的老马",他会是什么样的感觉,你就可以想象地出这匹澳大利亚马的感觉了。我看到他眼白在黑暗中闪着光。

"喂,你这个进口的马拉加公驴的儿子,"他龇着牙说,"我要让你知道,在我妈妈这边,我和墨尔本杯的获奖者卡宾有关系。在我家乡,我们不习惯被儿童气枪、射豆枪炮兵连的那些长着鹦鹉嘴巴、猪脑袋的骡子欺凌。你准备好了吗?"

"站起来!"比利尖叫道。他们两个都用后脚站立起来,面对着面。我正等着一场激烈的打斗呢,这时在黑暗中一个咯咯的低沉的声音往右边喊着:"孩子们,你们在吵什么呢?安静点。"

两个野兽都从鼻子里发出愤慨的哼哼声后趴下了,因为马和骡子听到大象的声音都受不了。

---

sacred *adj.* 神圣的　　inclined *adj.* 有……的意向　　sprawl *v.* 伸开四肢躺
stuff *n.* 言语　　stamp *n.* 踩脚

丛林的故事

"It's Two Tails! " said the troop-horse. "I can't stand him. A tail at each end isn't fair! "

"My feelings exactly," said Billy, crowding into the troop-horse for company. "We're very alike in some things."

"I suppose we've inherited them from our mothers," said the troop horse. "It's not worth quarreling about. Hi! Two Tails, are you tied up?"

"Yes," said Two Tails, with a laugh all up his trunk. "I'm picketed for the night. I've heard what you fellows have been saying. But don't be afraid. I'm not coming over."

The bullocks and the camel said, half aloud, "Afraid of Two Tails—what nonsense! " And the bullocks went on, "We are sorry that you heard, but it is true. Two Tails, why are you afraid of the guns when they fire?"

"Well," said Two Tails, rubbing one hind leg against the other, exactly like a little boy saying a poem, "I don't quite know whether you'd understand."

"We don't, but we have to pull the guns," said the bullocks.

"I know it, and I know you are a good deal braver than you think you are. But it's different with me. My battery captain called me a Pachydermatous Anachronism the other day."

"That's another way of fighting, I suppose?" said Billy, who was recovering his spirits.

THE JUNGLE STORY

"是'双尾巴'！"军马说，"我真受不了他。两头都有尾巴真不公平！"

"我也这么觉得，"比利说，一边挤到军马旁边做伴，"我们在有些方面很相像。"

"我想我们都是从我们的母亲那里继承来的。"军马说，"这没什么好争论的。嗨！'双尾巴'，你被拴牢了吗？"

"是的，"'双尾巴'回答道，一边笑着仰起鼻子，"我晚上都是拴住的。我听到你们说的话了。但是别害怕，我不会走过来的。"

公牛和骆驼低声说，"怕'双尾巴'——什么胡话！"公牛继续说，"我们很抱歉，你听到了，但是这是事实。'双尾巴'，为什么他们开火的时候你会怕大炮啊？"

"嗯，"'双尾巴'说，一边用一条后腿蹭另一条后腿，就像一个小男孩在念诗，"我不十分了解你们是否能懂。"

"我们不懂，但是我们得拉大炮。"公牛说。

"我知道，而且我知道你们比自己认为的还要勇敢得多。但是我就不一样了。我炮兵连的连长有一天称我为厚皮肤的、不合时代的家伙。"

"我想，那是另外一种战斗的方式吧？"比利说，他又恢复了精神。

---

imported *adj.* 进口的　　related *adj.* 有联系的，相关的　　accustomed *adj.* 习惯的
company *n.* 同伴　　recover *v.* 重新获得，恢复　　spirit *n.* 精神，情绪

丛林的故事

"You don't know what that means, of course, but I do. It means betwixt and between, and that is just where I am. I can see inside my head what will happen when a shell bursts, and you bullocks can't."

"I can," said the troop-horse. "At least a little bit. I try not to think about it."

"I can see more than you, and I do think about it. I know there's a great deal of me to take care of, and I know that nobody knows how to cure me when I'm sick. All they can do is to stop my driver's pay till I get well, and I can't trust my driver."

"Ah! " said the troop horse. "That explains it. I can trust Dick."

"You could put a whole regiment of Dicks on my back without making me feel any better. I know just enough to be uncomfortable, and not enough to go on in spite of it."

"We do not understand," said the bullocks.

"I know you don't. I'm not talking to you. You don't know what blood is."

"We do," said the bullocks. "It is red stuff that soaks into the ground and smells."

The troop-horse gave a kick and a bound and a snort.

"Don't talk of it," he said. "I can smell it now, just thinking of it. It makes me want to run—when I haven't Dick on my back."

460

THE JUNGLE STORY

"你当然不知道那是什么意思,但是我知道。它的意思是介于马和驴之间,那就是我的处境。我能够在脑袋里看见当一个炮弹爆炸的时候,会发生什么事情,而你们公牛就不能。"

"我能,"军马说,"至少能看到一点点。只是我努力地不去想它罢了。"

"我能看到的比你多了,而我总去想它。我知道得好好照顾自己,一旦我生病了,没有人知道该怎么医治我。他们所能做的就是停止给我的驱赶者发佣金,直到我好了。我不能信任我的驱赶者。"

"啊!"军马说,"这就能解释一切了。我能信任迪克。"

"你可以把一大群的迪克放在我背上,都不能让我觉得好过点。我知道不舒服的滋味,但我不知道没有它怎么继续生活下去。"

"我们不理解,"公牛说。

"我知道你们不懂。我不和你们说了,你们不知道血是什么。"

"我们知道的。"公牛说,"它是红色的东西,会渗入到地里,还有臭味。"

军马踢了一下,跳了一下,还喷了下鼻子。

"别谈这个了,"他说,"只要一想到它,我就能闻到这个味道。它让我想跑——当迪克不在我背上的时候。"

---

cure *v.* 治疗　regiment *n.* 大群　　soak *v.* 浸泡,吸收　　smell *v.* 发出臭味

461

丛林的故事

"But it is not here," said the camel and the bullocks. "Why are you so stupid?"

"It's vile stuff," said Billy. "I don't want to run, but I don't want to talk about it."

"There you are! " said Two Tails, waving his tail to explain.

"Surely. Yes, we have been here all night," said the bullocks.

Two Tails stamped his foot till the iron ring on it jingled. "Oh, I'm not talking to you. You can't see inside your heads."

"No. We see out of our four eyes," said the bullocks. "We see straight in front of us."

"If I could do that and nothing else, you wouldn't be needed to pull the big guns at all. If I was like my captain—he can see things inside his head before the firing begins, and he shakes all over, but he knows too much to run away—if I was like him I could pull the guns. But if I were as wise as all that I should never be here. I should be a king in the forest, as I used to be, sleeping half the day and bathing when I liked. I haven't had a good bath for a month."

"That's all very fine," said Billy. "But giving a thing a long name doesn't make it any better."

"H'sh! " said the troop horse. "I think I understand what Two Tails means."

"You'll understand better in a minute," said Two Tails angrily.

THE JUNGLE STORY

"但是这里没有血啊,"骆驼和公牛说,"你为什么这么蠢啊?"

"血是肮脏的东西,"比利说,"我不想跑,但是我也不想谈论它。"

"你们在那里啊!""双尾巴"摇着尾巴说道。

"当然了。我们整个晚上都在这儿,"公牛说道。

"双尾巴"跺着脚直到他身上铁环叮当响个不停。"哦,我不和你们说了。你们看不见头脑里的东西。"

"不。我们用四只眼睛看,"公牛说,"我们径直往我们前面看。"

"只要我能那样看,就根本不需要你们去拉那些大炮了。如果我能像我的连长那样——他能在开火前在脑袋里看到东西,然后全身发抖,但是他知道得太多就跑不了了——如果我能像他一样,我就能拉炮了。但是如果我能那样聪明的话,我就不会在这儿了。我就该是森林之王了,就像我过去那样,睡上大半天,想洗澡就洗澡。我都已经一个月没好好洗个澡了。"

"那都很好,"比利说,"但是给个东西取个长长的名字,并不会让他舒服。"

"嘘!"军马说,"我想我懂'双尾巴'的意思了。"

"过会儿你会更加明白的,""双尾巴"生气地说,"现在你就跟我解

463

丛林的故事

"Now you just explain to me why you don't like this! "

He began trumpeting furiously at the top of his trumpet.

"Stop that! " said Billy and the troop horse together, and I could hear them stamp and shiver. An elephant's trumpeting is always nasty, especially on a dark night.

"I shan't stop," said Two Tails. "Won't you explain that, please? Hhrrmph! Rrrt! Rrrmph! Rrrhha! " Then he stopped suddenly, and I heard a little whimper in the dark, and knew that Vixen had found me at last. She knew as well as I did that if there is one thing in the world the elephant is more afraid of than another it is a little barking dog. So she stopped to bully Two Tails in his pickets, and yapped round his big feet. Two Tails shuffled and squeaked. "Go away, little dog!" he said. "Don't snuff at my ankles, or I'll kick at you. Good little dog —nice little doggie, then! Go home, you yelping little beast! Oh, why doesn't someone take her away? She'll bite me in a minute."

"Seems to me," said Billy to the troop horse, "that our friend Two Tails is afraid of most things. Now, if I had a full meal for every dog I've kicked across the parade-ground I should be as fat as Two Tails nearly."

I whistled, and Vixen ran up to me, muddy all over, and licked my nose, and told me a long tale about hunting for me all through the camp. I never let her know that I understood beast talk, or she

464

THE JUNGLE STORY

释一下你为什么不喜欢这样！"

他开始以最高的嗓门怒吼起来。

"闭嘴！"比利和军马一起喊道，我能听到他们跺脚和发抖的声音。大象的吼叫总是很烦人，特别是在一个漆黑夜里。

"我不会闭嘴的，""双尾巴"说，"你不解释一下吗？呼啦噗！咻噗！咻噗！咻啦！"接着他突然停了下来，我听到黑暗中有啜泣的声音，我知道维克森终于找到我了。她和我一样清楚地知道，如果说在这个世界上有一样最让大象害怕的东西，那就是一条吠叫的小狗。所以她停下来威吓拴在木桩上的"双尾巴"，绕着他的大脚边狂叫着。"双尾巴"不断地挪着位子，尖叫着。"走开，小狗！"他说，"别在我的脚踝旁嗅来嗅去，不然我就踢你啦。好小狗——可爱的小狗！回去吧，你这狂吠的小家伙！哦，为什么没人把她带走呢？她马上会咬我的。"

"在我看来，"比利对军马说，"好像我们的朋友'双尾巴'怕好多东西。要是我每次在阅兵场上踢了一条狗都会换来一顿好吃的，我都该和'双尾巴'这么肥了。"

我吹了下口哨，维克森跑到了我的面前，全身上下都是泥。她舔着我的鼻子，告诉我她在营地里到处找我。我从没让她知道我能听懂动

---

nasty *adj.* 使人不愉快的　　shuffle *v.* 不断改变位置　　ankle *n.* 踝　　whistle *v.* 吹口哨
lick *v.* 舔

would have taken all sorts of liberties. So I **buttoned** her into the breast of my overcoat, and Two Tails shuffled and stamped and growled to himself.

"**Extraordinary**! Most extraordinary! " he said. "It runs in our family. Now, where has that nasty little beast gone to?"

I heard him feeling about with his trunk.

"We all seem to be **affected** in various ways," he went on, blowing his nose. "Now, you gentlemen were **alarmed**, I believe, when I trumpeted."

"Not alarmed, exactly," said the troop-horse, "but it made me feel as though I had hornets where my saddle ought to be. Don't begin again."

"I'm frightened of a little dog, and the camel here is frightened by bad dreams in the night."

"It is very lucky for us that we haven't all got to fight in the same way," said the troop-horse.

"What I want to know," said the young mule, who had been quiet for a long time—"what I want to know is, why we have to fight at all."

"Because we're told to," said the troop-horse, with a snort of contempt.

"Orders," said Billy the mule, and his teeth snapped.

"Hukm hai! " (It is an order!), said the camel with a gurgle, and

THE JUNGLE STORY

物的语言,否则的话她就对我放肆随便了。于是,我把她抱到胸口,扣在大衣里。"双尾巴"不停地挪着脚步,跺着脚,低声吼叫着。

　　"不可思议!太不可思议了!"他说,"它是我们家族世代相传的。咦,那个脏兮兮的小东西跑到哪里去了?"

　　我听到他用他的象鼻子到处嗅来嗅去。

　　"我们似乎都被各种各样的方式影响,"他继续说道,鼻子里吹着气,"我相信,当我吼叫的时候,你们这些绅士都受了惊吓。"

　　"没吓到,真的,"军马说,"但是它让我觉得,本来该放马鞍的地方,好像有许多大黄蜂。别再吼了。"

　　"我怕小狗,而这儿的骆驼晚上怕做恶梦。"

　　"我们很幸运,不需要以同一种方式打仗,"军马说。

　　"我想知道的是,"已经沉默了半天的年轻的骡子开口说话了——"我想知道的是,到底我们为什么要打仗呢?"

　　"因为命令我们去打仗,"军马轻蔑地哼着说。

　　"命令,"骡子比利说,他的牙齿喀嚓一下合上了。

　　"呼啃-嗨!"(这是命令!),骆驼咯咯地说。"双尾巴"和公牛重复

---

button v. 扣　　　**extraordinary** adj. 不同寻常的　　　**affect** v. 影响　　　**alarm** v. 惊恐

丛林的故事

Two Tails and the bullocks repeated, "Hukm hai! "

"Yes, but who gives the orders?" said the recruit-mule.

"The man who walks at your head—Or sits on your back—Or holds the nose rope—Or twists your tail," said Billy and the troop-horse and the camel and the bullocks one after the other.

"But who gives them the orders?"

"Now you want to know too much, young un," said Billy, "and that is one way of getting kicked. All you have to do is to obey the man at your head and ask no questions."

"He's quite right," said Two Tails. "I can't always obey, because I'm betwixt and between. But Billy's right. Obey the man next to you who gives the order, or you'll stop all the battery, besides getting a **thrashing**."

The gun-bullocks got up to go. "Morning is coming," they said. "We will go back to our lines. It is true that we only see out of our eyes, and we are not very clever. But still, we are the only people tonight who have not been afraid. Good-night, you brave people."

Nobody answered, and the troop-horse said, to change the conversation, "Where's that little dog? A dog means a man somewhere about."

"Here I am," yapped Vixen, "under the gun tail with my man. You big, **blundering** beast of a camel you, you upset our tent. My

THE JUNGLE STORY

了一遍,"呼唷–嗨!"

"但是是谁发的命令呢?"刚入伍的骡子问。

"走在你前面的那个人——或者是坐在你背上的那个人——或者是拉着你鼻子上的绳索的人——或者是捻着你的尾巴的人,"比利、军马、骆驼和公牛一个接一个地说。

"但是是谁给他们发的命令呢?"

"你想知道的太多了,年轻人,"比利说,"这是找挨踢的一个方法。你所要做的只是听从你头上的那个人的命令,别问问题。"

"他说的对,""双尾巴"说,"我不能总是遵守命令,因为我即非马也非驴。但是比利是对的,听从你身边的人发出的命令,否则你会让整个炮兵连停顿下来,而且你会被痛打一顿的。"

两头公牛站起来要走了,"就快天亮了,"他们说,"我们要回我们的队伍里去了。的确,我们只会用眼睛看,我们不是非常聪明。但是,我们是今晚惟一不感到害怕的人。晚安了,勇敢的人们。"

没有人回答他们,为了转换话题,军马开口了,"那个小狗去哪里了?有条狗就意味着附近有人。"

"我在这儿,"维克森叫到,"在大炮尾部和我的主人在一起。你这

---

thrashing *n.* 痛打　　ammunition *n.* 弹药

469

丛林的故事

man's very angry."

"Phew! " said the bullocks. "He must be white! "

"Of course he is," said Vixen. "Do you suppose I'm looked after by a black bullock-driver?"

"Huah! Ouach! Ugh! " said the bullocks. "Let us get away quickly."

They plunged forward in the mud, and managed somehow to run their yoke on the pole of an **ammunition wagon**, where it **jammed**.

"Now you have done it," said Billy calmly. "Don't **struggle**. You're hung up till daylight. What on earth's the matter?"

The bullocks went off into the long hissing snorts that Indian cattle give, and pushed and crowded and slued and stamped and slipped and nearly fell down in the mud, grunting savagely.

"You'll break your necks in a minute," said the troop-horse. "What's the matter with white men? I live with 'em."

"They—eat—us! Pull! " said the near bullock. The yoke snapped with a twang, and they **lumbered** off together.

I never knew before what made Indian cattle so scared of Englishmen. We eat beef—a thing that no cattle-driver touches — and of course the cattle do not like it.

"May I be **flogged** with my own pad-chains! Who'd have thought of two big lumps like those losing their heads?" said Billy.

470

个跌跌撞撞的大家伙骆驼,扰乱了整个军营。我的主人非常生气。"

"呦!"公牛说,"他一定是白人吧!"

"当然是了,"维克森回答,"你认为我是由黑皮肤的赶牛人照看的吗?"

"哗!噢呦!啊呀!"公牛说,"我们快点走吧。"

他们在泥地里往前冲,设法拉动陷在泥地里的弹药车车辕上的牛轭。

"好啦,你们已经尽力了,"比利平静地说,"别费力气了。你们非等到天亮了不可。到底是怎么回事啊?"

公牛发出长长的咝咝的喷鼻声,这是印度牛特有的。他们努力地往前推,急速地前进,突然往旁边一滑,连忙跺了跺脚,又滑了一下,几乎要在泥地里摔倒了,嘴里还生气地咕哝着。

"你们马上会把脖子折断的,"军马说,"白人怎么了?我和他们住在一起。"

"他们——吃——我们!拉呀!"近处的公牛说。牛轭突然砰地一下折断了,他们一起跟跟跄跄地站住了。

我以前从来不知道是什么让印度牛这么害怕英国人。我们吃牛肉——那是没有一个赶牛人会碰的东西——当然牛也不会喜欢。

"我要挨自己的脚链的鞭打了!谁会想到这么两个傻大个会掉脑袋呢?"比利说。

丛林的故事

"Never mind. I'm going to look at this man. Most of the white men, I know, have things in their pockets," said the troop-horse.

"I'll leave you, then. I can't say I'm over-fond of 'em myself. Besides, white men who haven't a place to sleep in are more than likely to be thieves, and I've a good deal of Government property on my back. Come along, young un, and we'll go back to our lines. Good-night, Australia! See you on parade to-morrow, I suppose. Good-night, old Hay-bale! —try to control your feelings, won't you? Good-night, Two Tails! If you pass us on the ground tomorrow, don't trumpet. It spoils our formation."

Billy the Mule stumped off with the swaggering limp of an old campaigner, as the troop-horse's head came nuzzling into my breast, and I gave him biscuits, while Vixen, who is a most conceited little dog, told him fibs about the scores of horses that she and I kept.

"I'm coming to the parade to-morrow in my dog-cart," she said. "Where will you be?"

"On the left hand of the second squadron. I set the time for all my troop, little lady," he said politely. "Now I must go back to Dick. My tail's all muddy, and he'll have two hours' hard work dressing me for parade."

The big parade of all the thirty thousand men was held that

THE JUNGLE STORY

"没关系。我要去看看这个人。据我所知,大部分的白人,口袋里都有东西。"军马说。

"那么,我要离开你了。我不能说我自己特别喜欢他们,而且,那些没地方睡觉的白人很可能会作贼,我的背上就有许多政府的财产。来吧,年轻人,我们要回到我们的队伍里去了。晚安,澳大利亚!我想,明天检阅的时候见了! 晚安,老草包! ——设法控制一下你的情绪,行吗?晚安,'双尾巴'!如果明天操练场上从我们身边经过,别吼叫,那样会破坏我们的队形的。"

骡子比利拖着笨重的脚步走了,摆出老兵的姿态大摇大摆地一瘸一拐地走了。军马把脑袋伸到我胸口,我给了他一些饼干,而维克森,这个自大的小狗,对他撒了点小谎,说我和她养了几十四马。

"我明天要坐着我的狗拖车去参加检阅,"她说,"你会在哪里呢? "

"第二骑兵队的左侧。我控制我的队伍的行进速度,小姐,"他礼貌地回答,"现在我得回到迪克那儿去了。我的尾巴上都是泥,他要花上整整两个小时为我打扮,准备参加检阅。"

那天下午,举行了三万人的大检阅,维克森和我在靠近印度总督和阿富汗的埃米尔的地方。埃米尔头上戴着高高大大的黑色俄国羔羊

---

thrashing *n.* 痛打　　ammunition *n.* 弹药　　wagon *n.* 四轮马车,运货车
jam *v.* 使卡住,轧住　　struggle *v.* 挣扎　　lumber *v.* 笨拙地移动;缓慢地移动

afternoon, and Vixen and I had a good place close to the Viceroy and the Amir of Afghanistan, with high, big black hat of astrakhan wool and the great diamond star in the center. The first part of the review was all sunshine, and the regiments went by in wave upon wave of legs all moving together, and guns all in a line, till our eyes grew dizzy. Then the cavalry came up, to the beautiful cavalry canter of "Bonnie Dundee," and Vixen cocked her ear where she sat on the dog-cart. The second squadron of the Lancers shot by, and there was the troop-horse, with his tail like spun silk, his head pulled into his breast, one ear forward and one back, setting the time for all his squadron, his legs going as smoothly as waltz music. Then the big guns came by, and I saw Two Tails and two other elephants harnessed in line to a forty-pounder siege gun, while twenty yoke of oxen walked behind. The seventh pair had a new yoke, and they looked rather stiff and tired. Last came the screw guns, and Billy the mule carried himself as though he **commanded** all the troops, and his harness was oiled and polished till it **winked**. I gave a **cheer** all by myself for Billy the mule, but he never looked right or left.

The rain began to fall again, and for a while it was too misty to see what the troops were doing. They had made a big half circle across the plain, and were spreading out into a line. That line grew

THE JUNGLE STORY

毛帽子,中间有一个大大的钻石星星。检阅的第一部分是在灿烂的阳光下举行的,步兵团整齐地抬着脚走过,像一道道波浪,他们手里的枪也整齐划一,看得我们头晕目眩。然后骑兵走上前来,随着优美的"邦尼·邓迪",慢跑经过。维克森在狗拖车上竖起了她的耳朵。拿着长矛的第二骑兵队迅速通过了,接着是军马,他的尾巴就像纺过的丝绸一样,头被拉到胸前,一只耳朵在前,一只耳朵在后,为他的队伍控制速度,腿走起来像华尔兹那样平稳。接着过来的是大炮,我看到"双尾巴"和其他两头象排成一排,拉着发射四十磅重的炮弹的攻城加农炮,后面跟着二十对同轭牛。第七对有一个新牛轭,他们看上去相当僵硬、疲惫。最后过来的是螺旋式炮,骡子比利摆出一副姿态,似乎他指挥着整个军队,他的挽具上过油,擦得锃亮,闪闪发光。我为骡子比利欢呼起来,但是他既不往左也不往右看。

又开始下雨了,过了一会就变得雾朦朦的,看不清楚军队在做什么了。他们在平原上围起了半个大圈圈,然后慢慢展开成一条直线。那条线越来越长,直到从一翼到另一翼足足有四分之三英里长——一道由人、马和大炮组成的坚固的城墙。接着,它笔直地朝总督和埃米尔走

---

flog *v.* 鞭打　　property *n.* 财产　　spoil *v.* 破坏　　formation *n.* 队形
conceited *adj.* 自负的,自以为是的　　fig *n.* 无伤大雅的谎话
command *v.* 命令　　wink *v.* 闪耀　　cheer *n.* 欢呼

丛林的故事

and grew and grew till it was three-quarters of a mile long from wing to wing—one solid wall of men, horses, and guns. Then it came on straight toward the Viceroy and the Amir, and as it got nearer the ground began to shake, like the deck of a steamer when the engines are going fast.

Unless you have been there you cannot imagine what a frightening effect this steady come-down of troops has on the spectators, even when they know it is only a review. I looked at the Amir. Up till then he had not shown the shadow of a sign of astonishment or anything else. But now his eyes began to get bigger and bigger, and he picked up the reins on his horse's neck and looked behind him. For a minute it seemed as though he were going to draw his sword and slash his way out through the English men and women in the carriages at the back. Then the advance stopped dead, the ground stood still, the whole line saluted, and thirty bands began to play all together. That was the end of the review, and the regiments went off to their camps in the rain, and an infantry band struck up with—

The animals went in two by two, Hurrah!
The animals went in two by two,
The elephant and the battery mul', and they all got into the Ark
For to get out of the rain!

476

THE JUNGLE STORY

去。随着他们越走越近,大地开始摇晃起来,就像站在发动机转得太快的轮船的甲板上。

除非你在那里,否则你很难想象军队这样稳步的逼近对于观看者来说,有着怎样震撼的效果,即使他们知道这只是个检阅。我看着埃米尔。在这之前,他脸上都一直没有显露出任何一丝害怕的表情。但是现在他的眼睛开始越瞪越大,他拉紧了马背上的缰绳,看着他身后。过了一会,他好像要拔出剑,从他身后坐在马车里的英国男女中间杀出一条路。突然,行进的队伍停止了,整个大地静止了,整个军队一起行礼,三十个乐队开始齐声奏乐。检阅到此结束了,士兵们冒雨返回他们的营地。一个步兵团乐队开始演奏——

动物们成双成对地进去了,万岁!

动物们成双成对地进去了,

大象和炮兵连的骡子,他们全部进去了,进了方舟,

为了躲避那场雨!

---

wing n. 翼　 deck n. 甲板　 spectator n. 观众　 infantry n. 步兵

Then I heard an old grizzled, long-haired Central Asian chief, who had come down with the Amir, asking questions of a native officer.

"Now," said he, "in what **manner** was this wonderful thing done?"

And the officer answered, "An order was given, and they obeyed."

"But are the beasts as wise as the men?" said the chief.

"They obey, as the men do. Mule, horse, elephant, or bullock, he obeys his driver, and the driver his sergeant, and the sergeant his lieutenant, and the lieutenant his captain, and the captain his major, and the major his colonel, and the colonel his brigadier commanding three regiments, and the brigadier the general, who obeys the Viceroy, who is the servant of the Empress. Thus it is done."

"Would it were so in Afghanistan!" said the chief, "for there we obey only our own wills."

"And for that reason," said the native officer, twirling his mustache, "your Amir whom you do not obey must come here and take orders from our Viceroy."

THE JUNGLE STORY

接着,我听到一位跟着埃米尔来的,满头灰白色长头发的老中亚头领在问一个军官问题。

"那么,"他说,"这么了不起的事情是怎么办到的呢?"

军官回答说,"发出一个命令,然后他们就执行了。"

"但是动物和人一样聪明吗?"头领问。

"他们和人一样遵守命令。骡子,马,大象,或者公牛,都服从他的骑士的命令,骑士服从中士,中士服从中尉,中尉服从少校,少校服从上校,上校服从统率三个团的旅长,旅长服从将军,将军服从总督,而总督是女王的仆人。就是这样的。"

"要是阿富汗能这样就好了!"头领说,"因为那里我们只服从自己的意愿。"

"就是因为这样,"军官捻弄着自己的胡子说,"你们不服从的埃米尔必须到这里来,接受我们总督的命令。"

---

manner *n.* 方法

丛林的故事

Chapter 14   Parade Song of the Camp Animals

ELEPHANTS OF THE GUN TEAMS

We lent to Alexander the strength of Hercules,
The wisdom of our foreheads, the cunning of our knees;
We bowed our necks to service: they ne'er were loosed again,

—

Make way there—way for the ten-foot teams,
Of the Forty-Pounder train!

GUN BULLOCKS

Those heroes in their harnesses avoid a cannon-ball,
And what they know of powder upsets them one and all;
Then we come into action and tug the guns again—
Make way there—way for the twenty yoke,

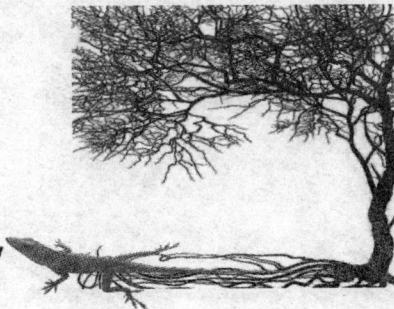

第十四章　营地动物进行曲

大炮组的大象们

我们把头脑的智慧,灵巧的膝盖,
借给亚历山大,大力神赫拉克勒斯,
我们低下脖子服役:它们永远不会被松开,——
前进——让路给十英尺长的队伍,
拉着四十磅重的炮弹的队列!

大炮公牛

那些带着挽具的英雄避开了一个炮弹,
他们对于炸药的了解让他们个个都心烦意乱;
接着我们采取行动,再次拖起大炮——
前进——让路给二十对同轭牛

---

cunning *n.* 灵巧

481

Of the Forty-Pounder train!

CAVALRY HORSES

By the **brand** on my shoulder, the finest of tunes,
Is played by the Lancers, Hussars, and Dragoons,
And it's sweeter than "Stables" or "Water" to me—
The Cavalry Canter of "Bonnie Dundee"!

Then feed us and break us and **handle** and **groom**,
And give us good riders and plenty of room,
And launch us in column of squadron and see
The way of the war-horse to "Bonnie Dundee"!

SCREW-GUN MULES

As me and my companions were scrambling up a hill,
The path was lost in rolling stones, but we went forward still;
For we can wriggle and climb, my lads, and turn up everywhere,

THE JUNGLE STORY

拉着四十磅重的炮弹的队列！

骑兵队的马

以我肩上的烙印发誓，最美妙的曲子，
是由骑兵、轻骑兵和重骑兵演奏的，
对我来说，这比"马厩"或者"水"更令人高兴——
骑兵慢步曲"邦尼·邓迪"！

把我们喂得饱饱的，训练、驾驭、照料我们，
给我们好的骑手和足够的空间，
把我们投入到骑兵队的纵队中去，你们会看到，
战马的行进——伴随着"邦尼·邓迪"的曲子！

螺旋式大炮的骡子们

当我和我的同伴们爬上一座小山，
山径在滚滚山石中消失了，但是我们仍继续前进；
因为我们能蜿蜒而行，能攀爬，我的伙伴们，出现在每一个角落，

---

brand *n.* 烙印   handle *v.* 驾驭   groom *v.* 照料

483

Oh, it's our delight on a mountain height, with a leg or two to spare!

Good luck to every sergeant, then, that lets us pick our road;
Bad luck to all the driver-men that cannot pack a load:
For we can wriggle and climb, my lads, and turn up everywhere,
Oh, it's our delight on a mountain height, with a leg or two to spare!

COMMISSARIAT CAMELS

We haven't a camelty tune of our own,
To help us trollop along,
But every neck is a hair trombone,
(Rtt-ta-ta-ta! is a hair trombone!)
And this our marching-song:
Can't! Don't! Shan't! Won't!
Pass it along the line!
Somebody's pack has slid from his back,
Wish it were only mine!

THE JUNGLE STORY

哦,登上山顶让我们欣喜若狂,还有一两条腿可以歇着!

那么,祝福每一个让我们来选择道路的中士;
愿所有不能负重的驾驭者倒霉:
因为我们能蜿蜒而行,能攀爬,我的伙伴们,出现在每一个角落,
哦,登上山顶让我们欣喜若狂,还有一两条腿可以歇着!

给养的骆驼们

我们没有自己的骆驼之歌,
一路鼓舞我们这些邋遢的人,
但是每个脖子都是一管长号
(哩嗒–嗒–嗒–嗒! 是一管长号!)
这就是我们的进行曲。
不能! 不要! 不会! 不愿!
沿着队伍把这个传过去!
有人的包裹从背上滑落了,
希望它是我的!

485

丛林的故事

Somebody's load has tipped off in the road—
Cheer for a halt and a row!
Urrr! Yarrh! Grr! Arrh!
Somebody's catching it now!

ALL THE BEASTS TOGETHER

Children of the Camp are we,
Serving each in his degree;
Children of the yoke and goad,
Pack and harness, pad and load.
See our line across the plain,
Like a heel-rope bent again,
Reaching, writhing, rolling far,
Sweeping all away to war!
While the men that walk beside,
Dusty, silent, heavy-eyed,
Cannot tell why we or they,

THE JUNGLE STORY

有人的负重掉到了路上——
为停顿吵闹而欢呼！
呦！耶！咯！啊！
已经有人领会了！

所有的动物一起

我们是营地里的孩子，
在各自的职位上效力；
牛轭的孩子们和刺棒，
包裹和马鞍，脚爪和负重。
看我们的部队穿过平原，
就像绑脚的绳索再次弯曲，
前进，蜿蜒移动，行进到远方，
一路奋勇前进去打仗！
尽管走在旁边的人们，
风尘仆仆，一言不发，眼皮沉重，
他们不知道为什么我们或者他们，

丛林的故事

March and suffer day by day.
Children of the Camp are we,
Serving each in his degree;
Children of the yoke and goad,
Pack and harness, pad and load!

THE JUNGLE STORY

每天都要前进,受苦难。
我们是营地里的孩子,
在各自的职位上效力;
牛轭的孩子们和刺棒,
包裹和马鞍,脚爪和负重!